NORTHERN ILLINOIS HUSKIES FOOTBALL

DAN VERDUN

FOREWORD by Joe Novak

NIU PRESS / DEKALB IL

Published by the Northern Illinois University Press, DeKalb, Illinois 60115
Manufactured in the United States using acid-free paper.

Design by Shaun Allshouse

Library of Congress Cataloging-in-Publication Data

Verdun, Daniel.

Northern Illinois Huskies football / Dan Verdun; with a foreword by Joe Novak.

p. cm.

Summary: "This highly illustrated book chronicles the history of
Northern Illinois University football, from its founding to the present day.
The book highlights important moments, memorable games, and lasting football traditions
at the school, and details the role of favorite players as well"—Provided by publisher.

Includes bibliographical references.

ISBN 978-0-87580-455-2 (hardback) — ISBN 978-1-60909-060-9 (e-book)

1. Northern Illinois University—Football—History. 2. Northern Illinois Huskies
(Football team)—History. I. Title.

GV958.N584V47 2012

796.332'630977328—dc23

2011046882

All photos courtesy of NIU unless otherwise noted

To my mother, Marion, and my late father, Paul

To my wife, Nancy, and my children, Tommy and Lauren

CONTENTS

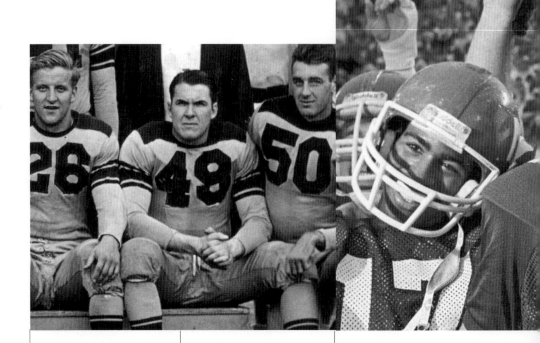

EXTRA POINTS

APPENDICES

BIBLIOGRAPHY AND RESOURCES

FOREWORD

Joe Novak, Head Football Coach, 1996–2007

NIU Football. Potential. Those words have been linked together for years. The only problem is, the word *potential* means untapped abilities. For years, football coaches would look at Northern Illinois and think, "That could be a good job."

Prior to 1969, when NIU made the decision to move into Division I, the Huskie football tradition was strong. From 1929 to 1954, Chick Evans' record as head coach was 132-70-20. From 1956 to 1968, Howard Fletcher's record was 74-48-1, including an NCAA College Division National Championship in 1963. Many great players came through NIU during those years. The most well-known and probably the best player in NIU Football history was George Bork, who played from 1960 to 1963. George, recently inducted into the College Football Hall of Fame, helped put NIU Football on the national scene with his record-setting passing performances in Coach Fletcher's unique (at that time) wide-open offense.

Huskie Stadium, sometimes called the House That Bork Built, was opened in 1965, and soon the move to Division I would take place. The pre-1969 years truly were years of many great seasons, as well as players. Names such as Reino Nori, Hugh Rohrschneider, Tom Beck (also in the College Football Hall of Fame), Bob Heimerdinger, Fran Cahill, and John Spilis, as well as Bork, gave NIU a rich and powerful tradition leading up to the move to Division I football.

Playing Division I football means you are in competition with teams like Notre Dame, Michigan, Alabama, Southern California, Texas, and Oklahoma—so you had better be serious about it! Granted, NIU wasn't going to be exactly on a par with those teams, but it would require a total university commitment to be successful at all in that division. The university administration, board of trustees, fundraisers, athletic department and alumni had better all be pulling in the same direction, or success would be very spotty at best.

Unfortunately, in the 27-year span from 1969 to 1996, NIU had only seven winning seasons, and only two seasons with more than 7 wins (Bill Mallory's 10-2 season in 1983 and Jerry Pettibone's 9-2 season in 1989). It was true that there were many reasons why the football successes had fallen off, but it was obvious that the transition to Division I football had not been an easy one.

In December of 1995, NIU president John La Tourette and Athletics Director Cary Groth offered me the position of head football coach. I had interviewed once before, in 1985, when Jerry Pettibone was hired (a wise choice, as it turned out), but I was disappointed when I wasn't chosen. I moved along in my career, and at age 50 in 1995, I wasn't sure I was going to get the opportunity to be a head coach. I really wanted to have the chance to run my own program and always looked at NIU and its potential as a great job for me. I had spent many years recruiting the Chicago area, knew the high school coaches there, was familiar with NIU, and felt I could do a good job. I was thrilled to be given the opportunity to lead the Huskies when the head coaching job was offered to me—it was truly a dream come true.

That dream felt more like a nightmare for the first three years, though, as it was a disaster on the football field. Three wins in three years does not make you a candidate for a contract extension! After the third season, and a record of 3-30, I did a lot of soul searching. I questioned everything and everybody—but mostly myself. I had come into the job with a philosophy of strong discipline and a strong work ethic. That did not sit well with many of the players we inherited in the fall of 1996, and subsequently 25 to 30 players left the program. I was okay with that, because I wanted guys who would take coaching, work hard, and were good character people. I had seen this philosophy work many years for my boss, Bill Mallory. It was what I believed in. Fortunately, during those first three years, we recruited some very good players, such as future NFL players Justin McCareins and Ryan Diem, who helped us turn things around.

After the 1998 season, I did a lot of reflecting. Maybe I was too "old-fashioned"? Maybe I should "loosen up"? I decided to stay the course. I figured, if we were to fail, I was going to do it my way. I wasn't going to compromise. I was hired to turn the Huskie football program around, and I'd have to do it my way. I stayed strong with my beliefs in how to run a successful football program, and I believe that was the primary reason we turned things around.

In 1999, we started out 0-4 but won five of our last seven games, and things looked better for us. President La Tourette and Cary showed great faith in me at that time and awarded me a contract extension. We could move ahead with our work. The 2000 season produced a winning record; 2001 brought another winning season with a near victory against Big Ten champion Illinois. After the Illinois game, our players were very upset. They felt that playing them close wasn't good enough—and I felt we had turned a huge corner with our expectations. The 2002 season produced an 8-4 season with a victory over Wake Forest in our opening game and a narrow defeat (no comment!) to Wisconsin in a game we thoroughly outplayed them. Again, our players were very unhappy with that outcome.

Our 2003 season was, of course, a magical year for us. The opening game victory over Maryland in DeKalb was amazing! I had a dream when I took the job that we would one day have a sold-out Huskie Stadium, a ranked opponent, on national TV, resulting in a Huskie win. It all fell into place when Maryland came into the game ranked No. 14 in the country, Fox TV was televising the game nationally on Thursday night before Labor Day weekend, and three hours before kickoff someone came into my office to tell me fans were scalping tickets on Annie Glidden Drive—we had a sellout. Wow! Three out of four ... all we needed was a win. Then, I saw the Maryland team in their warm-ups. Another wow! That was one of the best-looking teams I had ever seen. They took the opening kickoff and marched right down the field and scored. It was like we weren't even on the field. "Well," I thought to myself, "three out of four isn't bad." But our kids had come through a lot that off-season, dealing with the tragic deaths of Shea Fitzgerald and Jawan Jackson, which was the hardest thing I had to deal with during my tenure. The team responded by coming back that night and playing hard. P.J. Fleck made an amazing catch in the back of the end zone, dragging his feet in-bounds on a throw by Josh Haldi, and Steve Azar hit a big field goal late in the game to send it into overtime. When Dan Sheldon broke a tackle in overtime to score, and we had the amazing interception to seal the win, my dream was fulfilled.

Alabama, with 12 national titles, was soon to follow—another great win for us. To beat Alabama in Tuscaloosa was unbelievable! I consider it our best win ever. There were many heroes at Alabama, including Josh Haldi, Dan Sheldon, Mike Turner, and Steve Azar, and a very stout defense led by Nick Duffy, Randy Drew, and Akil Grant. We were at the top of the college football world.

The week after Alabama, we beat Iowa State at home. That win gave us three victories over BCS teams . . . a No. 12 ranking in the country . . . a No. 10 slot in the first-ever BCS rankings. However, the games took a toll, as we lost some very key players for the year. The toughest loss was when Nick Duffy, surely the leader of our defense, suffered a broken leg at Central Michigan. The biggest disappointment that year was that our 10-2 team received no bowl bid. I was devastated for our players.

Once again, I was awarded a four-year contract extension. I really felt at that time I would finish out that contract and call it a career. I loved what I was doing, but after time, a change is good for all involved.

In 2004, we received our first bowl bid, to the Silicon Valley Football Classic in San Jose. We had a big win in a driving rain over a very good Troy University team. In 2005, we were once again denied a bowl bid that our team deserved, having won the MAC West Division title. The 2006 season brought another bowl bid, to the Poinsettia Bowl in San Diego, but a sound defeat to a very good TCU team.

Our 2007 season started with a date with Iowa in sold-out Soldier Field. I had pretty much made up my mind that my time had come to step aside at the end of that season. I felt the foundation was strong, even though we suffered through a 2-10 season. We had redshirted most of our freshmen, and I felt the program would rebound quickly.

It did. Jerry Kill came in and took the Huskies to three bowl games in three years. That made it five bowl games in seven years—and nine winning seasons in the previous eleven years. The NIU potential was finally falling into place.

I was blessed to have many great coaches work for me at NIU. A lot of those men have moved on and are having success at other places. I was also blessed to have many great players, several of whom have played in the NFL. Many others didn't go on to pro football, but they were great players for NIU. A lot of those kids came to us with a chip on their shoulder; they thought they should have been recruited by Southern Cal or Ohio State. That was okay—I liked players with a desire to prove people wrong.

We made a living with walk-on players, too—guys who wanted to prove they could play Division I football. Some of our walk-ons were: Chris Finlen, Larry Williams, Brian Atkinson, Randy Drew, Brad Cieslak, Travis Moore, Alex Krutsch, Chad Spann and Steve Azar—names that Huskie fans know well. That's a pretty good group, and there were others. Our program thrived on young people like them. Most of those players have moved on to be good husbands, fathers and very productive people.

I had a lot of fun working with all those great coaches and players and am very proud of the men we had representing our program. We also had a very loyal, hard-working support staff, including sports information director Mike Korcek, associate A.D. Robert Collins, athletics trainer Phil Voorhis, photographer Scott Walstrom, equipment managers Dick Townsend and Linda Krone, and our gracious secretaries, Julie Edwards and Joyce James. Those people made my job easier on a daily basis.

My wife, Carole, and I lived a total of 16 years in DeKalb. It's a wonderful community with a lot of very supportive people and loyal Huskie fans. We left behind many great friends when we retired to North Carolina, so we return to the area a couple of times a year and really enjoy seeing our friends there. The DeKalb-Sycamore community was very good to me and my family.

Recent coaches Dave Doeren and Rod Carey were great hires for NIU. Things look bright for the future of Huskie Football. It's a consistent winner now; there is stability in the program. With the help and support of everyone involved, Huskie football should and can be strong. Its *potential* can be fulfilled.

Thank you to Dan Verdun for writing this book and highlighting the individuals and events that have been part of the NIU Football tradition.

GO HUSKIES!!

ACKNOWLEDGMENTS

As with any project of this magnitude, there are so many people to thank. First and foremost would be my wife, Nancy, and children, Tommy and Lauren. They have been understanding and supportive all the way through the late night phone calls and early morning writing sessions, and I thank them for making life special each and every day.

This would also not have been possible without the unfailing support and love of my parents, Marion and the late Paul Verdun. Throughout my life my mom has always been there for me. She truly has made me what I am today. My father introduced me to the wonderful world of sports and, more importantly, taught me about life. Not a day passes that I don't miss him. Like most of us, I never realized just how much those two people did for me as I was growing up until I began raising my own kids. Thanks also to my brothers, Jeff, Don and Ron. Yes, I still remember how mad you were growing up in a one-TV household when Dad sided with me and the World Series won out over shows like *The Dukes of Hazzard*. Hey, it all paid off—this book is proof of that.

This book would not have been possible without the efforts of a multitude of people at NIU Press. Starting with the initial contact by Sara Hoerdeman, I have been blessed to have worked with such wonderful and talented people throughout the project. I wish to publicly thank Kenton Clymer, Sara, Mark Heineke, Alex Schwartz, Susan Bean, Barbara Berg and Shaun Allshouse. The book you are holding in your hands (or reading electronically) exists because of all the hard work and dedication from the folks at NIU Press.

A huge thank-you goes out to my close friend Barry Bottino for all his advice, guidance and support along the way. Thanks for listening to me ramble on time after time about this, Mister B.

Other friends have contributed in more ways than they will ever know. So, thanks to Tom Doran, John Eisenhour, Mike Fitzgerald, Al Lagattolla, Tim Lee, Jeff Long and Jeff Strohm.

Huge thanks go out to each former coach and athlete who took time out of his life to open the memory bank and share with a complete stranger. This book is about you. Hopefully you will enjoy reading it as much as I did writing it.

This book would not have been possible and certainly not as complete without the assistance of Mike Korcek, the 1970 NIU graduate who served as the school's sports information director until 2009. Simply put, this book would not have been written if it were not for Mike Korcek. There is no one on this earth who knows more about NIU athletics than Mike. He gave freely and willingly of his time. The coaches and players I interviewed along the way had kind words and praise for him. Mike truly bleeds cardinal and black.

Behind all the media reports that hit newspapers, magazines, radio and TV shows along with Internet sites are the people of the sports information offices and media relations departments.

From the NFL ranks, my thanks go out to Mike Corbo of the Bears; Craig Kelley, Vernon Cheek and Pam Humphrey of the Colts; Rich Dalrymple and Jancy Briles of the Cowboys; Vince Freitas, Bill Johnston, Jamaal LaFrance and Morad Shah of the Chargers; Reggie Roberts of the Falcons; Rob Crane of the Packers; and David Hall of the 49ers. From the CFL came help from Jamie Cartmell of the BC Lions; Kelly Forsberg of the Saskatchewan Rough Riders; and Mitch Bayless and Melenee Mehler of the Calgary Stampeders.

Invaluable assistance came from members of the media. Thus, I'd like to recognize and thank the following for their help: Rick Armstrong of the *Aurora Beacon-News*; Bob Asmussen of the *Champaign News-Gazette*; Taylor Bell, formerly of the *Chicago Sun-Times*; Bill Baker, play-by-play voice of NIU athletics; David Kaplan of WGN Radio and Comcast Chicago;

Michael MacCambridge, author of so many landmark sports histories; Murray McCormick of the *Regina Leader-Post*; Bob McGinn of the *Milwaukee Journal Sentinel*; Fowler Connell of the *Danville Commercial News*; and Len Ziehm of the *Sun-Times*.

Fellow sports historians and writers Bob Gill, John Maxymuk and Roger Snell offered not only support and information but also key pieces of advice and insight.

Joan Metzger of the Regional History Center at Founders Library was a tremendous help to me. In fact, all of the NIU information you see for transitional decade pages in this book is thanks to her research.

Jay Orbik and Don Butler of the NIU Media Services and University Relations deserve a huge thanks as well. Nearly all of the photographs in this book are courtesy of Scott Walstrom. Scott, who has worked with NIU Media Services and University Relations as a photographer since the late 1980s, did most of the legwork to unearth all these images. In addition, many of the pictures you see were taken by Scott.

NORTHERN ILLINOIS UNIVERSITY HUSKIES

INSTITUTION FOUNDED—1895

LOCATION—DeKalb

FOOTBALL ESTABLISHED—1899

COLORS—Cardinal & Black

WEBSITE—http://www.niuhuskies.com

MASCOT—Victor E. Huskie

NATIONAL CHAMPIONSHIP—1963 (NCAA College Division)

HIGHEST NFL DRAFT PICK—Larry English, San Diego Chargers, 1st round, 16th overall

FAMOUS ALUMNI IN OTHER SPORTS—Rick Cerrone (baseball), Ned Colletti (baseball), Tim Gullikson (tennis), Tom Gillikson (tennis), Fritz Peterson (baseball), Larry Young (baseball umpire)

FAMOUS NON-SPORT ALUMNI—Joan Allen (actress), Terry Boers (journalist/sports radio host), Dan Castellaneta (voice of Homer Simpson), Jimmy Chamberlain (musician), Tammy Duckworth (politician), Andrew Harris (musician), Steve Harris (actor), Wood Harris (actor), J. Dennis Hastert (former Speaker of the House), E.E. Knight (author), Justin Mentell (actor), Anthony Padilla (pianist), Robert Reed (business journalist/commentator), Paul Sereno (paleontologist), Kurt Sutter (actor/writer/producer)

INTRODUCTION

Northern Illinois University was founded in 1895. Just four years later, the school fielded its first football team. Over the course of the next ten decades, the Huskies have captured the hearts and imaginations of a loyal following of students, alums and fans across the region, state and nation. Moreover, the Huskies' berth in the 2010 International Bowl in Toronto sent NIU north of the border and expanded the nationality of cheering fans.

Traditions abound throughout NIU football. From nationally ranked cheerleading squads to Band Day to fans shaking their car keys during kickoffs, Huskie fans have long been a major part of the Saturday scene (or a weeknight if TV dictates it). There are plenty of spellbinding stories:

- The national championship team of 1963 led by quarterback and basketball star George Bork, who is enshrined in the College Football Hall of Fame

- NIU running star Mark Kellar's jersey was retired and buried in a time capsule on campus following his final game

- The 1983 team that won the California Bowl and was inducted into the NIU Athletic Hall of Fame en masse

- LeShon Johnson, the aspiring rodeo star who finished sixth in the Heisman Trophy race

- Thomas Hammock, the star running back whose career was derailed one game into his senior season by a heart ailment

- P.J. Fleck, the Kaneland High School standout, grabbed the final scholarship available and turned into one of the all-time clutch receivers in Huskie history

- Dan Sheldon, the former Burlington Central speedster, turned a five-yard pass route into the game-winning touchdown in the Huskies' upset of Maryland in 2003

- Eddie Davis, the former Huskie defensive back, who now seems to be on the verge of induction into the Canadian Football League Hall of Fame

- The wild & brief tenure of ESPN analyst Lee Corso as NIU head coach

- New Orleans Saints' head coach Sean Payton, who nearly became a Huskie

- The origins of Northern's first Homecoming in 1903, seven years before the University of Illinois "created" the concept

- Players who have had their numbers retired by NIU

- Huskies drafted by professional football teams

- Illinois High School Association Hall of Fame members

- Super Bowl winners

- Pro Bowl players

- Former Huskies who made their post-football life in the fields of education and business

- Those who played for or coached with legends such as Bud Wilkinson, Woody Hayes, Ara Parseghian, John Pont, Bo Schembechler, Barry Switzer, Joe Paterno and Jim Tressel

THEY ARE LEGENDARY NAMES IN NIU HUSKIE HISTORY

- George Bork
- Randy Clark
- Larry English
- P.J. Fleck
- Doug Free
- Chandler Harnish
- Bob Heimerdinger
- Sam Hurd
- LeShon Johnson
- Jordan Lynch
- Bill Mallory
- Justin McCareins
- Joe Novak
- Todd Peat
- Jack Pheanis
- Mike Sabock
- Hollis Thomas
- Tim Tyrrell
- Michael Turner
- Garrett Wolfe

The stories about these individuals span every decade from the 1940s to the present day. They focus not only on their glory days of college football but also on what occurred before and since. Many of these men also played professionally. You name a league and it is here: the NFL, the CFL, the USFL and the many forms of Arena ball. Furthermore, Bork spent time in the long-forgotten Continental Football League, while Johnson played in the short-lived XFL.

This book has been painstakingly researched through newspaper and magazine archives and online sites and databases. Ad-ditional information has been supplied via the sports information departments and alumni offices. So I could be sure to write an accurate and more personal chronicle, interviews were conducted with more than 50 coaches, players, administrators, sports historians and media members. After all, first-hand accounts are often the most riveting and insightful.

Football remains our nation's most popular sport, and the appeal of this book is far-ranging. In addition to the alumni and local enthusiasts, many people who never attended NIU will have an interest in discovering or reliving the merits of this fine football program. With the book centering on players and coaches over the past seven decades of football history, readers will find something to enjoy.

The Internet age has made many things easier. An NIU alum now living in California can listen to the beloved Huskies online. A fan from North Carolina can follow the Huskies via the NIU website year round. A proud graduate can turn the volume up when Michael Turner utters "Northern Illinois" during the player introductions of a "Sunday Night Football" telecast. No longer do you have to purchase a media guide; it's available free in downloadable form. Huskie wear can be purchased with relative ease from a home computer.

So, what qualifies me to write this book (a question more than a few people asked along the way)? Well, for starters, I competed in a bowling tournament at NIU as an eighth grader. I have relatives and friends who went to NIU, and I've been in "local establishments" in DeKalb.

Seriously though, I attended graduate school at NIU in the 1990s. At the same time, Jeff Strohm—a good friend of mine from undergraduate days—was a Huskie men's assistant basketball coach. I spent many a day and night hanging out with Jeff around the NIU athletic facilities. We often went to football games together.

I've seen the likes of LeShon Johnson, Michael Turner, P.J. Fleck, Garrett Wolfe, Larry English, Chad Spann and Chandler Harnish play on a regular basis. I was in the stadium when the Huskies grabbed national headlines by shocking Maryland on that glorious Thursday night. I was there when Wolfe ran wild against Western Michigan on the day before Thanksgiving three years later.

I remember the junior college transfer years under Charlie Sadler, the early struggles as Joe Novak rebuilt the NIU program and the hirings of Jerry Kill and Dave Doeren.

I have taught language arts and social studies for nearly a quarter century. Currently, I teach in Naperville District 204. On the side, I have written feature stories for the likes of *The Aurora Beacon-News, Charleston Times-Courier, Lincoln Courier,* profootball researchers.org and collegehockeynews.com. In addition, I am writing a book about Eastern Illinois University football.

The idea for "Northern Illinois Huskies Football" has always been floating around inside my head. I finally took the time to let it work its way out.

True, I couldn't include everyone I wanted for the book. So, when you say, "Hey, where is so-and-so?!" know that I made attempts. For example, I got in touch with former Huskie

Hollis Thomas on the phone one Sunday afternoon. "Call me back tomorrow," Thomas said. "I'm watching the NBA playoffs with some friends." After three unsuccessful follow-up calls, I surmised that Hollis Thomas had no interest in my potential book. Sometimes the game plan works to perfection. More often than not, it has to be altered. And while Erin Andrews wasn't on hand to ask me about halftime adjustments, know that there were plenty along the way.

I was able to interview many of the individuals in the book. If a chapter ends with the Four Down Territory sidebar, know that I was able to interview that particular coach or player and that it is their words that supply the information. Some gave short responses; others rambled.

This book's purpose is to bring together, for the first time, a collection of NIU football lore. If you're a graduate, you'll enjoy reading about your alma mater. If you're a fan, there's plenty here for you as well.

Thank you for taking the time to read this book. I truly appreciate it, and I hope that the journey through the NIU Huskies' history you are about to embark upon will be as much fun for you to read as it was for me to research and write.

A BRIEF HISTORY OF NORTHERN ILLINOIS HUSKIE FOOTBALL

Northern Illinois University fielded its first football team in 1899. That inaugural team (nicknamed the Profs) was led by Coach John L. Keith, who also was both a player and a professor of pedagogy (education). Keith had been a part of the game as a graduate student at Harvard.

Northern Illinois State Normal School (NISNS) then had only 25 male students enrolled. Thus, "football was the most difficult (sport to start) . . . and only with Professor Keith as one of the players were they able to field a team," wrote Earl W. Hayter in his book "Education in Transition—The History of Northern Illinois University."

"The football season was half gone when the idea occurred to that ingenious man, Mr. Keith, that the NISNS might get up and support a team," "The Norther" yearbook reported in the spring of 1900.

Keith, listed at 5 foot 9 and 136 pounds, became the team's quarterback. The first victory in the program's history came on November 10, 1899, when NISNS defeated DeKalb High School 16-0.

Two years later, Keith's team registered its first intercollegiate victory. On November 2, 1901, Northern Illinois shut out North Central College of Naperville 10-0. James I. Frederick, listed as the starting left tackle, ran for a 75-yard touchdown. Halfback Sanford Givens scored the other touchdown. In that era, touchdowns were only worth five points when

the point-after kick was missed. Northern Illinois finished that season with a 6-1 record.

In 1902 Keith's team declared itself the "Champion Normal Team of the State" by virtue of a 10-0 victory over Eastern Illinois and a 5-1-1 record on the season. "The Norther" called it "defending The Castle," a reference to Altgeld Hall, the original campus building. (Keith went on to coach football and basketball at Illinois State Normal School in 1907.)

In 1903 NISNS moved to its home for the next 60 football seasons—the rustic 400-seat Glidden Field was on East campus next to the Kishwaukee River, where the Art and Music buildings are presently located.

Willard W. Wirtz took over the football program in 1910. He posted a 33-17-1 record through the 1916 season. His son, also Willard W., would later serve as the secretary of labor in John F. Kennedy's administration.

The Northern Illinois program continued playing an independent schedule through the 1919 season before joining the Illinois Intercollegiate Athletic Conference. During the 1920s, the NIU athletic teams were often referred to as the "Cardinals."

NIU briefly left the conference in 1925, but returned to the IIAC (Illinois Intercollegiate Athletic Conference) in 1928. NIU struggled through its first winless season in 1928.

However, the team bounced back the following year under new head coach George "Chick" Evans. The Huskies recorded a 6-1-1 record. A

The 1900 NISNS football team practices northeast of what is now called Altgeld Hall. At that time, it was the only building on campus and bore no name. This photo originally appeared in the 1901 Norther yearbook. (Regional History Center)

year later, Evans' team again produced a winning record. By 1938, NIU won its first IIAC title. During this time, the team was referred to as "Evansmen" after their coach. The Huskie mascot was officially introduced in 1940.

Still under Evans' leadership, NIU captured three more championships in 1944, '46 and '51.

During the 1930s, NIU welcomed its first two African-American student-athletes, Elzie Cooper (1933–1936) of Rochelle and Chet Davis (1935–1939) of Aurora. Davis was known for his elusive running style and described as "spectacular" and "dazzling" in football. "In Chet Davis," reported the NIU student newspaper, "the team has a scoring threat from any spot on the field."

Davis led the track team in scoring (113 1/4 points) on the Little 19 Conference outdoor team champions (1939), plus captured Little 19 outdoor individual titles in the high jump (1936) and 100-yard dash (1938). He played on Little 19 Conference team champions in

three sports—football, basketball and track.

The Huskies made their first bowl game appearances in 1946 and '47. First, NIU played in the Turkey Bowl and followed that with a berth in the Hoosier Bowl.

In 1950, the conference added Central Michigan and Eastern Michigan and officially became the Interstate Intercollegiate Athletic Conference.

While the conference changed, NIU's success did not. With quarterback Bob Heimerdinger leading the NCAA College Division in total offense in 1950 and '51, NIU was a high-flying team to watch. Heimerdinger's talented arm helped the Huskies to an unbeaten 1951 season as NIU won the conference championship and earned yet another bowl invitation. Heimerdinger's No. 12 was the first jersey retired by the university.

Meanwhile, former Huskie defensive end Larry Brink was making a name for himself in the National Football League. Brink, who played at NIU from 1945 to 1947 and was the first Huskie ever selected in the NFL Draft, was a three-time All-Pro selection with the Los Angeles Rams in the early 1950s.

After a brief dry spell in the latter part of the 1950s, the fortunes of NIU football again turned when Howard Fletcher was hired as head coach.

Fletcher led the Huskies to three conference championships, including an Associated Press College Division national championship in 1963. Fletcher installed a pass-oriented offense that showcased the throwing skills of gifted quarterback George Bork.

Northern left the IIAC in 1966 and became an independent. In 1969, NIU joined Idaho, Pacific and San Diego State in the University Division of the NCAA. At the time, NIU was only the third Division IA institution in the state and one of only 118 nationwide.

In its fourth year of major college football, NIU finished with a 7-4 record under head coach Jerry Ippoliti. The Huskies won four of their final games that season, including a 28-7 thrashing of defending Mid-American Conference champion Kent State.

NIU joined the MAC (Mid-American Conference) in 1973, the year running back Mark Kellar led the nation in rushing with 1,702 yards.

Wide receiver Dave Petzke rewrote the NIU record book in 1978. Petzke led the NCAA with a school and MAC record 91 receptions. That total was 29 catches better than the runner-up.

The Huskies won their first MAC title in 1983 under the guidance of head coach Bill Mallory. NIU then claimed its first major bowl victory by defeating Cal State-Fullerton in the California Bowl to cap that landmark season.

NIU left the MAC in 1986. Competing again as an independent from 1987 to 1992, the Huskies turned to former Oklahoma assistant coach Jerry Pettibone. Having cut his teeth on wishbone football, Pettibone brought the run-oriented offense to DeKalb.

The offense proved to be successful. Pettibone's 1989 NIU team won nine games. Led by elusive quarterback Stacey Robinson, the Huskies racked up 733 yards in a 73-18 blowout of nationally rated Fresno State in 1990.

The Huskies were members of the Big West Conference from 1993 to 1995. Running back LeShon Johnson was the star of that era. In 1993, Johnson led the nation in rushing and finished sixth in the Heisman Trophy balloting. Though he played just two years as a Huskie, Johnson ran for an incredible 3,314 yards.

NIU returned to independent status in 1996 before being readmitted into the MAC in 1997.

Quarterback/halfback Chet Davis (15) starred for the Huskies during the 1930s. Davis also excelled in basketball and track. He was inducted into the Huskie Hall of Fame in 1987.

Football
Mineral Water Bowl

Game

With The Theme — CHRISTIAN ATHLETES

Roosevelt Field

Excelsior Springs, Mo.

Southwest Mo. State

Springfield, Mo.

VS

Northern Ill. University

DeKalb, Illinois

George Bork

25c

Game Time 2:00 p. m.

SATURDAY, NOVEMBER 30, 1963

NCAA Sanctioned

This poster, featuring NIU quarterback George Bork, promotes the 1963 NCAA College Division national championship.

Joe Novak, the defensive coordinator under Mallory in 1983, returned to DeKalb as the NIU head coach in 1996. Novak faced the task of rebuilding a struggling Huskie program. Novak also struggled, winning just three games his first three seasons.

However, the NIU administration stuck with Novak, who followed many of the ideals he had learned under Mallory. In 1999, the Huskies won five games. In 2000, NIU started a string of seven consecutive winning seasons.

After narrowly missing a spot in the MAC championship game in 2002, Novak's Huskies grabbed national attention in 2003. With a roster that included future pro players Michael Turner, Randee Drew, Doug Free and P.J. Fleck, NIU shocked nationally ranked Maryland to open the season. The Huskies later registered victories over Alabama and Iowa State. NIU was ranked No. 10 nationally when the first Bowl Championship Series rankings came out.

Despite finishing the year with a 10-2 record, NIU was not invited to a bowl game.

Novak's Huskies did receive bowl bids in 2004 and 2006. The '04 team took home the Silicon Valley Classic trophy behind the running of Garrett Wolfe and the passing of Josh Haldi.

The Joe Novak era ended when the head coach retired following the 2007 season. NIU won 63 games under Novak.

NIU then hired Jerry Kill, the highly successful head coach at Southern Illinois University, to succeed Novak. In 2009, Kill's Huskies defeated Purdue in West Lafayette and appeared in their second consecutive bowl game. A year later, NIU knocked off its second straight Big Ten opponent with a 34-23 victory at Minnesota.

Kill's 2010 Huskies won the MAC West title and earned a berth in the conference championship game. However, shortly after NIU's loss to Miami in the MAC title game, Kill announced he had accepted the head coaching job at the University of Minnesota, a school his Huskies had defeated earlier in the fall.

Assistant coach Tom Matukewicz took over the NIU helm and guided the Huskies to a 40-17 rout over Fresno State in the Humanitarian Bowl in Boise, Idaho.

Former University of Wisconsin defensive coordinator Dave Doeren was hired as the Huskies' head coach following Kill's departure. Doeren posted a 23-4 record, won two MAC titles and earned two bowl appearances in his time in DeKalb. Doeren's 2012 team earned the first-ever BCS bowl berth by a MAC school.

N THE EARLY YEARS

(1899–WORLD WAR II)

IIAC

There was a time when NIU faced the other three Illinois directional schools and Illinois State in conference play. The league was known for many years as the Illinois Intercollegiate Athletic Conference (IIAC).

"It was great," said Bob Heimerdinger, NIU quarterback and the conference's 1951 Most Valuable Player. "It was made up of the people you knew from high school, and you saw them every year."

Heimerdinger added that the IIAC's strength was the men who ran it.

"They were the whole ball of wax. In those days those men were everything. They coached the sports, and they ran the PE departments."

Those men included Heimerdinger's coach, George "Chick" Evans. Others were Maynard "Pat" O'Brien of Eastern, Ray "Rock" Hanson and Vince DiFrancesca of Western, and Ed Struck of ISU. Southern was coached by Glenn "Abe" Martin (1939–1949), Bill Waller (1950–1951) and William O'Brien (1952–1954).

"It was just those five state schools when I played," said 1947 conference MVP Red Miller of Western. Miller later coached the Denver Broncos in Super Bowl XII.

"Northern and Southern were the biggest schools, ISU was in the middle and Western and Eastern stayed about the same size," said Lou Stivers, captain of Eastern's 1948 conference champions.

"(The IIAC) was every bit as tough as the Mid-American Conference," said Jack Pheanis, who played with Heimerdinger and later coached under both Evans and Howard Fletcher at NIU. "The Mid-American was better at publicizing themselves. They also had a number of people on all the (NCAA) committees."

One of the attractions of the IIAC was its wide-open play.

"The Big Ten was known for its running game," said Pheanis, who began his playing career at the University of Illinois. "The IIAC was a passing league."

Jack Dean played halfback for NIU's 1963 national championship team and later served as the head coach at Eastern.

"(The IIAC) was special because people don't realize how many great players came out of that league," Dean said. "You look at Western. They had guys like (future AFL star) Booker Edgerson and (first-round NFL Draft pick) Leroy Jackson. You went down to Southern and they were always loaded.

"Eastern Michigan had Hayes Jones, who was an Olympic hurdler (who won gold in the 110-meter hurdles in the 1964 Games). Central Michigan was just so tough in football."

When asked just how strong the IIAC was, Dean used an analogy: "I consider it very close to what the Mid-American Conference is today."

According to a 1970 article in *The NCAA News,* the league claimed most of the Illinois institutions of higher education. It was nicknamed the "Little Nineteen," though in 1928 it had a membership of 23 schools.

Former Illinois State track coach Joe Cogdal noted that the IIAC had roots dating back to the 1870s, when a number of schools banded together for oratorical contests. Cogdal was associated with the conference for 43 of its 62 years of existence.

The first intercollegiate football game was played in 1881 between ISU and Knox College. By 1894 a football association was established.

The conference was officially formed in April 1908 with eight charter members—Illinois State, Illinois Wesleyan, Bradley, Millikin, Monmouth, Knox, Lombard College and Illinois College.

The first track meet was held on May 22, 1908. The league expanded rapidly. Eastern and Western joined in 1912 and 1915, respectively.

In 1920, the name "Illinois Intercollegiate Athletic Conference" was adopted. Conference membership reached a peak of 23 schools in

1928 when virtually all of the small colleges of Illinois were included.

Private schools withdrew during the 1930s, until in 1942 only the five state schools remained.

In 1950, the league became the "Interstate Intercollegiate Athletic Conference" when Central Michigan and Eastern Michigan joined, upping membership to seven schools.

In 1961, Eastern Michigan and Southern Illinois withdrew. Shortly thereafter, NIU began to consider the idea.

"We are experiencing growing pains all right," said Evans, the NIU athletic director, in a 1963 *Sports Illustrated* story. "We're expanding so fast that we are getting too big for the rest of our conference. We like them, but they might not like us pretty soon. We have to decide what our future policy is going to be."

Three years later, in 1966, Evans' words became fact as NIU withdrew from the IIAC.

By decade's end, the IIAC was no more. The conference officially disbanded at the end of the 1969–1970 academic year.

While Northern became a Division IA football program in 1969, the rest of the state schools played at the Division II and then I-AA (now called the Football Championship Subdivision) levels.

ILLINOIS INTERCOLLEGIATE ATHLETIC CONFERENCE FOOTBALL CHAMPIONS

1913—Eastern Illinois
1914—Eastern Illinois, Millikin
1915—Illinois College
1916—Millikin
1917—Lombard
1918—No Champion
1919—Unknown
1920—Unknown
1921—Unknown
1922—Unknown
1923—Unknown
1924—Bradley
1925—Bradley, Monmouth
1926—Bradley, Monmouth
1927—Bradley
1928—Eastern Illinois, Millikin
1929—Knox, Lombard
1930—Millikin
1931—Monmouth
1932—Illinois Wesleyan, McKendree
1933—Illinois Wesleyan
1934—Augustana, Millikin
1935—Millikin, Monmouth
1936—Illinois Wesleyan, St. Viator
1937—Bradley, Illinois College, Illinois State
1938—Northern Illinois
1939—Illinois State, Western Illinois
1940—Carthage (Wisc.), Illinois State
1941—Northern Illinois, Illinois State
1942—Western
1943—No Champion
1944—Northern Illinois
1945—Illinois State
1946—Northern Illinois
1947—Southern Illinois
1948—Eastern Illinois
1949—Western Illinois

INTERSTATE INTERCOLLEGIATE ATHLETIC CONFERENCE FOOTBALL CHAMPIONS

1950—Illinois State
1951—Northern Illinois
1952—Central Michigan
1953—Central Michigan
1954—Central Michigan, Eastern Michigan
1955—Central Michigan, Eastern Michigan
1956—Central Michigan
1957—Eastern Michigan
1958—Western Illinois
1959—Western Illinois
1960—Southern Illinois
1961—Southern Illinois

1962—Central Michigan
1963—Northern Illinois
1964—Northern Illinois, Western Illinois
1965—Northern Illinois
1966—Central Michigan
1967—Central Michigan, Illinois State
1968—Central Michigan, Illinois State
1969—Western Illinois

NIU HUSKIES NAMED IIAC PLAYER OF THE YEAR

1935—Reino Nori, HB
1938—Tego Larsen, G
1946—Duane Cunz, G
1950—Bob Heimerdinger, QB
1959—Lew Flinn, QB
1962—George Bork, QB
1963—George Bork, QB
1964—Jack Dean, HB

REINO NORI, LARRY BRINK, OTHER EARLY HUSKIE PROS

While his glory days came in the 1930s, Reino Nori remains one of the greatest players in NIU football history.

According to a story on the NIU Web site by former sports information director Mike Korcek, Nori was "the best Northern Illinois University football player at the midpoint of the program's history. The diminutive 5-foot-6, 155-pounder was the Huskies' No. 1 athlete during the 1899–1949 era. Hands down."

Korcek's story noted, "The legacy of 'The Phantom Finn'—the nickname used by local newspapers in his day—will always stand the test of time. Nori was the only athlete in Northern Illinois history to earn 17 varsity letters in five sports."

Nori, who passed away in 1988, lettered one year in wrestling and four years in football, basketball, baseball and track. He was an all-conference guard in basketball in 1935–1936 and an all-conference broad jump champion in 1934. A DeKalb native, Nori played third base on the baseball team and ran back and forth between the diamond and the track.

"We heard stories about how he would run at a track meet and then go play baseball all in the same day," said former NIU athletic director Bob Brigham in a 1988 *Northern Star* story by Mike Morris.

Nori was the first Huskie, or "Fighting Prof" as they were called in the 1930s, to play in the National Football League.

"Reino was tiny," Brigham told Morris. "He was not a big guy. You would look at Reino and you'd never believe he could ever play professional football—especially quarterback."

In college, Nori had been used mainly as a halfback, but his versatility and skills allowed NIU head coach George "Chick" Evans to use his star at many positions.

"He was fast, and he could do everything," said Brigham, who was coached by both Evans and Nori, an NIU assistant following his pro football days.

"He could pass, punt—he could do it all. He was just a gifted athlete."

Nori's 99-yard touchdown run against Wisconsin-Whitewater on November 17, 1934, still stands atop the NIU record book.

The play occurred with less than a minute and a half left in the game with Northern clinging to a 7-0 lead. Whitewater had pinned "the DeKalb Teachers" down on their own one-yard line with a punt.

According to a story in the November 18, 1934 edition of the *DeKalb Daily Chronicle,* Nori spotted a hole in the middle of the Whitewater line.

"(Nori) shifted his hips, ducked along the sideline and evaded the five would-be tacklers, hitting the open field at about the 50-yard line and outdistancing all the Whitewater men to the goal," read the newspaper's account.

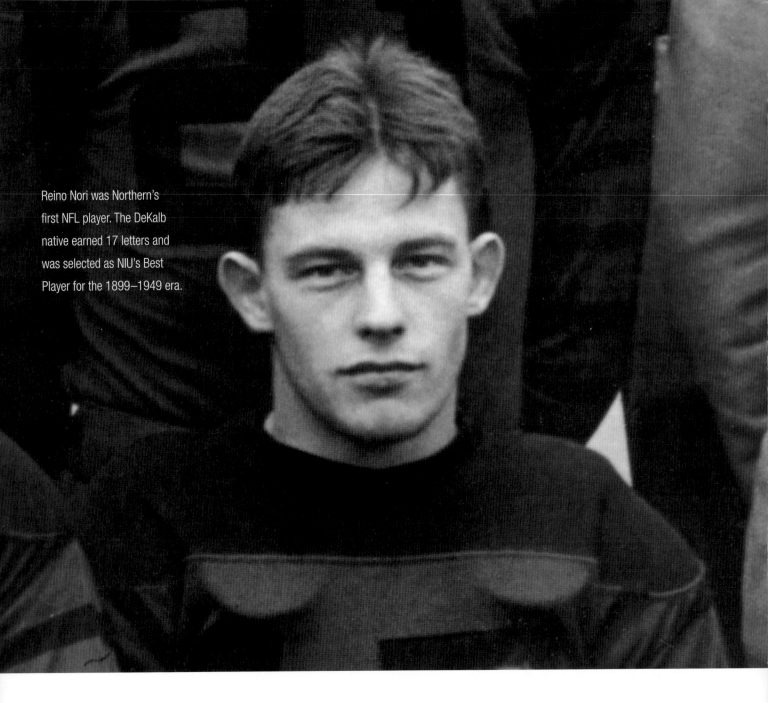

Reino Nori was Northern's first NFL player. The DeKalb native earned 17 letters and was selected as NIU's Best Player for the 1899–1949 era.

Nori's own account was included in "The Best of the First Century" of the 2004 NIU Media Guide. The play was chosen as the greatest in Huskie history.

"A punt went dead on our one," Nori said. "We planned to try to get the ball out to about the four or five so we could get off a kick. Well, a hole opened up in the middle and before I knew it I was out to the 30 and I look around and that was all there was to it."

Nori was renowned for his speed and determined running. In a dual track meet against the University of Chicago, he tied for first place in the long jump with Jay Berwanger, the first winner of the Heisman Trophy. Nori also competed against famed Olympic gold medalist Jesse Owens of Ohio State University.

"(That is) indicative of the national type of athlete he was," Korcek said of Nori. "Think of the scope. A Little 19 athlete vs. Big Ten athletes."

Nori was the school's first Little 19 Conference Player of the Year in football. His name still ranks on the leader boards for some NIU offensive categories.

Nori was also the first Northern Illinois

State Teachers College player to appear in the *Chicago Tribune*'s famed College All-Star Game at Soldier Field.

Detroit Lions' head coach Potsy Clark came to DeKalb to see Nori firsthand. The two met on the cinder track where Clark asked, "Son, do you want to play professional football?"

According to the book "Charlie Sanders's Tales from the Detroit Lions" by Charlie Sanders and Larry Paladino, Clark was quite high on Nori in training camp.

"Nori is faster than Ernie Caddel," Clark was quoted in a story by Bob Murphy of the *Detroit Times* in 1936. "He looks to be one of the most glittering Lion recruits in camp."

Clark was so smitten with Nori that he traded for the back the following year when the former Lions coach took over the Brooklyn Dodgers. Clark was impressed with Nori's running, passing, kicking and blocking.

Clark said, "He has everything I wish for in a quarterback. He is an alert field general, spots even the slightest weaknesses in the enemy defense, and then knows exactly what to do about it. He is one of the fastest men on our squad, and he is hard to catch in the broken field."

According to his book "Strong Arm Tactics: A History and Statistical Analysis of the Professional Quarterback," Rutgers-based sports historian John Maxymuk lists Nori as the leader in comeback victories for the 1937 NFL season.

In all, Nori played three NFL seasons for the Lions (1936), Dodgers (1937) and Chicago Bears (1938). He later played with Camp Grant, a military team that regularly played both college and military opponents during World War II.

Nori later served as an assistant coach under Evans during the 1940s.

* * * * *

While the 1940s brought war to America, it also brought other Northern stars into the NFL. NIU sent Charlie Behan and Toimi Jarvi onto pro rosters. Behan caught four passes for 63 yards in 1942 as a Detroit Lion. Jarvi played the 1944 and '45 seasons with the Philadelphia Eagles and the Pittsburgh Steelers respectively.

* * * * *

Larry Brink, like Reino Nori, was a charter member of the Huskie Hall of Fame in 1978. Brink played football at NIU from 1945 to 1947. He earned First Team All-IIAC recognition as an end his senior season.

Brink made Huskie history by becoming the first NIU player drafted by an NFL team. The Los Angeles Rams selected him in the 17th round of the 1948 draft. Brink was the 150th overall pick.

Brink, listed at 6 foot 5 and 236 pounds, became a three-time All-Pro selection with the Rams in the early 1950s.

* * * * *

Many former Huskies found roster spaces in the world of minor league football.

"In the 1960s, the United Football League, the Pro Football League of America and the Continental Football League all had teams representing Chicago, and the PFLA also had other teams in the general vicinity," said minor league football historian and author Bob Gill. "Dozens of players from Eastern, Western, Southern and Northern Illinois played for those teams."

According to Gill, those former NIU players included Roland Beckham, Abe Booker, George Bork, Jim Caldwell, Ron Christian, Derril Corbett, Jack Dean, Jim Gilbert, Mike Maehl, Richard Marks, Dave Mulderink, Alex Pikuza, Hugh Rohrschneider, Bob Stark and Roger Stark.

Rohrschneider led the Atlantic Coast League in receiving in 1964.

"I'm sure many more players from Illinois

Larry Brink, who played at NIU from 1945 to 1947, was the first Huskie ever selected in the NFL draft. Brink became a three-time All-Pro selection with the Los Angeles Rams in the early 1950s.

schools played in the Central States League (successor to the Tri-States League, which changed its name in about 1962), since its teams were concentrated around the Great Lakes, but I don't have rosters for that league. It was a lower level, with teams in smaller towns and players making less money, but was still interesting—something like the Carolina League in baseball today. In that analogy, the Continental League or the Atlantic Coast League would be the equivalent of the International League or the Pacific Coast League," said Gill, author of two books on minor league and independent football.

GEORGE "CHICK" EVANS

George "Chick" Evans' name is one of the most recognizable in the history of Northern Illinois University athletics.

While 1929 is remembered by many as the year of the stock market crash that plunged America into the Great Depression, it marks the time when Evans arrived at NIU.

Evans took over the NIU program as its football coach, a position he would hold for the next 26 years.

When he finally stepped down in 1954, Evans left with more victories than any other head coach in NIU football history. He posted a 131-70-20 record. In addition, Evans' teams won the Illinois Intercollegiate Athletic Conference championship five times (1938, 1941, 1944, 1946 and 1951).

"He was well ahead of his time. He believed in the forward pass," said Jack Pheanis, who played for and coached with Evans.

His '51 team went 9-0-0 and received a bid from the Tangerine Bowl. The Huskies were led by Little All-America quarterback Bob Heimerdinger and split end Fran Cahill. Cahill was the school's second National Football League draft pick. He was taken by the New York Giants in the 19th round of the 1952 draft.

The '51 Huskies were highlighted by seven first team All-IIAC players. In addition to Cahill being drafted, two others were signed as NFL free agents.

NIU capped its perfect regular season with a thrilling 27-26 comeback victory at Nebraska-Omaha.

However, the Huskies could not accept their Tangerine Bowl bid. NIU's governing body, the State Teachers College Board, turned down the bid because it would have extended the season seven weeks.

Though it seems hard to believe in this day and age, Heimerdinger and a few of his teammates actually lived under the same roof as Evans.

"I had just been discharged from the Navy and was late coming to Northern," Heimerdinger explained. "I had no arrangements for housing. Chick took me to his house and I wound up living upstairs with three or four other fellas.

"There wasn't much room, but we each had a bed. There was a shower in the basement. It was very convenient to campus as most things were back then."

Heimerdinger recalled paying $3.75 per week for the housing.

"Once in awhile, usually during the off-season, the door downstairs would open up and Chick would yell up, 'Pancakes in five minutes!' I lived there for three years."

Mike Korcek, who has been around NIU athletics for more than 40 years, interviewed Evans as a college sophomore.

"Chick was a strong, bold personality, and had the vision to lead us to the University Division in football (in 1969 after his retirement) and affiliation with the Mid-American Conference (in 1973). We (NIU) were starting to play the MAC schools in most of our sports in my student days and Evans told me that the Mid-Am was the route for us to go and that you could not 'manufacture' a better league of

George "Chick" Evans is one of the most recognizable names in the history of NIU athletics.

similar programs and the MAC was nationally recognized at that level," Korcek said.

Like Heimerdinger, Pheanis viewed Evans as much more than just his coach or an administrator.

"He was just like a father to me," said Pheanis. "I used to babysit his sons, Bob and George. I visited him in San Diego before he died.

"Chick Evans was a wonderful, wonderful man."

BOB BRIGHAM

Robert J. Brigham spent a half century involved in Northern Illinois University athletics.

A native of Marion and a graduate of Chicago Bowen High School, Brigham began his studies at NIU in 1946 after serving in the United States Navy during World War II.

According to former NIU sports information director Mike Korcek, Brigham lettered three times in football and became the fullback as a member of the famed "Pony Backfield." He set the school's single-game, single-season and career rushing records during his playing days.

During his record-setting 242-yard performance against Washburn in 1948, Brigham injured his knee. Not only did Brigham stay in that game, Korcek noted, but he finished out the rest of that season with the injury. This was remarkable, since it was decades before arthroscopic surgery.

In addition to football, Brigham also earned a varsity letter as a wrestler.

After graduating from NIU in 1950, Brigham landed a coaching and teaching position at downstate Tuscola High School. He returned to DeKalb in 1955 as an NIU assistant football coach. A year later, Brigham took the reins of the Huskie wrestling team. His program would produce five national individual champions and 11 All-Americans. Brigham posted an 82-45-6 record in dual meets.

Brigham was also an assistant for legend-

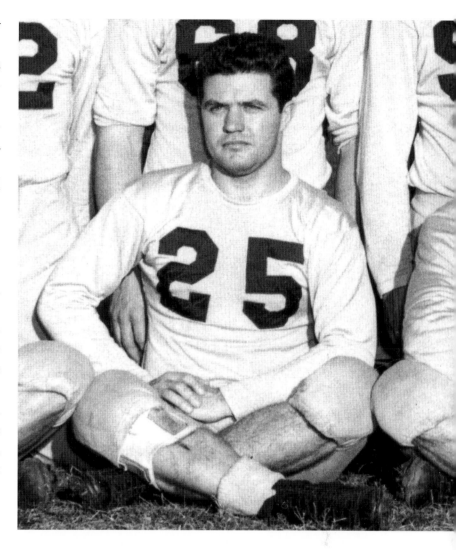

ary football head coach Howard Fletcher during the national championship season of 1963.

In September 1968, Brigham was named NIU athletic director and physical education department chair. He succeeded NIU legend George "Chick" Evans in those capacities.

Under Brigham, the NIU football program elevated to what the NCAA then called "University Division" status in 1969. This level is the equivalent of today's Division I-A level.

In addition, Brigham upgraded the Huskies' schedule. NIU played the likes of Wisconsin, Northwestern, Boston College, West Virginia, Nebraska, Miami, Minnesota, Kansas State and Iowa during his tenure.

"Bob convinced Wisconsin athletic director

Bob Brigham spent a half century involved in NIU athletics. The playing surface at Huskie Stadium bears his name.

Elroy Hirsch to play the Huskies in the early 1970s," Korcek said. "That was a major moment for Northern Illinois football, acceptance by the Big Ten in that early Division I era."

Perhaps more importantly, the Huskies joined the Mid-American Conference on his watch.

Bud Nangle, another NIU Hall of Famer and former sports information director, said, "While Chick opened the door, so to speak, Bob is the one who took the program through it."

Under Brigham's leadership, NIU installed the state's first major college Astroturf field at Huskie Stadium in 1969. The Huskie program received NCAA tournament bids in baseball, men's soccer, men's basketball, men's golf and men's gymnastics. NIU also won the MAC football title and the California Bowl in 1983.

In 1987, Brigham took control of the university's compliance responsibilities as a special assistant to the president until his retirement at age 77 in 2001.

Brigham was inducted into the NIU Physical Education Hall of Fame and the NIU Athletic Hall of Fame. In 1991, he received the F.R. "Bud" Geigle Outstanding Service Award from the NIU Foundation.

Before the Huskies' 2003 season opener, the playing surface at Huskie Stadium was named in his honor.

"It is a natural and an overdue tribute to Dr. Bob," said then-NIU athletic director Cary Groth. "I cannot think of a more loyal and devoted Northern Illinois alum. He served his alma mater with distinction, dignity, integrity, and perseverance. You really cannot say enough about his many contributions to NIU intercollegiate athletics and this institution. We all felt this was the most appropriate way of recognition."

NIU ENROLLMENT—217 (1900)

TUITION—No tuition was charged

AVERAGE COST FOR ROOM & BOARD—$3.25 per week

NIU PRESIDENT—John Williston Cook (1899–1919)

CONFERENCE—Independent

NEWS OF THE DECADE—President William McKinley assassinated; Panama Canal Treaty signed; Theodore Roosevelt elected; earthquake and fires devastate San Francisco; one million immigrants pass through Ellis Island; Matthew Henson and Robert Peary reach North Pole

NOTABLE MOVIES OF THE DECADE—"The Great Train Robbery," "The Gibson Goddess," first newsreels

NOTABLE BOOKS OF THE DECADE—"The Wonderful Wizard of Oz," "The Tale of Peter Rabbit," "The Hound of the Baskervilles," "The Call of the Wild," "The Jungle," "A Room with a View"

NOTABLE MUSICAL ACTS OF THE DECADE—Sergei Rachmaninoff, Enrico Caruso, Isadora Duncan, Richard Strauss, Sergei Diaghilev's "Les Ballets Russes"

NIU FOOTBALL BY THE DECADE: 1910s

NIU ENROLLMENT—359 (1910)

TUITION—No tuition was charged

AVERAGE COST FOR ROOM & BOARD—$4.50 to $4.75 per week

NIU PRESIDENT—John Williston Cook (1899–1919)

CONFERENCE—Independent

NEWS OF THE DECADE—U.S. passes Mann Act; Titanic sinks; federal income tax authorized by 16th Amendment; Pancho Villa eludes General John J. Pershing; World War I; worldwide flu epidemic; Prohibition ratified

NOTABLE MOVIES OF THE DECADE—"Keystone Kops," "The Squaw Man," "The Birth of a Nation," "The Tramp," "The Little Princess"

NOTABLE BOOKS OF THE DECADE—"The Innocence of Father Brown," "Riders of the Purple Sage," "O Pioneers!," "My Antonia," "Tarzan of the Apes," "Of Human Bondage," "Spoon River Anthology," "Chicago Poems"

NOTABLE MUSICAL ACTS OF THE DECADE—Irving Berlin, W.C. Handy, Scott Joplin, George M. Cohan, George Gershwin, Jerome Kern

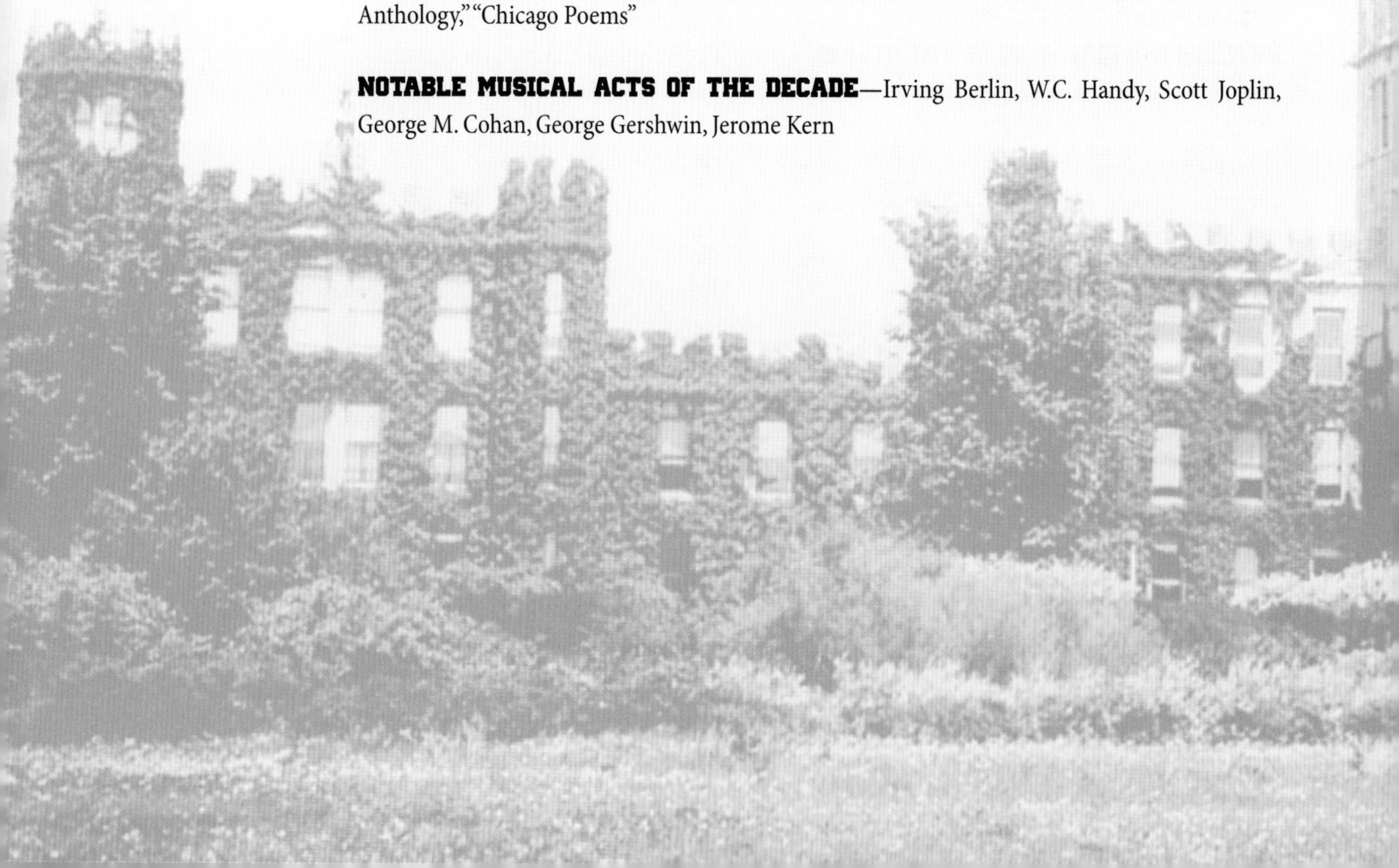

NIU FOOTBALL BY THE DECADE: 1920s

NIU ENROLLMENT—335 (1920)

TUITION—No tuition was charged

AVERAGE COST FOR ROOM & BOARD—$6.50 per week at Williston Hall (1920)

NIU PRESIDENT—James Stanley Brown (1919–1927); Joseph Clifton Brown (1927–1929)

CONFERENCE—Illinois Intercollegiate Athletic Conference (1920–1924); Independent (1925–1927); Illinois Intercollegiate Athletic Conference (1928–1949)

NEWS OF THE DECADE—Red scare breaks out; Sacco and Vanzetti executed; Ku Klux Klan spreads terror; Teapot Dome Scandal rocks government; nation's eyes on Scopes monkey and Fatty Arbuckle trials; Charles Lindbergh flies solo; Al Capone reigns; stock market crash

NOTABLE MOVIES OF THE DECADE—"The Jazz Singer," Harold Lloyd and Charlie Chaplin comedies, Tom Mix westerns, "The Mark of Zorro," "The Phantom of the Opera," "The Sheik," "The Virginian"

NOTABLE BOOKS OF THE DECADE—"The Great Gatsby," "The Sun Also Rises," "All Quiet on the Western Front," "Babbitt," "The Sound and the Fury," "Lady Chatterley's Lover"

NOTABLE MUSICAL ACTS OF THE DECADE—Louis Armstrong, Irving Berlin, Duke Ellington, Bix Beiderbecke, Al Jolson, Bessie Smith, Rudy Vallee, Rodgers and Hart, Hoagy Carmichael, Fanny Brice, the Charleston

NIU FOOTBALL BY THE DECADE: 1930s

NIU ENROLLMENT—760 (1930)

TUITION—No tuition was charged

AVERAGE COST FOR ROOM & BOARD—$8.50 per week at Williston Hall (1930)

NIU PRESIDENT—Karl Langdon Adams (1929–1948)

CONFERENCE—Illinois Intercollegiate Athletic Conference (1928–1949)

NEWS OF THE DECADE—FDR pushes the New Deal; Adolf Hitler rises to power; Admiral Byrd explores; Amelia Earhart disappears; Jesse Owens grabs Olympic gold and glory; Prohibition ends

NOTABLE MOVIES OF THE DECADE—"Dracula," "King Kong," "The Hunchback of Notre Dame," "A Day at the Races," "The Mummy," "The Wizard of Oz," "Mutiny on the Bounty," "Mr. Smith Goes to Washington"

NOTABLE BOOKS OF THE DECADE—"The Good Earth," "Gone with the Wind," "How to Win Friends and Influence People," "Brave New World"

NOTABLE MUSICAL ACTS OF THE DECADE—Benny Goodman, Cole Porter, Duke Ellington, Bing Crosby, Glenn Miller, Ella Fitzgerald, Irving Berlin, George Gershwin, Johnny Mercer, Aaron Copland

NIU FOOTBALL BY THE DECADE: 1940s

NIU ENROLLMENT—1,173 (1940)

TUITION—No tuition was charged

AVERAGE COST FOR ROOM BOARD FEES & SUPPLIES $380 (1940)

NIU PRESIDENTS—Karl Langdon Adams (1929–1948); Leslie Arnold Holmes (1949–1967)

CONFERENCE—Illinois Intercollegiate Athletic Conference (1928–1949)

NEWS OF THE DECADE—Japan attacks Pearl Harbor; World War II fought; Israel established; Marshall Plan enacted; Berlin Blockade imposed; Iron Curtain goes up; Jackie Robinson breaks color barrier

NOTABLE MOVIES OF THE DECADE— "Citizen Kane," "Casablanca," "It's a Wonderful Life," "The Philadelphia Story," "The Maltese Falcon," "The Pride of the Yankees," "Notorious," "Oklahoma," "Miracle on 34th Street"

NOTABLE BOOKS OF THE DECADE—"The Naked and the Dead," "A Bell for Adano," "A Tree Grows in Brooklyn," "Native Son," "Nineteen Eighty-Four"

NOTABLE MUSICAL ACTS OF THE DECADE—Glenn Miller, Harry James, Frank Sinatra, Mel Torme, Duke Ellington, Nat King Cole, Ella Fizgerald, Count Basie, The Andrews Sisters, Woody Guthrie, Tommy Dorsey, Jimmy Dorsey, The Ink Spots, Bing Crosby, Billie Holiday, Artie Shaw

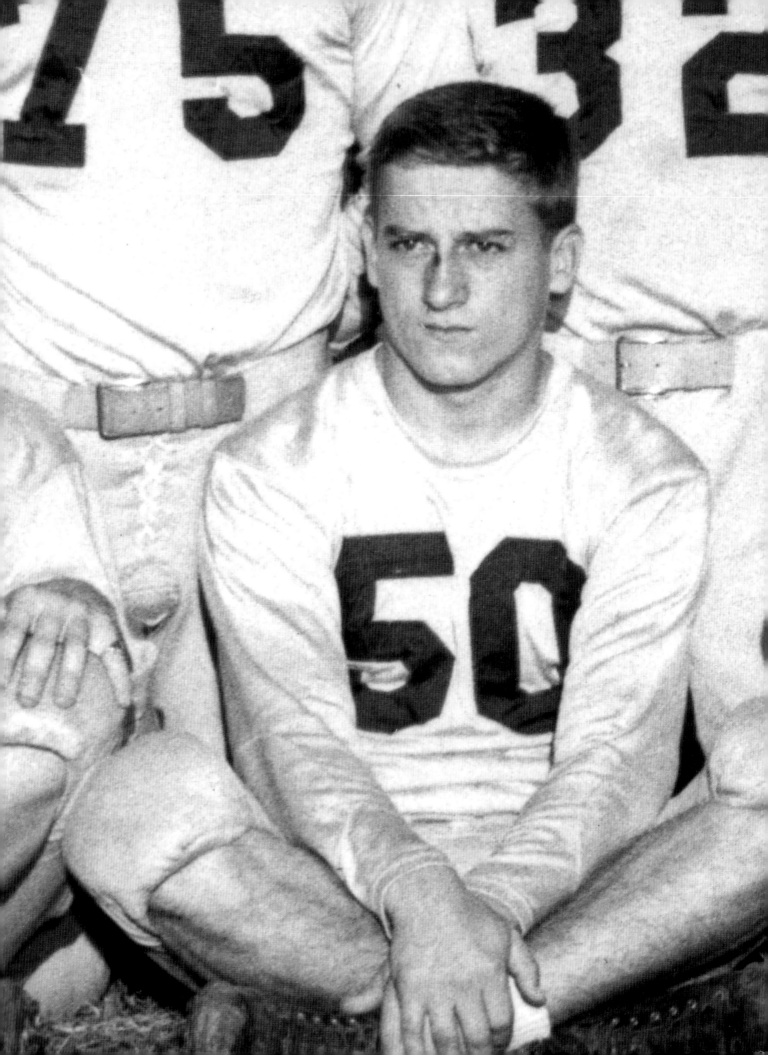

N THE 1950s

NIU FOOTBALL BY THE DECADE: 1950s

NIU ENROLLMENT—1,986 (1950)

AVERAGE COST FOR ROOM BOARD FEES AND SUPPLIES—$600–$750

NIU PRESIDENT—Leslie Arnold Holmes (1949–1967)

CONFERENCE—Illinois Intercollegiate Athletic Conference

NEWS OF THE DECADE—Cold War sets in; civil rights emerge; Sputnik launched; quiz show scandals rock nation

NOTABLE MOVIES OF THE DECADE— "Ben-Hur," "The Bridge on the River Kwai," "Singin' in the Rain," "From Here to Eternity," "Rebel Without a Cause," "Vertigo"

NOTABLE BOOKS OF THE DECADE—"The Catcher in the Rye," "On the Road," "Lord of the Flies," "Atlas Shrugged," "Naked Lunch," "The Power of Positive Thinking"

NOTABLE MUSICAL ACTS OF THE DECADE—Elvis Presley, Chuck Berry, Buddy Holly, Jerry Lee Lewis, Miles Davis, Fats Domino, Nat King Cole, John Coltrane, Frank Sinatra

BOB HEIMERDINGER

Huskie Illustrated, NIU's game day program, ranks Bob Heimerdinger at the top of the school's great post–World War II quarterbacks.

Known as the "Huskie Humdinger," the 5 foot 9, 160-pounder went down in NIU football history for a number of "firsts."

Heimerdinger became the school's first national statistical champion—winning the College Division total offense title in both 1950 (1,782 yards) and 1951 (1,775 yards). Following his senior season in which the Huskies went unbeaten, won the conference championship and earned a bowl bid, Heimerdinger's No. 12 was the first uniform retired by the university.

"It is a great honor," Heimerdinger said from his DeKalb home. "I'm very proud of that. It's something that will be there forever."

Yet, he was quick to point out it didn't happen alone.

"A million things and many people led to that number being honored," Heimerdinger said.

After starring at Riverside-Brookfield High School, Heimerdinger's path to NIU was made clear to him.

"Back in those days most of the recruiting was done by former Northern players and alums," he explained. "Well, my high school teacher and coach whose name was Barney Dudley saw me when I was home on leave from the Navy. He was from Earlville (southwest of DeKalb) and had played basketball at Northern. Anyway, he said, 'I'll take you to the school you'll go to when you get out of the Navy.'"

Thus, Heimerdinger enrolled at NIU.

"Back then, it was a teachers' college," he said. "It's amazing the way things have evolved. It's changed so much. We weren't even close to 3,000 for enrollment in those days."

Heimerdinger played under legendary head coach George "Chick" Evans and his staff.

"All the coaches were terrific," he said. "They were the program. They coached every sport in addition to their teaching responsibilities. I put those guys on a pedestal.

"Chick was pretty phenomenal. He had a winning record forever. Chick always looked at the pro game. He wanted to be like the pros."

Heimerdinger flourished in Evans' system. He topped the nation in passing yardage (1,710) and touchdowns (16) his senior season. He ran for a 78-yard score against Nebraska-Omaha in 1949. He also ranked ninth in the country with a 38.3 punting average.

Heimerdinger's senior season proved to be the perfect cap to his Huskie career.

"After our first game (a 20-7 victory over Wisconsin-Whitewater), Chick had a meeting in town with one of the local groups. I can't remember if it was the Kiwanis or Lions Club or whatever. Chick brought a couple of us players along and had us talk. I said this year is going to be different. We had over 100 yards in penalties that first game. I said we'd be giving it out rather than taking it."

Heimerdinger's words proved to be prophetic. NIU steamrolled through the season with a perfect 9-0-0 record and won the Interstate Intercollegiate Athletic Association title.

"Our defense was just incredible," he noted.

The offense wasn't bad either. Heimerdinger completed 103 of his 225 pass attempts for a national-best 1,710 yards. He earned First Team Little All-America honors. He was selected as the conference Player of the Year.

The most memorable play of the season came on November 17. Facing a crucial fourth-and-10 situation in the fourth quarter against Nebraska-Omaha, Heimerdinger scrambled up the middle, dodged three defenders and picked up 24 yards.

"If there was a big play that season, that was it," said teammate Fran Cahill. "I can still remember being downfield trying to get free and watching 'Heimer' duck everybody in the backfield. It seems like it took forever, like one of those slow-motion films."

Quarterback Bob Heimerdinger (50) led the Huskies to a 9-0-0 record and Interstate Intercollegiate Athletic Association title in 1951. Heimerdinger was the first NIU player to have his jersey retired.

Yet, all these years later, Heimerdinger still remembers his teammates and their contributions to the Huskies' success.

"There were so many of my teammates who were just quality individuals in addition to being good football players," he said.

Heimerdinger spoke of Cahill, the Huskies' leading receiver during the '51 season.

"Fran was from Utica and played his high school ball at LaSalle-Peru," Heimerdinger said. "He was a great wide receiver. He's in the Northern Hall of Fame. Fran played baseball when they were conference champs two years running."

Following Cahill's passing in the early 2000s, Heimerdinger and others created an award in his name.

"It goes to the wide receiver at Northern who best represents the spirit of Fran," Heimerdinger explained. "He doesn't have to be the best receiver, but he does have to show he's willing to give it his all."

Following Northern's perfect 1951 season, the team received three bowl invitations. The first came from the Corn Bowl, which was played in Bloomington around Thanksgiving in those days. Another came from the Cigar Bowl, but the third came from from Tangerine Bowl, which was played in Florida closer to New Year's Day.

"Chick Evans put it to a team vote," Heimerdinger said. "Well, of course, the Tangerine Bowl won out."

However, Northern's Board of Regents vetoed the trip because it extended the football season too long and there was concern about the number of classes the players would miss.

"So, we didn't go anywhere," Heimerdinger said. "It was disappointing. In our minds, we would have won it."

Upon graduation, Heimerdinger took a teaching and coaching job at Leyden High School in Franklin Park for two years. Then, he found himself at DeKalb High School.

"I coached sophomore football and basketball and was also the golf coach," he remembered.

Soon after, Heimerdinger became the Barbs' head football coach.

In the late 1960s, Heimerdinger became the freshman football coach at Northern under Howard Fletcher and later Richard Urich.

"My son Mike was in high school at that time," Heimerdinger said. "Everyone says he can't wait to coach his own kid. I was not that way."

Heimerdinger explained that he had learned firsthand just how difficult it was to coach a son from seeing his friends and colleagues go through it.

"Mike was a good athlete," Heimerdinger said. "He wound up going to Eastern (Illinois) to play football for Jack Dean, who had played for me at the high school."

While at Eastern, Mike Heimerdinger met a backup quarterback who shared the same first name—Mike Shanahan. The two would end up leading the Denver Broncos to consecutive Super Bowl titles two decades later. The junior Heimerdinger later became the offensive coordinator for the Tennessee Titans and New York Jets.

"A friend of mine's dad worked for the (DeKalb) *Chronicle* and we were at a Northern Illinois football game," Mike Heimerdinger recalled in 2009. "I must have been in seventh grade or so. They were honoring All-Americans from Northern Illinois. I remember seeing my dad on the field. I said, 'What's he doing out there? He never played football.'"

Heimerdinger's friend's father then took him into the university's field house and showed him Bob Heimerdinger's retired jersey.

"It was the only one that was retired at the time," Mike Heimerdinger said. "(He never said a word about it), that was my father."

Baseball proved to be Mike Heimerdinger's sport as a collegiate athlete. A center fielder, he still holds the Eastern career record for stolen bases.

"And that's from the days of 30-game schedules, not the 60 they play today," pointed out his father.

About the time his son was enjoying success on the diamond, the senior Heimerdinger was getting his fill of college coaching.

"There was a big push for Northern to move on to bigger things," Heimerdinger recalled. "They left the IIAC. I was too old in my mind at that point to put in the required time. You'd begin your day at six in the morning and stay there until the head coach was ready to go home, usually around midnight. Then it would be back up at six the next day and ready to go.

"If I were younger, I may have continued, but at that point, it wasn't for me."

Fortunately for Heimerdinger, there was a job teaching math available at DeKalb High School.

"I did some coaching as an assistant, but it was nothing like what was going on at the college level," he said.

Eventually, Heimerdinger became the high school's athletic director. He retired in the mid-'80s, but after a year at home "driving my wife crazy," Heimerdinger took a job in the NIU equipment room.

"It was a great way to meet great people," he said.

Jerry Pettibone was the NIU head football coach at that time.

"What a job he did," Pettibone said. "The kids admired him so much. Whenever I wanted to check the pulse of the team, I'd ask Bob what was going on."

Heimerdinger also thought a great deal of Pettibone.

"He made everyone feel like family," he said.

It was also in the equipment room that Heimerdinger, the former star, really grew attached to the walk-ons.

"Those kids go through everything the scholarship kids do and will never set foot on the field," Heimerdinger said. "But, they go out and do it every day. Those are the kids that make good in life because they can take anything that comes their way."

After six years in the equipment room, Heimerdinger supervised physical education student teachers for NIU.

"After that, I finally retired for good," he said.

These days, Heimerdinger enjoys golfing and his grandchildren.

"Our four other children all live in the area," he said. "We have 16 grandchildren. We stay busy attending their activities."

So, how much has football changed since Heimerdinger's glory days as the NIU quarterback in the late 1940s and early '50s?

"It's so different," he said. "Back then, there was no weight room. There was no off-season conditioning. You'd play the season and then go to the library or wherever until spring practice came around. It's gotten so crazy. Even the high schools have made it year-round. It's gotten so that there's no time for a kid to be a kid."

Bob Heimerdinger should know. He's been around kids all of his life.

And, once upon a time, Heimerdinger was a kid himself: a kid who made his name and his fame as the first great NIU quarterback in the post-WWII era.

FOUR-DOWN TERRITORY

Favorite Football Movie—"Rudy"—After seeing all those walk-ons while I worked in the equipment room, I'm a sucker for a sentimental story.

First Car—A 1940 or '41 Mercury that burned oil when it wasn't even running.

Worst Summer Job—It wasn't necessarily bad, but it was the one I knew the least about. The AD (athletic director) at Leyden High School got me a job at the local country club as a bartender. I didn't drink, and I didn't know how to make the drinks.

Favorite Subjects in School—Geography, I love maps, and math.

JACK PHEANIS

For nearly all of his adult life, Jack Pheanis has been associated with Northern Illinois University.

"I love this school and always will," said the 81-year-old Pheanis in the spring of 2010. "You've got the best right here."

Pheanis' opinion should be highly respected. He retired in 2002 as the person with the longest coaching tenure of anyone in NIU athletic history. Pheanis played for Northern and later coached football, basketball and golf for the university. He was inducted into the NIU Athletic Hall of Fame in 1988.

Pheanis grew up in Chicago Heights during the 1930s and '40s.

"At that time, Chicago Heights was bigger than Northern when I came here," he said. "Chicago Heights was about 20,000 people and Northern was around 2,000 students."

Though his family wasn't Catholic, they sent him to parochial grade school.

"My parents wanted those nuns to straighten me out," he said.

Pheanis' grade school experience also exposed him to athletics.

"There were eight Catholic grade schools in Chicago Heights in those days," he said. "We had teams for softball, basketball and track. We had uniforms and the whole bit."

After seeing Pheanis compete as a sprinter, Mt. Carmel High School went after him.

"It was an all boys' school in those days," he said. "They taught me the basics of football. They taught me how to block and how to tackle."

Mt. Carmel also taught him strict discipline.

"You want to know how badly I wanted out of there?" Pheanis said. "I almost joined the Marines to get out of there."

Sure enough, Pheanis brought home induction papers for his father to sign when he turned 16.

"My dad took the papers and tore them up," Pheanis said. "He probably saved my life because that was the time when the Marines were going from island to island fighting (in World War II)."

However, Pheanis' father did allow him to transfer to Bloom High School.

"We won a mythical state championship at Bloom," Pheanis said. "I was an option quarterback, a running back and linebacker."

Though he was recruited by the likes of Illinois, Colorado, Illinois State and Iowa State, Pheanis joined the Army after graduation.

"I served 15 months in Korea," he said.

After his honorable discharge in 1948, Pheanis enrolled at Illinois on the G.I. Bill.

"So many guys came back from the war on the G.I. Bill. I knew that I wasn't going to play until maybe I was junior," Pheanis said.

When word got out that he was interested in transferring, Northern assistant coach John "Red" Pace contacted him.

Jack Pheanis coached at NIU from 1957 to 2002. Pheanis is the only four-time NIU Hall of Famer. He was inducted individually as an athlete, as head coach of the 1976 men's golf team, as an assistant football coach for the 1963 team and as a fullback on the 1951 football team.

"Pace was also an NFL official," Pheanis said.

Shortly thereafter, Pheanis got a telephone call from NIU head coach George "Chick" Evans.

"He helped me move everything I had out of the fraternity house I was living in down at Illinois," Pheanis recalled. "We loaded it up in his old Hudson and he drove me all the way to DeKalb. Mr. Evans, that's what I call him because he was my coach, found me a place to live."

Pheanis played fullback for Evans' Huskie teams from 1950 to 1952. He led the team in rushing as a senior.

"I mainly was a blocker and played linebacker on defense," he said.

Quarterback Bob Heimerdinger recalled the work ethic and enthusiasm that Pheanis brought to the team.

"He was not very big, but he had a lot of energy," Heimerdinger said. "Since we threw the ball so much he ended up blocking more than anything else. When we did run, it was usually a trap play up the middle with Jack."

The Huskies won the 1951 Illinois Intercollegiate Athletic Conference championship with a perfect 9-0-0 record.

"The G.I. Bill equalized things. We were every bit as good as Illinois, it's just that we didn't have the numbers they did," Pheanis said. "I feel comfortable saying that because that's where I came from."

NIU received an invitation to play in the Tangerine Bowl in Florida.

"That was special because in those days there were only five or six (major) bowl games at that time," Pheanis said.

However, NIU's governing body, the State Teachers College Board, turned down the bid because it would have extended the season seven weeks.

"That wasn't it (so much as) what it cost in those days (to send a team to a bowl)," Pheanis said. "We also had a (university) president who was very academic-minded. We were on quarters back then, and he didn't want us missing class for any bowl game."

Pheanis added that many of the players left Northern because of the bowl game decision.

"We would have been strong again in 1952 and beyond if those guys hadn't taken off for other places," he said.

In recent years alarm bells have been raised concerning the dangers of concussions sustained on the football field. It seems nearly every major sports publication and talk show has done something on the topic.

So what is to be done? Pheanis eagerly weighed in with his opinion.

"The answer to that is simple," Pheanis said. "When I played, there were no facemasks. Hitting was just as vicious then, but we learned to tackle the proper way. We tackled with our arms and shoulders, not our heads.

"There was no head-to-head (contact) talk back in my days. Without the facemask I don't care who he is, a player will protect his face. You don't want your nose and teeth getting smashed."

Pheanis earned his bachelor of science in education degree in 1952 and his master of science in education in 1954. Both degrees came from NIU. Pheanis began his career in 1953 as the head football coach and athletic director at Warren Township High School in Gurnee. He also coached at McHenry High School.

"When I told my dad I wanted to coach, he said, 'Are you crazy? Coaches don't make any money.' Well, even though my dad wasn't Catholic, he was very good friends with a priest. I told him, 'That priest doesn't make any money either.' That seemed to help my dad understand," Pheanis said.

He next had an offer to coach at Rich High School.

"It was going to be quite a pay increase

for me," he said. "Then Mr. Evans came and told me he wanted me to coach at Northern. I couldn't say no to a guy who was like my father."

Thus, Pheanis returned to DeKalb in 1957 and began as a graduate assistant. Pheanis served as head freshman coach in both football and basketball.

Pheanis cut his teeth under Evans.

"Chick Evans was ahead of his time," Pheanis said. "He always said you pass three times and then you kick. His philosophy always stayed with me."

He later applied that philosophy as an assistant under Howard Fletcher.

"I was the backfield coach and offensive coordinator and recruiter," Pheanis said. "We used Chick's offense. He gave me a book on the spread offense and told me to read it. 'This is the future,' Chick said."

The future turned into three straight IIAC titles and the 1963 NCAA College Division national championship.

"I recruited George Bork," Pheanis said of the Huskies' College Football Hall of Fame quarterback. "George could really throw the ball."

Pheanis recalled one game in which Illinois State came up with a defensive strategy to thwart Bork and the Huskies.

"They didn't rush anybody," Pheanis said. "All of our running plays were traps. Well, when they didn't rush anybody that was so confusing to Bork. The linemen were looking around for somebody to block. Bork would run around to the left and then back to the right (looking for a receiver). It stalled our offense for a time. We eventually got things going and won the game, but give Illinois State credit, they hung with us."

Pheanis hoped that either he or fellow assistant John Wrenn would be named head football coach when Fletcher retired.

"John and I were great friends," Pheanis

said. "We both wanted one of us to get the job. Maybe that's why they hired somebody else."

That somebody else was Richard Urich.

Meanwhile, Pheanis also coached the NIU golf team.

"In those days, assistants coached other sports," he said. "John Wrenn coached wrestling and tennis—he had those Gullikson brothers (Tim and Tom). I had golf."

In 1959, Pheanis' Huskies won the NCAA College Division Midwest Regional. His 1960 team captured the IIAC links crown.

"I recruited golfers like I recruited football players," he said. "I'd go and see them play. Other coaches just looked at the scores in the newspaper.

"I worked at (being a golf coach). I studied the game. I learned all the shots. I got to really love golf."

During his tenure, NIU won seven league team championships, including two Mid-American Conference titles. Pheanis was named conference Coach of the Year six times. He helped produce two major-college All-America selections, four NCAA Tournament qualifiers and 17 all-conference selections.

"I served on many NCAA committees," he noted.

Pheanis finally retired as the Huskie golf coach in May 2002. He then became the university's director of special projects and golf coach emeritus.

His "retirement" ended a 46-year run on the Huskie coaching staff.

"It was time," Pheanis said of his retirement. "But I love this job so much and it was difficult to give it up. I transferred here in 1950 from Illinois and I immediately fell in love with the campus, the teachers and the whole place. That NIU magic hit me back in 1950."

FOUR-DOWN TERRITORY

Favorite Football Movie—"Knute Rockne: All-American."

First Car—When I got out of the military I got a Ford convertible. It was yellow. I took it to Northern. It was a big hit with the girls on campus. Ha ha!

Worst Summer Job—My dad got me a job working construction. He always got me a hard job because he believed in conditioning. He wanted me to be in shape when football got around. The hardest job I had was when I was 16 I worked at a feed mill. I had to catch these 100-pound bags and stack them in box cars. They came down about two a minute. I got to where I could throw them. If you missed throwing them into place, then you had to pick them up off the floor and stack them again. I was pretty strong after that job.

Favorite Subjects in School—In grade school it was recess. At Northern I had a football theory class. Chick (Evans) gave me a B in class. He said, "I can't give all As and some of the others need the grade more than you do."

N THE 1960s

NIU FOOTBALL BY THE DECADE: 1960s

NIU ENROLLMENT—7,042 (1960)

AVERAGE COST FOR ROOM BOARD FEES AND SUPPLIES— $850–$900 (1959–1961)

NIU PRESIDENTS—Leslie Arnold Holmes (1949–1967); Rhoten Alexander Smith (1967–1971)

CONFERENCE—Illinois Intercollegiate Athletic Conference

NEWS OF THE DECADE—Civil rights fight continues; John F. Kennedy, Martin Luther King Jr. and Robert F. Kennedy assassinated; Vietnam War; the Moon Landing caps decade

NOTABLE MOVIES OF THE DECADE—"West Side Story," "The Longest Day," "Cleopatra," "The Great Escape," "The Sound of Music," "Dr. Zhivago," "The Graduate," "Bonnie and Clyde," "Butch Cassidy and the Sundance Kid," "Easy Rider," "Hello Dolly!"

NOTABLE BOOKS OF THE DECADE—"The Electric Kool-Aid Acid Test," "To Kill a Mockingbird," "Slaugtherhouse-Five," "In Cold Blood," "Catch-22"

NOTABLE MUSICAL ACTS OF THE DECADE—Bob Dylan, The Beatles, The Rolling Stones, The Doors, Jimi Hendrix, Janis Joplin, Cream, The Beach Boys, The Grateful Dead, Jefferson Airplane, Marvin Gaye, The Supremes, Led Zeppelin, The Who, Buffalo Springfield

TOM BECK

Tom Beck's 2004 entry into the College Football Hall of Fame came as a complete surprise—literally.

"A reporter called me from the *Detroit Free Press*," said Beck, who had coached at Grand Valley State in Michigan. "He told me that his editor had told him to call me and get my reaction to being admitted into the Hall of Fame.

"I told him, 'I think you are mistaken.' It was the first I had heard about it."

The reporter told Beck that he would call the National Football Foundation to verify his Hall selection and call the former NIU Huskie back. A short time later, the reporter did just that.

"What had happened was that we had moved and the National Football Foundation had mailed the announcement to my old address," Beck said.

The official paperwork eventually arrived at Beck's new address. Thus, the 1961 NIU graduate joined George Bork as the second Huskie to be enshrined into the College Football Hall of Fame.

"It was tremendous," said Beck. "It was a weekend that I will never forget. (Induction) was something I never aspired to. I never thought of it. I never dreamed of it.

"So many people are responsible. One person can't do it by himself. That's true for anyone; Joe Paterno, Bear Bryant, anyone. In fact, I've often thought the Hall of Fame should include assistant coaches."

Beck gained even more satisfaction "representing the small schools" at his induction ceremony that included the likes of Joe Thiesmann (Notre Dame), Barry Sanders (Oklahoma State), Jimbo Covert (Pittsburgh) and Hayden Fry (Iowa).

Beck's road to the Hall of Fame began with his birth on December 21, 1940. He attended Lake View High School in Chicago, where he captained the football and basketball teams.

"I had also played baseball growing up, but at that time, there was spring practice for football so I gave up baseball," Beck explained.

Beck suffered through an injury-plagued prep football career.

"I broke three different bones in three different years," he said.

As a result, Beck didn't receive any offers to play college football. Moreover, he was a young high school graduate.

"I was 16 my last football season," Beck said. "I went to Northern because it was close to home. I walked on the football team."

As a freshman in 1958, Beck played quarterback for the NIU junior varsity.

"Facemasks and mouthpieces were just coming in," he said. "We were playing Joliet Junior College down in Memorial Stadium (in Joliet). I was rolling out near the sideline and just got a pass off when one of their linemen grabbed me by the single bar (of the helmet) and threw me down."

Beck not only tumbled to the ground, but his jaw also struck the concrete on a nearby track and field pit.

"I cracked eight teeth and had two knocked out," he said. "I still have dental problems to this day."

Beck wasn't unique to the era.

"We had all kinds of guys who had these removable bridges for their teeth," he said. "They would take them out when they played. They would be out there with these big gaps in their smiles."

As a sophomore in 1959, NIU head coach Howard Fletcher moved Beck ahead of a returning upperclassman on the depth chart.

"I backed up Lou Flynn, who did a really good job at quarterback that year," he said.

Beck soon teamed with NIU All-Century member Al Eck to form the "Beck-to-Eck" passing combination.

Beck helped the Huskies in a number of ways. He played in the defensive backfield,

Tom Beck was selected as NIU's best two-way player. Following a brilliant coaching career, Beck was inducted into the College Football Hall of Fame.

returned punts, held for extra points and served as the safety on kickoff coverage.

"I played literally 59 minutes of the game," he said.

With the emergence of Bork as the team's No. 1 quarterback, Fletcher moved Beck to running back.

"I went in motion a lot," he said. "I threw passes from the halfback position. I accepted (my new role)."

Nearly 50 years after he last suited up for the Huskies, Beck still easily recalled some of his most memorable games and plays.

"We beat Western Illinois (23-22) on Homecoming in 1961," he remembered. "I took a handoff from Bork in the spread (formation) and threw a touchdown pass to Gary Stearns to put us ahead."

Beck, the last two-way player in NIU football history, recalled how worn out he was after tossing the winning touchdown.

"I played a monster back position in that game," he said. "Fletcher told me to go wherever (WIU running back and future NFL first-round draft pick) Leroy Jackson went. I was exhausted."

Beck also remembered playing a game in Carbondale against Southern Illinois.

"Fletch put in a safety blitz (for the game)," Beck said. "Our defensive linemen were to engage their offensive line. I was to shoot the gap between their offensive guard Paul Beaston and their offensive tackle Houston Antwine. Those two guys weighed in at something like 250 and 280 (pounds). I was about 165. I remember thinking, 'What if our linemen don't get those guys engaged?' I never did call the safety blitz that game."

In another game against SIU, Beck said Fletcher punted the ball away on first down the entire second half.

"It rained like you wouldn't believe," he said. "It was a deluge. Fletch kept kicking the ball away until Southern made a mistake (receiving the ball). And they eventually did and we wound up winning."

Beck's final game also stands out in his memory, but not for his performance or the final result.

"We were playing Eastern Michigan," Beck said. "We improvised a play with a fake kick. I took the snap and rolled out and threw a touchdown pass to (lineman) Butch Maloney. Fletcher wasn't too happy with me, but I thought Butch deserved something for all the hard work and sacrifice he had made in his career."

Beck finished his NIU career as an all-conference selection on both offense and defense. In addition, he was an Academic All-American.

"I'm proud of that fact," he said. "Most people want to be remembered for something. I feel good that the coaches felt like I could play both

ways and that I was good enough to do it."

With his degree in hand, Beck began his coaching career by landing a job at West Leyden High School for 1962.

"My salary was $5,100 and I also got $1,900 for coaching three sports," Beck said. "I was married with our first kid on the way. My wife

and I said that when I got to $10,000, we'd have it made! Our budget allowed us $10 a month for entertainment, maybe a movie and an ice cream afterward."

In 1965, Beck became a head coach at Lake Zurich High School. He spent two years there before returning to take the same position at West Leyden.

In 1970, Beck moved to the collegiate ranks when he became the head coach at St. Procopius College, which changed its name to Illinois Benedictine College the following year.

"They had suffered 18 straight losing years," he said.

Beck and his staff quickly showed its ability to turn around programs. In five seasons as the Eagles' head coach, Beck won 37 games.

"We led first NAIA and then NCAA Division III football in total offense and passing offense," he said.

With Beck's success in hand, NIU athletic director Bob Brigham reached out to him.

"He brought me in as offensive coordinator and implied that the next (NIU) head coach would be a Northern man," Beck said.

Beck spent much of the 1975 season clashing with defensive coordinator Pat Culpepper.

"We were oil and water," Beck said.

When Jerry Ippoliti was removed as Huskie head coach, Brigham hired Culpepper as his replacement. Beck was passed over.

Thus, Beck returned to Division III as the head coach at Elmhurst College. The Blue Jays had posted just two winning seasons in the last 22 years.

Once again, Beck and his staff righted the ship. Elmhurst won 50 games and two conference championships over the course of the next eight seasons. In addition, his teams again led the nation in total offense and scoring offense.

"I'm real proud of our success," Beck said. "I never thought I'd leave there."

But, leave he did. Following a loss in the final 26 seconds of a game to conference rival and D3 powerhouse Augustana, Beck received an offer to move into the pro game.

"I was perhaps vulnerable (from the loss to Augustana), and I took the job," he said.

The job was an assistant coach with the Chicago Blitz of the United States Football League for the 1984 season under head coach Marv Levy.

"It was short-lived because the league folded right after that," Beck said.

In 1985, Beck beat out 64 other candidates and was hired as the head coach at Grand Valley State in Allendale, Michigan. Yet again, Beck had the Midas touch. He led the Lakers to 50 victories, two conference titles and two playoff berths in six seasons.

During the 1987 season, Beck was inducted into the NIU Athletic Hall of Fame.

"The ceremony was on a Friday night," Beck said. "I wasn't going to go because we had a game the next day."

When Grand Valley State's director of development got word about Beck's plan, she put her foot down.

"She said, 'You've got to go to something like that! I'll drive you there and back. You can sleep the entire time if you want.' I really have to thank her for that," he said.

Beck's success at Grand Valley led Lou Holtz to hire him as offensive coordinator at Notre Dame in 1991.

"A lot of pro scouts and player personnel people I knew tried to talk me out of it," Beck said. "But it was Notre Dame, and it was hard to turn down."

What may seem like a dream job to many soon turned into a negative situation.

"At first Lou Holtz was good to me," Beck said. "It was great in the beginning. I called most of the plays."

The day prior to the Irish opener against Indiana University, former Super Bowl–winning coach turned NBC color analyst Bill Walsh interviewed Beck.

"We beat Indiana (49-27) and Bill Walsh complimented me on the TV broadcast," Beck said. "The next day Holtz told me that I couldn't talk to the media."

Beck also had clashes with Irish offensive line coach Joe Moore.

Consequently, Beck left South Bend to take the offensive coordinator position at the University of Illinois under Lou Tepper the following season.

"Lou Tepper was a defensive coach by nature and didn't like to take chances (on offenses)," Beck said. "He had three offensive coordinators in four years."

As with Notre Dame, Beck also has issues with some of the other Illini assistants.

"Maybe I wasn't made for the Division I level," he said. "I felt like I could be a real asset as an assistant. There are guys stabbing you in the back to move up the coaching ladder. I felt I was a better head coach than assistant."

Thus, Beck left coaching. He spent time as a scout for the Buffalo Bills and Chicago Bears. He later became an analyst for two Web sites that covered Notre Dame football.

"I gave that up during Charlie Weis' time as (Irish) head coach," Beck said.

Ironically, Brian Kelly—Weis' replacement at Notre Dame—got his start in coaching as a graduate assistant under Beck at Grand Valley State.

"I miss football," Beck said. "I don't miss the long hours, but I do miss the camaraderie and friendships. I golf every Thursday with a group of former high school and college coaches. We spend the day reminiscing."

Beck takes pride not only in Brian Kelly, but also in other former players and assistant coaches who have advanced in the game.

"I'm really pleased," he said. "I'm going to some (of their) games. You always are excited when guys you had succeed."

These days, Tom Beck spends his retirement years enjoying time with his wife Joyce.

"I play golf and tennis. I paint. I've had some of my work in art shows and sold some paintings," he said. "Life continues to be good to me."

FOUR-DOWN TERRITORY

Favorite Football Movie—There are a number that I like. "The Blind Side" is the most recent one. I really enjoyed that one. "Rudy" is a little hokey but I liked the message. The one with Ronald Reagan ("Knute Rockne: All-American"). I enjoy those old black-and-white films. The one with Dennis Quaid as the Grey Ghost that was based on Billy Cannon ("Everybody's All-American"). "Brian's Song" is another.

First Car—I was just married in 1961, and we bought a car. I got it from Jim Moran, the Courtesy Man. It was a 1957 or '58 Renault Dauphine. My wife and I took our honeymoon up to the Dells and Black Hills. We blew a head gasket in South Dakota. I never thought I'd make it back in time for fall practice. I was a team captain and thought how mad Coach Fletcher would be. But, we were able to get back on time.

Worst Summer Job—I never really had a worst job. I worked as a driver's helper for Pepsi Cola. I'd help carry in cases of pop to the local bars and stores. I was a stock boy for a time. I worked one night a week for Pizza Villa (in DeKalb). When the night was over I got to take home a pizza and a quart of pop. I'd wake my wife up and we'd have a meal in the middle of the night.

Favorite Subjects in School—I never liked history in high school, but in college I had this rather young teacher. He was a graduate of Annapolis, you know the Naval Academy. He made history come alive. Today I read historical novels and biographies. I also liked kinesiology. I had Dr. Bob McAdam for that.

HOWARD FLETCHER

Howard Fletcher is widely viewed as the most successful head coach in the history of Northern Illinois football.

"He was the man who initiated the modern era of football here," said Huskies' head coach Joe Novak at the time of Fletcher's passing. "He was a real innovator, the forerunner of today's wide-open offenses."

Former assistant coach Jack Pheanis said Fletcher's offense was a direct descendant of George "Chick" Evans, the NIU head coach Fletcher played under.

"Fletcher allowed his assistants to run whatever they liked," Pheanis said. "Chick Evans had always stressed throwing the ball."

Fletcher, who died at age 88 in a Florida hospice facility near his retirement home in Fort Myers in 2001, posted a 74-48-1 record at NIU. That included the 10-0-0 season of 1963 when the Huskies won the Interstate Intercollegiate Athletic Conference. After winning the Mineral Water Bowl, NIU was declared the NCAA College Division national champion by both the Associated Press and NAIA.

A 2009 *USA Today* article selected Fletcher's tenure as NIU's "golden years." The ESPN College Football Encyclopedia chose him as the best coach in Huskie history.

"His football mind was so far ahead of others at that time," said George Bork, Fletcher's All-American quarterback. "Nobody threw the ball the way we did back then."

Tom Beck, who played for NIU from 1959 to 1961, said Fletcher had read TCU head coach Dutch Meyer's book on the shotgun offense.

"That influenced him, certainly," said Beck, "but Fletch was ahead of his time."

According to a 1963 article by Gwilym Brown in *Sports Illustrated,* Fletcher "realized that he had something very special when Bork came to college, and he provided his team with an offense to take advantage of the passing—the shotgun. The ends are split wide, the two halfbacks and the fullback arrayed close behind the line of scrimmage, and Bork, as isolated as a tree on a bare prairie, takes his station eight to ten yards back of center."

Fletcher's offense generally had five receivers out in pass patterns. His linemen were noted for being mobile and effective in their pass protection.

"We ran just enough to keep them honest," Bork said in a 1999 *Chicago Tribune* article by Bonnie DeSimone. "Fletch's philosophy was, 'We came here to throw the ball.' I would just run around until someone got open."

According to DeSimone's story, Fletcher made liberal use of the reverse and often threw three downs out of four from the shotgun formation.

In fact, Fletcher communicated on a regular basis with another purveyor of the formation, Pro Football Hall of Fame coach Tom Landry of the Dallas Cowboys.

Utilizing Fletcher's innovative offense, Bork passed for 3,077 yards and 32 touchdowns in 1963. Those numbers were astounding totals for that era.

"That was fun to watch," said the late Mike Heimerdinger, an NFL offensive coordinator and also the son of NIU Hall of Fame quarterback Bob Heimerdinger. "Fletcher had Bork in the shotgun and throwing the ball all over the place. It's what you see in today's offenses."

Longtime Huskies' sports information director Mike Korcek, who also attended NIU as a student in the late 1960s, noted, "Fletch's style—the Blitz T formation—and Bork leading the country in passing—made us the BYU of the 1960s. Attempting 68 passes in one game (accomplished in 1963) was unprecedented at the time."

Jack Dean, a DeKalb native, played for Fletcher on the 1963 national championship team.

"We did, however, not disrespecting anyone else, have the best coaching the school ever

Howard Fletcher is widely considered to be NIU's most successful football coach. His Huskies won the 1963 NCAA College Division national championship.

had," Dean said. "Fletch was unbelievable! He was so far ahead of himself on offense. We ran all the spread stuff that the college teams run now. Somehow, I really do not know how, Fletch got into all of our minds that we just were not going to lose. Everybody went on the field knowing that we were going to win and that was all that was acceptable.

"Our defense was good because our offense practiced against them every day. We had great assistant coaches in Jocko Wrenn (defense), Jack Pheanis and Mark Dean. Fletch was low-key, a great listener, but very firm when he had to (be)."

Dean added that Fletcher gave very few pep talks.

"(Fletcher) once said he didn't because if he did, Mike Henigan and Jack Dean would jump out the window trying to get to the field. We had our pre-game in old Still Gym on the second floor," Dean said. "In our biggest game Fletch gave a low-key talk and then said, 'Gentlemen, let's go out there and knock their cocks off.'"

Prior to his time at NIU, Fletcher coached at the high school level in West Chicago and Cincinnati.

Fletcher, a Streator native, earned all-conference honors as a tackle at NIU in 1938 and '39 under Evans. He then transferred to the University of Illinois and played under Bob Zuppke.

Yet, NIU faithful will always remember him for his highly successful stint as the Huskies' head coach.

"There was a special coach-player relationship," said Bork years later. "You thought so much of him that you never wanted to let him down."

John Spilis, the gifted NIU receiver of the 1960s, said, "Howard Fletcher was like a father to me like he was to so many players. I loved playing for him. He had a great, great sense of humor. Even in the toughest of times, he always found time to smile."

Asked if he remembers Fletcher more as a man than as a coach, Spilis said, "I'd agree with that. That sounds about right."

GEORGE BORK

In the late 1950s and early '60s there was a TV western called "Have Gun—Will Travel." That title seems fitting to describe quarterback George Bork's career.

"He was a brilliant passer," said Darrell Mudra, who coached Bork in the Canadian Football League in 1966. "He didn't really have a strong arm, but he could get the ball into all sorts of places."

Bork arrived at Northern after starring in both football and basketball at Arlington Heights High School. Yet, it was the hardwood that first appeared to be his destiny. The 6 foot 1 Bork was recruited by the likes of Michigan, Northwestern and Wisconsin for his long-range shooting ability.

"I went to visit Michigan (on a recruiting trip)," said Bork from his Illinois home in the late summer of 2009. "It was first class all the way."

"The following week I went to visit Northern. (Head football coach) Howard Fletcher took me in his jeep for a tour of the campus. We wound up with a barbeque back at his house."

In the end, Bork was persuaded by the prospects of playing both football and basketball in DeKalb. The other schools wanted him to play only basketball.

"I (also) just felt comfortable there," Bork said of Northern. "They were the only school to tell me I could play both sports."

Neither NIU nor Bork ever regretted the decision.

When starter Tom Beck was sidelined with an injury in 1961, the sophomore Bork took over at quarterback. He would hold the position for the next three seasons. In fact, when Beck returned, he was converted into a halfback.

Meanwhile, Fletcher, a Streator native who had played tackle for the legendary Bob Zuppke at Illinois, installed the Shotgun Spread offense.

"He had run the shotgun before," said Bork.

However, with Bork at the controls, the offense soared to new heights. In his 1999 story for the *College Football Historical Society Newsletter* titled "George Bork: Northern Illinois' Aerial Ace," writer John Greenburg quotes Fletcher: "I based it on the 'Spread Formation Football' coached by TCU's Dutch Meyer, but I had the offensive line in real tight line splits. We also ran a lot more shotgun plays than TCU did."

Soon, Bork was slinging the ball around to a variety of receivers. This came at a time when offenses were dominated by running plays.

"I had two main (targets)," Bork said. "Gary Stearns and Hugh Rohrschneider. Gary got injured his senior year, but he was our speed receiver. Hugh was 6 foot 6. I'd throw the ball up and he'd go get it."

In 1962, Bork's junior year, Northern rolled to an 8-2 record. With Bork setting nine national records, the team won the Interstate Intercollegiate Athletic Conference title.

"Our conference had a rule that you could only accept a bid to a bowl game if it was played before Thanksgiving," Bork recalled. "We really only had one choice."

That choice was the Mineral Springs Bowl in Excelsior Springs, Missouri. Northern's opponent would be Adams State (Colorado)

George Bork was the first 3,000-yard passer in NCAA history.

coached by Mudra, Bork's future CFL boss.

"We were excited just to be there," said Bork. "But they (Adams State) kind of hoodwinked us."

Mudra insisted the game be played with "iron man" one-platoon rules, which some conferences were still using at the time. Thus, Bork played defensive back as well as quarterback in the bowl game.

"There wasn't any free substitution," Bork said. "There were guys playing positions they'd never played before. It was the Twilight Zone."

Mudra and Adams State defeated Northern 23-20. The loss would serve as motivation for the 1963 season.

Bork spent the summer prior to his senior year working harder than ever. He even drove to Chicago to run on the beach near Lake Michigan in hopes of increasing his endurance and strengthening his hamstrings.

It all paid off as Bork put together a season for the ages. He completed 244 of 374 attempts for 3,077 yards. He was the first to surpass the 3,000-yard plateau in college football history.

"Now (quarterbacks) get it in pretty fast fashion," said Bork. "Sure, I'm proud (to have been the first)."

The season also produced Bork's most memorable game.

A member of the College Football Hall of Fame, George Bork quarterbacked the 1963 NCAA College Division national champion Huskies.

"We had lost a close game to Central Michigan in 1962," he said. "But, in '63, we came back to get them."

Fletcher recalled the key IIAC game in Greenburg's story: "We were down 22-20 with a minute and 33 seconds left. George took 'em 72 yards for the winning touchdown and put it in the end zone with ten seconds left on the clock. He hit on 10 of 15 passes on that drive."

Bork finished the game with a record-setting 43-for-68 performance. Stearns, his roommate, caught 17 balls.

"That's the best scoring drive I've ever seen in person, on film, or on TV," Fletcher said.

Bork's numbers caught national attention. *Sports Illustrated* ran a three-page feature about him titled "A Big Man in Any League." Bork and his Northern teammates found their way into *Time* magazine. CBS aired game highlights nationally. Bork was interviewed on NBC Radio. Pro scouts from the likes of the Green Bay Packers, Dallas Cowboys and San Francisco 49ers came to see him play.

The Northern marching band spelled B-O-R-K and played the song "You Gotta Be a Football Hero" at halftime. He was a two-time First-Team Little All-America.

An undefeated season brought Northern a return invitation to the Mineral Springs Bowl. This time around, the opposition would be Southwest Missouri State, and two-platoon football would be played.

"Southwest Missouri could really hit," Bork said. "They punished you."

By game's end, it was Bork who handed out the most punishment. The senior earned the Mineral Bowl's Most Outstanding Back award by completing 27 of 41 passes for 327 yards and three touchdowns.

More importantly to Bork, Northern won the game 21-14. Although it was overshadowed by his gaudy passing numbers, Bork sealed the victory by pinning Southwest Missouri on its own two-yard line with a punt.

The triumph gave Northern the NCAA College Division national championship.

"That 1963 season is my greatest memory (of my career)," said Bork.

Longtime NIU sports information director Mike Korcek told the *Chicago Tribune* in 1999, "We're Division I now because of that season and that team."

Moreover, Huskie Stadium was built and opened for the 1965 season thanks to the success of the '63 team. It became known as "The House That George Built."

With the national championship in the books, Bork was selected to play in the North-South All-Star Game along with Rohrschneider. In fact, Bork started the game ahead of future NFL quarterback Jack Concannon of Boston College.

Bork left NIU with 6,782 career passing yards. That mark stood until Chandler Harnish surpassed Bork during the 2011 season.

Despite all the records, an unbeaten season and mounds of exposure, Bork wasn't drafted by any NFL team. No doubt, his small size (6 foot 1, 178 pounds) was a determining factor. Thus, Bork signed with the Montreal Alouettes of the Canadian Football League.

"I played four years up there for three different coaches, which was a bit unsettling," Bork said. "The game is so different, but I enjoyed it."

Jack Dean was a teammate of Bork's on the 1963 NIU team that won the national championship. Like Bork, Dean, a DeKalb native, later played in the CFL.

"George Bork, this is the best player ever to play at Northern," Dean said. "I coached at Northern. I played with (1962) Heisman Trophy winner Terry Baker at Edmonton. He could not carry George's water. I was with USC All-American Bill Nelson at Pittsburgh, and he could not carry George's water. I was with Sonny Jurgenson at Washington. Yeah, Sonny was better than George, but George was in his class. Sonny threw the ball **very** hard. George threw a softer ball but as accurate as anyone I have seen. I also played against George in Canada. We had to play both ways up there as U.S. citizens, and George burned me at cornerback.

"The NFL passed on him because he wasn't 6 (foot) 4, but they wouldn't now. He was a **winner**."

After being cut in Montreal, Bork signed with the Chicago Owls of the Continental League in 1968. The league took its name from the proposed Continental Baseball League of a decade earlier, which had forced Major League Baseball into expansion.

The ContFL, as it came to be known, was a forerunner of the World Football League in the 1970s and the United States Football League in the '80s. Bill Walsh, Sam Wyche, Kenny Stabler and Otis Sistrunk all got their starts in the ContFL.

"It fell into place," Bork said. "If you remember the College All-Star Game where the college stars played the NFL champion . . . well, I always had a big desire to play in Soldier Field."

Bork got his chance with the Owls, three seasons before the NFL's Chicago Bears moved from Wrigley Field to Soldier Field.

The highlight of his Continental League career came against the powerhouse West Virginia Rockets.

"They were flying high and we were struggling, playing about .500 football," Bork said. "Well, everything went right and we upset them."

When the Continental League folded, Bork knew his career was over.

"I had arm trouble," he said. "It started in Canada. A quarterback who can't throw isn't much good. It was the end of the line."

Often overlooked because of his prowess on the football field is Bork's time on the basketball court.

In a 2001 *Daily Herald* article, Northern sports information director Mike Korcek told writer Bob Frisk, "The same right wrist that threw for 6,782 yards as a quarterback also flicked those jump shots for 1,114 career points in three Huskie basketball seasons."

Bork was inducted into the NIU Athletics Hall of Fame in 1983. His No. 11 jersey was retired in 1996.

Then, in 1999, Bork was inducted into the College Football Hall of Fame in South Bend, Indiana. He calls it the greatest honor of all his accomplishments.

"It was an incredible thrill," Bork said. "You walk along and see all the busts and think 'What in the world am I doing here?' It's such an honor. It was first class all the way. The class I went in with was incredible. There was Jim McMahon and Herschel Walker and a number of others.

"My wife (Merlin) said if she had to choose between her wedding weekend and the College Football Hall of Fame weekend, it's the Hall of Fame weekend."

Bork began teaching during his playing days in Canada. He retired after a 38-year teaching career that included four years north of the border.

"My wife was an elementary teacher," Bork said. "My three daughters are all teachers. Two of their husbands are teachers."

During his career in education, Bork coached at Prospect High School. In fact, his golf team won the school's first team state championship.

Since retiring, Bork and his wife have spent their time golfing and traveling.

"Our goal is to play golf in all 50 states," Bork said. "We've played in all but one."

Which state have the Borks yet to hit the links in?

"Nevada, as hard as it is to believe, Nevada," Bork chuckled.

The couple takes a vacation about "once a month." Their travels have included Alaska, South Africa and Europe.

"If it weren't for our family and (six) grandchildren, we'd probably live near Glacier National Park," Bork said.

"What do you mean **probably**?!" his wife interjected.

So maybe it isn't "Have Gun—Will Travel." Maybe it should be "Have Time—Will Travel."

FOUR-DOWN TERRITORY

Favorite Football Movie—I don't really have one. I did like "Rudy."

First Car—A 1957 Chevy.

Worst Summer Job—My dad was a printer. He got me a job at a factory. I had to stand over a conveyor belt and put envelopes for Christmas cards into boxes. The conveyor went twice as fast as I could keep up. My parents said I'd wake up from nightmares about the job. It was like that "I Love Lucy" episode.

Favorite Subject in School— Math.

JACK DEAN

Growing up in DeKalb, Jack Dean dreamed of playing college football.

"It was a very small town in those days," Dean said from his home in Arizona during the summer of 2010. "Everybody knew everybody. You played all the sports: football, baseball, basketball and track. You detassled corn in the summer. High school football was big."

Dean played his high school football for Bob Heimerdinger, the former record-setting NIU quarterback of the 1950s.

"He was a great coach, a great guy and a great influence on people," Dean said.

Heimerdinger's DeKalb teams also enjoyed success.

"My junior year, we were pretty good," Dean said. "Quite a few guys went on to play college football."

Dean noted that George Donnelly later played on the University of Illinois' Rose Bowl team with Dick Butkus. In addition, James Donnelly (George's brother) also played for the Barbs.

"(He) is a judge in DeKalb now," Dean said.

Bobby Evans, another DeKalb High graduate and the son of NIU legend Chick Evans, was the Huskies' center.

While George Donnelly was off to the Big Ten, Dean was just looking to play anywhere.

"I was about 145 pounds when I graduated high school," Dean recalled. "I had offers from a lot of small schools. I had offers to play baseball, but it was football that I wanted to play in college. That was always my dream you might say."

That dream was made possible by legendary NIU head coach Howard Fletcher.

"He was tremendous," Dean said. "He told me, 'I don't care how big you are, you can play college football.' I found a home."

Joining Dean at NIU were former DeKalb High teammates Lynn McCann and brothers Mike and Terry Henigan.

"Dick Bower was also on the DeKalb team and was set to play college football but tore up his knee," Dean said. "It's pretty remarkable for a high school our size."

Dean soon found a spot in the NIU backfield.

"Howard Fletcher had us running the spread way back then," Dean said. "He was so far ahead of his time. We were doing that back in 1962."

As the Huskies' halfback, Dean didn't see the ball much in Fletcher's high-powered passing offense spearheaded by College Football Hall of Fame quarterback George Bork.

"I might carry the ball nine times a game because we threw all the time," Dean said. "I wanted to get my hands on the football too. I'd study the pass patterns and trajectories and whatnot. Sometimes I'd run out and grab the passes thrown for (end) Gary Stearns."

In a 1963 *Sports Illustrated* article, writer Gwilym Brown noted that Dean was "Bork's third favorite target." The article described

Jack Dean was the Interstate Intercollegiate Athletic Conference Most Valuable Player in 1964. A DeKalb native, Dean later was the head coach at Eastern Illinois University.

Dean as "a wispy, 5-foot-8 running back, who leads the team in rushing but seldom gets the opportunity to perform his specialty."

That '63 season brought a national championship to the Huskies. While Bork and the offense gobbled up the headlines, Dean also remembers the other side of the ball.

"Our defense was very, very good. They practiced against our offense every day. They were led by Mike Henigan. He was a very, very intelligent guy at linebacker."

Yet, above all else, Dean remembers the tight bond of the '63 Huskies.

"It was absolutely fantastic," he said. "There was never any bickering. I've never been involved with a group like that. We covered each other's backs."

Dean still maintains contact with "about a half dozen or so" teammates from his college days.

"We've stayed in touch all these years," Dean said. "Dave Broderick, our fullback, was the best man in my wedding. We lost (record-setting end) Hugh Rohrschneider way too young. He died of lung cancer at age 44."

Dean, the player who once dreamed of playing college football, also enjoyed a brief career in the professional game. He played a season in the Canadian Football League and also had looks from both the Pittsburgh Steelers and Washington Redskins.

"The CFL was probably better suited for me because of my skills," Dean said. "I was on what today they call the practice or taxi squad with the Redskins."

Dean also played for the Richmond Rebels of the Continental Football League.

When his playing career ended, Dean turned to coaching. He spent two years at Conant High School in Hoffman Estates.

Following a year as an offensive assistant at Wisconsin-Whitewater, Dean accepted an assistant coaching position at Eastern Illinois University.

"My connections in the old IIAC (Interstate Intercollegiate Athletic Conference) really helped me," Dean said. "Tom Katsimpalis was the AD (at Eastern) then. He offered me the job and I took it."

By accepting the position, Dean was taking on a monumental task. The Panthers had not produced a winning season since 1951.

"The program was in real bad shape," Dean said. "But I saw it as an avenue to get back (to NIU), which was my goal."

Dean served as the team's offensive coordinator for two seasons.

"We had a lot of success on offense," he said. "But we faced some pretty stiff competition."

Then in August 1972 Eastern head coach Clyde Biggers bolted Charleston for an administrative position at the University of Richmond.

"They made me head coach," Dean said. "I was 27 years old, not much older than my players."

Dean spent three seasons as the Panthers' head coach (1972–1974).

"We won no games that first year," he said. "We had to start from scratch. We went out and hit the recruiting trail."

Three of his most interesting recruits proved to be Mike Heimerdinger, Mike Shanahan and Ted Petersen.

"I grew up watching Jack play," Heimerdinger said.

In fact, Dean had played for Heimerdinger's father at DeKalb High School.

"Jack was undersized but nobody could catch him," Heimerdinger said. "My dad and I watched him play in Canada (in the Canadian Football League) on TV. Today, he'd be a slot receiver and a return man on punts and kickoffs."

Heimerdinger roomed with Shanahan, then a quarterback.

Shanahan's collegiate career ended when one of his kidneys had to be removed following an injury in the Panthers' spring game.

"He was real close to death," Heimerdinger said. "I remember sitting in the hospital and the priest came in to give him last rites. When you're young you never think anybody is going to die. That really put it into perspective."

Dean recalled, "That was a scary deal."

Shanahan spent five days in critical condition. One doctor later told his father it was the closest he had ever come to losing a patient who actually survived.

Dean delivered the news that Shanahan's playing days were over. Neither the doctors nor the university would allow him to play again.

"I was crushed," Shanahan said in his autobiography co-written with Adam Schefter. "I should have been thankful I was alive, but all I could think about was never playing football again."

If playing football again wasn't an option, then Shanahan was intent on doing the next best thing—coaching football.

"Mike started coaching right away," said roommate Mike Heimerdinger. "He was breaking down film."

In fact, both Shanahan and Heimerdinger began their coaching careers under Dean.

"Shanahan helped run the freshman team," Dean said. "By then Mike Heimerdinger had decided to pursue baseball as his sport. But he helped coach wide receivers and defensive backs.

"John Wrenn was also on that staff. He played for DeKalb and then at Western Illinois. He won state championships in Illinois and Arizona. Today, he's on the Arizona State coaching staff."

Meanwhile, Shanahan and Heimerdinger were together as the Denver Broncos won back-to-back Super Bowls titles in the late 1990s.

"Ted Petersen was a 6 foot 5, 185-pound tight end in high school," Dean said. "He didn't have any other offers, but I thought this big, old raw-boned farm kid (from Momence) can play. We played him at tight end first but he didn't have the greatest hands. We moved him to tackle and later he played guard."

"Jack was a very enthusiastic guy," Petersen recalled. "He had played for the Washington Redskins, which gave him credence. But, for whatever reason, not everyone bought into him and his program."

Petersen became a fourth-round draft pick of the Pittsburgh Steelers, making him the highest draft choice in Eastern history at that point.

Petersen wound up playing ten years in the NFL. He won two Super Bowl rings with the Steelers along the way before ending his career with Cleveland and Indianapolis.

Dean was replaced as Eastern coach following the 1974 season.

"You didn't have long-term contracts back then," he said. "You were year-to-year. (Eastern) decided to go in another direction."

In 1978, the Panthers won the Division II national championship under head coach Darrell Mudra. It was a bittersweet time for Dean.

"My first recruiting class was part of that national championship," he said.

Dean finally returned to NIU. He spent two seasons as a Huskie assistant.

"I was the defensive backs coach," he said. "I was 32 and the fastest guy on the team. That tells you something, but we had great kids as players."

Dean then decided it was time to begin a new phase of life.

"My wife had some physical problems with miscarriages and so forth," he said. "After spending time with so many other people's kids, I decided it was time to spend time with my own kids."

Dean worked in the construction business in the Moline area for "about the next six years."

However, times were tough.

"The grain embargo put in by President (Jimmy) Carter really hurt our business," he said.

Dean again switched careers, this time teaming up with former NIU teammate Jerry Andres. Dean left the Midwest and moved to Arizona.

"I managed golf courses for 26 years," he said.

Today, Dean teaches some business courses at a community college. He also manages a real estate company.

"I'm enjoying what I'm doing," he said. "I'm not one of those guys to sit around in retirement."

Though he moved two time zones away from DeKalb and NIU, Dean still feels the Huskie influence in his life.

"(Longtime college football coach) Dick Tomey was an assistant my last year at Northern," Dean said. "My son (Erik) played for Dick at the University of Arizona. He wasn't a starter, but was a pretty reliable reserve."

Moreover, Dean still keeps close tabs on NIU football.

"(In recent years) I've been going back for games," he said. "I've been to their bowl games. I was very impressed with Jerry Kill and his staff and his discipline. They had a locker with my name on it. I met the kid who had that locker. (NIU football is) still important to me."

FOUR-DOWN TERRITORY

Favorite Football Movie—I don't watch football movies. Once you've been there as a player and a coach you find most of those movies don't get it right. They're so far away from the way it really is. I just get frustrated watching them.

First Car—A Chevy Corvair. It had a rear engine in it. It was in the late '50s.

Worst Summer Job—The toughest job I had was managing the Hopkins swimming pool. I had to clean the deck in the morning. Then I'd give swimming lessons until noon. I'd work as a lifeguard until we closed at nine. Then I was the night watchman 'til around 11 or so. Those were some long days.

Favorite Subjects in School: Geography and anatomy. I really enjoyed maps. The only course I ever failed was accounting. It was the year we had the bowl game. I had a bunch of worksheets to do. I figured that the professor wouldn't even look at them. I did pretty well on the final, but he failed me because I didn't turn in those worksheets. The next semester some of my friends took the course. The professor told them that if any of them were planning on sliding by because they were athletes to think again. He told them how he failed a football player who didn't do his work because of a bowl game. That being said, most of the professors at Northern were very good to me. The ironic thing is that today one of the courses I teach is accounting.

JOHN SPILIS

The actions of a high school athletic director may well have altered the life of John Spilis and Northern Illinois University forever.

Spilis was a three-sport standout at Thornridge High School and the Most Valuable Player of the football team.

"I played basketball, football and track," said Spilis from his home in California. "I have big hands so I was probably better at basketball than football. But, I also realized that I wouldn't have gone as far in basketball (as I did in football)."

Despite his prep success, Spilis received no scholarship offers.

"Guys on our (high school) team were getting offers," Spilis recalled. "But I didn't get one."

Spilis later found out that his high school athletic director had been throwing away any letters from colleges interested in the 6 foot 3, 210-pound Spilis.

"He didn't like me for whatever reason," Spilis said. "Any letter that came in for me, he got rid of it."

Figuring that he would never again play football, Spilis enrolled at NIU.

"My dad wanted me to go at least one year to college," Spilis said. "My older sister (Joan) went to Northern so I went there."

One day Spilis was walking through the field house when Huskie freshman coach Roger Theder spotted him.

"He called me over and asked if I was going out for freshman football," Spilis said. "He set up a meeting with me, and the rest is history as they say."

Spilis joined the team, went through spring practice and impressed Howard Fletcher, the NIU head coach.

"He put me on full scholarship after that first semester was over," Spilis said. "It was amazing to me because my dad was only going to pay for the first year. I didn't know how I was going to pay for the next three years."

Fletcher also wrote Spilis a letter during the summer between his freshman and sophomore years.

"He said that I was going to be a starter in the fall," Spilis said. "In a year I had gone from someone who thought he'd never play again to someone who was going to start on the varsity as a sophomore. I never thought it was possible."

Spilis joined tight end Roland Roth and linebacker Jim Faggetti as the only sophomores to start for the Huskies in 1966.

"To this day, those are two of my best friends," Spilis said. "Starting that first varsity game really stands out (in my memory)."

With NIU making the shift from NCAA College Division status to a major college schedule, Spilis and his teammates struggled at times.

"We took our lumps for a couple years," he admitted.

opening kickoff 97 yards for a touchdown against Bowling Green State.

"I ran up the middle, got a couple of blocks at the point of attack and took off to the right," he recalled. "At about midfield I knew I had a pretty good shot (at scoring the touchdown)."

The early lead held up for NIU as the field conditions continued to deteriorate as the afternoon wore on.

"Bowling Green scored but flubbed the extra point," Spilis noted.

When the final gun sounded, NIU had posted a 7-6 win.

In a remarkable statistical oddity, Spilis caught 46 passes for three consecutive seasons. He ended his career with 138 receptions for 1,815 yards and 22 touchdowns. Spilis returned two kickoffs for scores.

His All-Century Team profile points out that Spilis "possessed great hands, an uncanny ability to catch passes in crowds similar to a basketball rebounder, and big-time speed for his size."

However, his senior season was the year before NIU officially entered major status. With the Huskies playing an independent schedule, Spilis earned no conference fanfare.

In addition, Spilis suffered a broken leg in his final game and missed playing in the postseason American Bowl.

"We were playing (16th-ranked) Ohio University," Spilis said. "I caught a pass and got hit. My leg was really bothering me after that. I remember thinking, 'Gee, I've never felt like this before.'"

Spilis noticed that he couldn't push off while running his routes. However, the team doctor didn't think the injury was serious.

"They taped it up at halftime," he said.

In the third quarter, Spilis hauled in his second touchdown catch. The score gave him the NIU career TD reception record, formerly held by Huskie Little All-Americas Al Eck and Hugh Rohrschneider.

John Spilis played in the College All-Star Game at Chicago's Soldier Field. He later played with the Green Bay Packers. (Photo by Mike Korcek)

However, Spilis played a key role when the Huskies earned their first victory over a "major" in 1968.

"It had been raining for a couple of days," Spilis remembered. "On the day of the game it was just pouring. There was standing water on the sidelines. It looked like a lake in spots."

That didn't stop Spilis as he returned the

"I got hit from both sides," Spilis recalled. "The pain was just tremendous. I literally passed out on the bench."

After suffering through a painful Sunday, Spilis demanded his leg be x-rayed on Monday.

"I still remember sitting in the room and hearing the nurse say, 'Doctor, you might want to come look at this.' I limped into the room where the x-ray was up. The fibula was cracked vertically for three or four inches. There were also small fragments."

Though the leg was indeed broken, Fletcher still believed Spilis had a future in the National Football League.

"He's a definite pro prospect," Fletcher said at the time. "I can only quote the pro scouts that have talked to me and they rate Spilis as one of the best receivers in the country."

According to former NIU sports information director Mike Korcek, Fletcher viewed Spilis as the best receiver in Huskie history.

The 1969 draft was not the event that it has morphed into in the contemporary NFL.

"It wasn't on TV or the radio," said Spilis. "You got word by a phone call."

Predraft speculation had either the Chicago Bears or Dallas Cowboys taking Spilis.

"Those are the teams that showed the most interest," Spilis said. "In fact, I heard later that Chicago was set to take me in the second round, but when (quarterback) Bobby Douglas was still available, they decided to take him."

Although Spilis had grown up in Chicago, he had rooted for the rival Green Bay Packers.

"I was captivated, like so many people, with (Vince) Lombardi," said Spilis. "I can still remember watching the game when the Packers played the NFL Championship against Philadelphia (in 1960). I was just sick when they lost."

Despite the loss, Green Bay soon established itself as pro football's dynasty of the 1960s. The Packers won NFL championships in 1961, '62, '65, '66 and '67. By 1969, when the Packers drafted Spilis in the third round as the 64th overall player chosen, Green Bay was beginning to decline.

"I met Vince after the draft, which was in January in those days. He was still the general manager of the team at that time, but then he left for Washington (to finish his career as the head coach of the Redskins)," Spilis said.

While in training camp, Spilis received an invitation to play in the annual College All-Star Game in Chicago against the defending Super Bowl champion New York Jets.

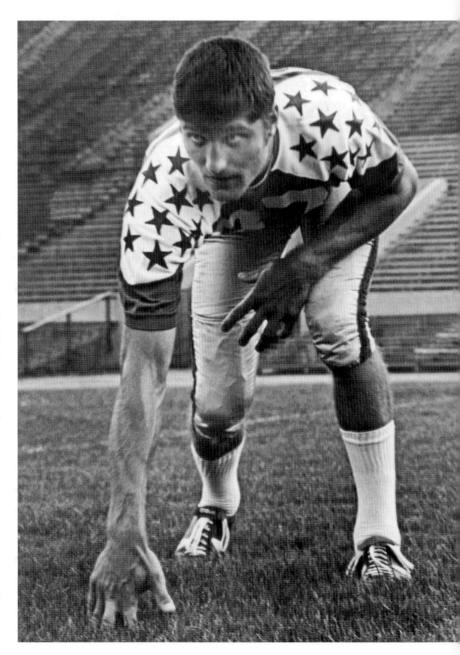

"A couple of receivers could not go," Spilis said. "So, I got to go."

The College All-Stars were coached by NFL legend Otto Graham.

"I knew about Otto from his glory days as quarterback of the Cleveland Browns," Spilis said. "He was just great."

Mike Korcek was a student at the time.

"I went to Soldier Field for the All-Star Game practice," Korcek said. "Spilis looked like Captain America in his All-Star uniform. Cool experience."

Spilis said that he didn't play much, but came away disappointed when the All-Stars lost 24-20 to the Joe Namath–led Jets.

"We had a touchdown called back because the officials said our player stepped out of bounds," Spilis said. "He didn't (step out of bounds), but that's what they called."

Though Spilis played for the team he grew up rooting for as a youth, his time with the Packers was bittersweet.

"My forte in college was catching the ball," he said. "The Packers had some really good veterans at receiver in Carroll Dale and Boyd Dowler. Marv Fleming was the tight end. Bart Starr was still playing quarterback.

"I was very seldom thrown the ball. I understand that with Bart having played with those guys for so long and being comfortable with them."

Spilis caught seven passes for 89 yards in his rookie season. A year later, he caught six balls for 76 yards. In his final season with Green Bay in 1971, Spilis hauled in 14 passes for 281 yards and a touchdown.

"It was a great experience, a dream come true," Spilis said of his years as a Packer. "I still go back to Green Bay every year. I'm still friends with my next-door neighbor from those days. In fact, I still take customers to one (Packer) game a year and he runs our tailgate."

When his playing days were over, Spilis worked briefly for Northwest Trust Bank and sold insurance.

"I really wasn't cut out for a desk job," he said.

Spilis then found his calling when Roth, his former NIU teammate, recommended that he apply for a sales position with a cement company. He worked at the job for ten years.

At that point, another former NIU connection entered his life.

"There was a girl from Northern Illinois I was following," Spilis said of his move to California. "She had been a pom-pom girl. I had dated her in college. She actually knew Howard Fletcher quite well."

The girl was Janice Jechort.

"We got reacquainted and here we are today," Spilis said. "We have a lot to talk about from those days at NIU."

Today, Spilis works for Mitsubishi Cement, a company he's been with for nearly 25 years.

"I love the business," he said. "It's not like working for bosses. It's more like working for friends."

In fact, Spilis returned to DeKalb with the vice president of the company in 2009.

"He's an Idaho graduate," Spilis explained. "He had taken me to a game there. I told him that I would return the favor when Northern played his school that fall."

Spilis estimated that he had not been back to NIU for nearly 20 years.

"I was really impressed with the way the school has grown up," he said.

Accompanied by his wife, Spilis also reunited with former sophomore starters Roth and Faggetti.

"We had a ball," he said.

Spilis remains both an NIU Athletics Hall of Fame inductee and All-Century Team member.

"Both are tremendous honors," he said. "There have been a lot of good ballplayers over the years at Northern Illinois. It's great to be included among them."

FOUR-DOWN TERRITORY

Favorite Football Movie—No, I don't watch sports movies. I've tried. People are always recommending them to me since I played ball. I've tried watching them on occasion, but I lose interest. I don't know why.

First Car—A 1963 Chevrolet Impala. It was metallic blue with blue rolled upholstery.

Worst Summer Job—Between my junior and senior years I worked at a construction company in DeKalb. The first day on the job they gave me a jackhammer and told me to break up a 16-inch concrete platform with reinforced steel bars. They wanted to see what I was made of. I worked there all summer. Another time we were building a church on the Sycamore Turnpike. The backhoe was broken so I had to dig the footings for the first two weeks. It was about eight or ten feet deep. When they finally got the backhoe fixed, it took about half a day to dig the other side. It may have been the worst job in some ways, but it was great in others. The guys I worked with were really good to me. I still respect them in so many ways.

Favorite Subject in School—History. I've always been a fan of history. Even to this day, most of what I read is historical nonfiction.

THE 1970s

NIU FOOTBALL BY THE DECADE: 1970s

NIU ENROLLMENT—22,817 (1970)

AVERAGE COST FOR ROOM BOARD FEES AND SUPPLIES— $1,800–$1,850 (1970)

NIU PRESIDENTS—Rhoten Alexander Smith (1967–1971); Richard James Nelson (1971–1978); William Robert Monat (1978–1984)

CONFERENCE—Independent, Mid-American Conference

NEWS OF THE DECADE—Four killed at Kent State; Patty Hearst kidnapped; Vietnam War ends; Woodward and Bernstein Watergate exposé; fuel in short supply; Camp David peace talks bring hope; Iranian hostages held

NOTABLE MOVIES OF THE DECADE— "Patton," "The French Connection," "The Godfather," "The Sting," "American Graffiti," "Jaws," "Rocky," "Annie Hall," "Star Wars," "The Deer Hunter," "Saturday Night Fever," "Apocalypse Now," "Kramer vs. Kramer"

NOTABLE BOOKS OF THE DECADE— "Deliverance," "Love Story," "Sophie's Choice," "Ball Four," "Dispatches," "All the President's Men," "Roots," "The Complete Book of Running"

NOTABLE MUSICAL ACTS OF THE DECADE—Pink Floyd, The Who, The Eagles, Carole King, Led Zeppelin, KISS, Fleetwood Mac, Elton John, Earth Wind & Fire

TOM WITTUM

Mike Korcek, NIU's longtime sports information director, has been around athletics all his life. Yet, when he remembers Huskie great Tom Wittum, sports are far from the only things that come to mind.

"The aspect of Tom that all of us remember the most is his modesty as a student-athlete and later in life," Korcek said in an e-mail. "A couple of years ago, Tom was a member of the 1972 baseball team that was inducted into the Northern Illinois Athletics Hall of Fame. Already enshrined as an individual, Tom, unbeknownst to most of us, had started his cancer treatments and did not want to attend the banquet and draw attention to himself (his hair had turned white due to the chemo) and away from the team.

"Typical Tom, instead he wrote a personal message to his teammates that was read to them by the coaches (Dave Mason and Wayne Franke) after the banquet on Friday night. There wasn't a dry eye among the group."

Most likely there wasn't a dry eye when Wittum passed away in January 2010. While his obituary focused on his days as a two-time Pro Bowl punter for the San Francisco 49ers during the 1970s, NIU fans remember Wittum as a bona-fide two-sport standout.

"Tom Wittum was a two-sport pro draftee," noted Korcek.

The Chicago White Sox selected Wittum out of Round Lake High School in the fifth round of the 1968 amateur draft. However, Wittum bypassed a shot at major league baseball to enroll at NIU.

"(Wittum became) one of Northern Illinois' first truly big-time athletes," said Korcek. "In that early Division I era in the late 1960s and early 1970s, you can put Tom Wittum with the all-time Huskie greats of that time—Jim Bradley, Billy Harris, Jerry Zielinkski, Mark Kellar, Larry Clark, Larry Johnson, Johnny B. Johnson, Pete Mannos, etc."

Wittum set 10 school records as a place-kicker and punter, including the career, single-season and single-game records for punts, punting yards and punting average.

"Football-wise, Wittum might have been the best all-around kicker (placekicker and punter) in school history, and that says a lot when you consider others who have played here," said Korcek.

As a skilled third baseman on the diamond, Wittum helped lead NIU to a 24-8 record in 1972, the first year the Huskies earned a berth in the NCAA baseball tournament.

"In baseball, I remember Tom hitting a home run that went off the west façade of Huskie Stadium," Korcek said. "Great third baseman, tremendous power hitter."

Yet, it was pro football that held Wittum's future. He was drafted by the 49ers in 1972. Wittum played in 70 National Football League games from 1973 to 1977. He averaged 40.8 yards a punt for his career. Wittum was twice named All-Pro.

Tom Wittum starred in baseball and football at NIU. Wittum was a two-time All-Pro in the NFL.

"Tom might have been the premier punter in the NFL prior to the arrival of Ray Guy in Oakland, and then he got hurt," Korcek said.

Wittum was injured in a serious 1978 car accident that left him with several broken bones. Ironically, with his playing days behind him, Wittum began a career as a driver's education instructor and coach for more than 30 years, mostly at Grayslake High School.

Wittum was survived by his wife, Cheryl, four children, four grandchildren and two sisters.

Korcek attended NIU as a student at the same time as Wittum.

"I nicknamed him 'The Toe,'" Korcek said. "When I contacted him years later about the Hall of Fame, I asked on the phone, 'Is Tom Wittum at home, I mean 'The Toe'? And he responded, 'This has to be Mike Korcek. . . .' Believe it or not, Tom remembered the nickname after all those years. He always made you feel good and important and he truly was the superstar. Terrible loss for all of us."

MARK KELLAR

When Mark Kellar peeled off his uniform following his final college game in 1973, his No. 31 jersey was retired by the university and placed in a time capsule near Altgeld Hall.

"It was put in there with a bunch of other things," Kellar said from his home in Minnesota. "They gave me one also. I have it here. (The time capsule) is to be opened after 75 years."

When that event occurs, NIU officials and historians will no doubt honor the greatness of Kellar, one of only four football players to have his number retired to date.

"That number (of players receiving that honor) will increase over time," said Kellar. "There are others who deserve it."

For the record, Kellar is joined by Bob Heimerdinger, George Bork and LeShon Johnson in what could be called the "Mount Rushmore of Northern Illinois football players."

Kellar arrived at NIU from Irving Crown High School in 1970.

"I was recruited by Northern Illinois (in football) and that was it," said the Carpentersville native. "I actually had more offers in track. I had about six if I remember correctly."

As a prep athlete, Kellar had been one of the top shot and discus throwers in the state. In fact, he was selected for an all-star track team that toured Germany in the summer following his high school graduation.

"We were there for six weeks," he said. "The first half of the tour we stayed with German families. The second half we stayed in hostels."

Kellar's personal bests were 61 feet in the shot and 183 feet in the discus.

"Track was a kick," he said. "I enjoyed it. I threw a little shot at Northern, but it was just too hard with spring football (to continue both sports). Plus, Northern had some really good throwers back then."

Though he had been recruited by Doc Urich, Kellar's glory days came under the guidance of NIU head coach Jerry Ippoliti.

"I really didn't get that close to Doc because I was with the freshman team and he was the varsity coach," Kellar said. "Jerry treated me well. He's my brother's father-in-law so there's still a connection somewhat."

After sitting out the mandatory freshman season per NCAA rules of the era, Kellar began his sophomore season with an ill-timed appendectomy.

"We had just played Wisconsin, which was the first game of my career," he said. "The next evening my abdomen got sore. That's what it turned out to be."

As a result, Kellar missed four games before returning to the Huskie lineup. He still managed to rush for 710 yards.

The following season, Kellar firmly established himself as an offensive force. Kellar

Mark Kellar led the NCAA in rushing in 1973. Kellar later played in the National Football League and World Football League.

rushed for 1,316 yards, good for sixth best among the country's leading ball carriers.

"I wouldn't consider it my breakout year," he said. "I knew what I was capable of doing. I just wanted to build on it from that. Jerry Latin came along. We were a nice running back pair. Jerry had a nice career. He was a great running back."

Kellar's senior season was one for the ages. He led the nation in rushing with 1,719 yards and 16 touchdowns. He averaged 5.9 yards per rush. In addition, Kellar racked up three 200-yard games. He earned honorable mention All-America status on four different lists.

Kellar finished his NIU career with 3,745 yards, 33 touchdowns and 20 100-yard games. He was the 18th player in major college football history to surpass the 3,000-yard mark.

"You carry that with pride," he said years later. "That's all you can do. It's important to me. It was a privilege to play for Northern Illinois University and to play for Jerry Ippoliti and with my teammates."

Rick Cerrone graduated from NIU in 1976. He spent more than a decade working as the director of media services for the New York Yankees. While at NIU, Cerrone worked as the sports editor for the *Northern Star,* the student newspaper.

"I interviewed Mark in our dorm one time," Cerrone recalled. "It was a big deal. All the guys were coming up and saying, 'Wow! Mark Kellar is here!'"

As of 2012, Kellar ranked fourth on the NIU career rushing list. Asked if he ever felt overlooked by successful Huskie running backs who followed in his footsteps such as LeShon Johnson, Michael Turner and Garrett Wolfe, Kellar replied, "You set something out there and let them go and break it.

"I don't feel lost in the shuffle at all. I lost four games my sophomore year because of the appendectomy. In all, I played 27 games. Take my 27 best games and compare it to theirs. I think I come out pretty well."

"They had four years of eligibility, which is huge. That first year is such an adjustment."

Kellar was invited to play in the North-South Shrine All-Star Game following the season.

"It was down in Miami," he said. "I really got to know (future Pittsburgh Steeler Hall of Fame linebacker) Jack Lambert (from Kent State, a Northern opponent). I wasn't really thinking about the next level like these guys are today."

To illustrate how much times have changed, consider this about the 1974 NFL Draft in which Kellar was taken in the fifth round by the Minnesota Vikings.

"I was walking back from class and one of my friends was working for a roofing company on campus," Kellar said. "He yelled down and told me I had been drafted by the Vikings."

Kellar, however, was also selected by the Chicago Fire of the fledgling World Football League. He opted to sign with the Fire.

"It was good money," he said. "It gave me an opportunity to build my game. I was staying at home and learning about pro football."

The Fire featured recognizable names such as wide receiver John Gilliam, a former Viking, and quarterback Virgil Carter, an ex-Cincinnati Bengal.

"We had a good team," Kellar said. "It was a great experience."

Kellar's season ended when he broke an ankle 12 games into the season. Still, Kellar led the Fire with nine touchdowns and finished second on the team in rushing with 778 yards. He also caught 28 passes for 342 yards and six touchdowns.

A year later, in 1975, Kellar began the season with the Chicago Winds. However, the team folded after only a few months of play and Kellar was assigned to the San Antonio Wings. A short time later, the entire WFL ceased operations.

"I had a two-year contract," Kellar said. "When the league folded, I still had my letter of credit from a bank. The team in San Antonio wasn't going to pay me, but I had that letter of credit with the bank so it worked out for me."

With the WFL gone, Kellar reported to Minnesota. The Vikings won the NFC title and advanced into the Super Bowl. Kellar, who had suffered the misfortune of breaking his other ankle that season, could only watch as the Oakland Raiders routed Minnesota 32-14.

Kellar spent two more seasons with the Vikings before retiring from football. He settled in Minneapolis, where he has worked in commercial finance.

"I lived in the Chicago area (Glenview) for nine years but came back here to Minneapolis in 2003," he said. "It's a nice place to live, to raise a family."

Kellar once told the *Chicago Tribune,* "I don't have much speed. When I run the 40 (yard dash) they have to use a calendar to time me."

When asked to describe his running style in 2010, Kellar said, "I had OK speed. It was better than average. I had great blockers. I didn't have a lot of moves. If there were defenders in my way waiting to be run over, then I'd run 'em over. I got off the snap pretty quickly and hit the hole. My goal was to get the ball and get through the hole as fast as I could."

Whereas most running backs that competed in track generally compete in events such as the sprints, Kellar's experience with the shot and discus paid off for him on the football field.

"I was always quick getting through the (throwing) circle with the shot and discus. It was the same way when I carried the ball," Kellar said.

A decade after his final collegiate game, Kellar was inducted into the NIU Hall of Fame.

"It was first class," he said. "I was very honored to go in. Northern's program has done nothing but grow. To be added to the Hall of Fame just tops it all off. I'm a lucky person. I'm in there with a lot of impressive people."

FOUR-DOWN TERRITORY

Favorite Football Movies—Boy, that's a tough one. I always liked "Semi-Tough." (From the background his daughter suggested "The Blind Side.") That was really good too.

First Car—It was a '67 MGB convertible. That was a great car.

Worst Summer Job—I worked in a gravel pit. It just wasn't any fun sitting down there doing that job.

Favorite Subject in School—Math.

RICK CERRONE

Rick Cerrone spent more than a decade in what *Sports Illustrated* called "the hottest seat in America" as the director of media relations for the New York Yankees.

Yet, it all began at NIU.

"In 1975, I did play-by-play for their (NIU football) games on the radio," said Cerrone, now a motivational speaker and media consultant. "The games were on WKDI. It was the first year (that NIU was) in the Mid-American Conference."

It also proved to be the last for Huskie head coach Jerry Ippoliti as NIU won only three games.

"The opener was with Long Beach State," Cerrone recalled. "Northern just got crushed (24-7)."

The next weekend, the Huskies played Northwestern at Dyche Stadium in Evanston. Prior to the game, Cerrone ran into Chicago radio personality Les Grobstein.

"He asked me what Northern's chances were, what the score would be," Cerrone said. "I told him, 'Anything they (NU) want it to be. We (NIU) have no chance.'"

Lo and behold, the Huskies stayed with Northwestern all the game. The Wildcats did manage a 10-3 victory.

Perhaps spurred on by the valiant showing, NIU won its next two games, MAC victories over Western Michigan and Kent State.

"All of a sudden, the team is 2-0 in the MAC and things are looking up," Cerrone said.

Following a pair of non-conference games,

NIU returned to a pivotal MAC showdown with Ball State.

"We lost 3-0 on a field goal with a couple of minutes left," Cerrone remembered. "Ball State missed the field goal, but there was a penalty on Northern. Ball State then made the field goal on the second attempt.

"That was it. We never won again."

One of the most disheartening losses came at Illinois State in November.

"We were losing the game, but had the ball inside their ten, maybe even inside their five," Cerrone said. "Jerry Golsteyn was the (NIU) quarterback. He later played with the New York Giants. I remember thinking, 'we're going to win this game.' Well. Golsteyn throws a pick six (interception that was returned for a touchdown). We lost. That was who we were that season."

How bad did the season get? After the Huskies were hammered 69-7 at Central Michigan, a decision was made not to have Cerrone broadcast the season finale from Idaho.

"I did the Jerry Ippoliti Show," Cerrone said. "We recorded it at seven in the morning on Thursdays. (After getting word about the final game) I let Jerry know that we wouldn't be making the road trip. He didn't seem to be fazed by that."

Ippoliti no doubt saw the handwriting on the wall. After a 25-24 loss to Idaho, Ippoliti resigned as NIU head coach.

Pat Culpepper replaced Ippoliti.

"The first thing Culpepper did was fire (former NIU quarterback and assistant coach) Tom Beck," Cerrone said. "Culpepper gets hired and five minutes later he fires Tom Beck. He (Culpepper) took the NI off the team's helmets and put that Huskie on it."

The game that stands out from Culpepper's first year is a 7-3 win over Illinois State in DeKalb—the lone victory by NIU that 1976 season.

Cerrone said, "The receiver ran a 10-yard out (pass pattern). He catches the ball, turns to the right on the scoreboard side of the field.

He does a little deke and goes 70 yards down the sideline for the victory."

Cerrone served as the sports editor for the *Northern Star* in the summers of 1974, '75 and '76.

"We published three times a week in the summer," Cerrone said. "I covered the Chicago Fire (of the World Football League) that summer. I remember going to their press conference that (former NIU star) Mark Kellar came out in the uniform."

Though the WFL folded the very next season, Cerrone had his first taste of professional sports—literally.

"I thought I'd hit the big time, free food," Cerrone laughed.

During his time with the *Northern Star*, Cerrone also interviewed Reino Nori, star back of the Huskies circa 1930s.

Following his graduation from NIU in 1976, Cerrone founded *Baseball Magazine* at the age of 23. As a means of increasing his publication's stature, Cerrone created a unique, high-profile awards program, which included the presentations of the official "Most Valuable Player" awards for the American and National League Championship Series and "Player of the Year" awards as selected by major league managers.

While still in his 20s, Cerrone joined the public relations staffs for two different Commissioners of Baseball, Bowie Kuhn and Peter Ueberroth.

In 1987, Cerrone created a groundbreaking nightly sports talk show on WNEW-AM in New York with co-host Richard Neer. The show's format, which included co-hosts and updates every 20 minutes, remains the model for today's sports programming on radio.

Cerrone then spent seven years (1987–1993) as the vice president of public relations for the Pittsburgh Pirates. He joined the Yankees in 1996. Over the course of the next 11 years, Cerrone was on hand for six World Series as well as the tragic events of 9/11.

Through it all, Northern Illinois University remains dear to his heart. In 2003, Cerrone was named to the *Northern Star* Hall of Fame. In 2009 he was elected to the NIU Board of the Alumni Association.

Cerrone continues to follow the exploits of the Huskie football team. In fact, that was never clearer than during NIU's incredible 2003 season under head coach Joe Novak.

When the Huskies opened their season by shocking Maryland, Cerrone went to extreme measures to watch the game.

"The front page of *USA Today* had hyped the game with Michael "The Burner" Turner. There were great expectations," Cerrone said. "We (the Yankees) had a day game against the White Sox."

However, Cerrone's plans were nearly derailed by several different circumstances.

"The White Sox had a practice of using aluminum bats (during batting practice), which you no longer can do," he explained. "A girl got injured by a line drive. I began to wonder if I would have to stay behind to tend to things."

However, the incident was taken care of and Cerrone joined the Yankees in Boston. He quickly found a sports bar.

"I was sitting there nursing a dinner," he said. "There was a long bar and two TVs. I asked if they were going to have the Maryland game on. I figured I had a better chance asking about the ACC team."

As things turned out, the sports bar had a back room with a big screen TV.

"The place was almost empty except for one table of eight or ten people who were clearly ACC fans," Cerrone said. "There was no sound up (on the TV) and I'm looking up in the corner of the screen for the score."

While NIU fell behind early in the game, Cerrone stuck with the Huskies. As the tide turned and the bar crowd began to grow, Cerrone was joined by others rooting for NIU.

"People had no idea who this team was," he said.

When Steve Azar's potential game-winning field goal was blocked at the end of regulation time, Cerrone had flashbacks to Huskie frustrations of earlier seasons.

"Here we go again was my thought," he said.

However, when NIU pulled off the upset of the nationally ranked Terrapins in overtime, Cerrone overheard an older couple asking who the victorious team was.

"I yelled out, 'That was the Northern Illinois University Huskies, thank you and good night!' and I walked out of the bar," Cerrone recalled.

Afterwards, a major newspaper sought him out for a quote.

"I said something like, 'This is the end of moral victories. We're not going to just take your money (and lose) any more,'" Cerrone said. "I still have the game on tape. My father taped it for me."

The next day at the ballpark, Yankees manager Joe Torre complimented Cerrone on the Huskies' headline-grabbing victory.

"He said, 'Hey, your team did all right last night but tell your kicker not to celebrate too soon,'" Cerrone said.

When the Huskies shocked tradition-rich Alabama three weeks later, Cerrone was forced to listen to the game via the Internet at Tropicana Field in Tampa.

"It was one of those early webcasts," Cerrone said. "They always say there's no cheering in the press box, but I said, 'I'm not cheering for this game. I'm cheering for **this**!'"

When NIU failed to get an invitation to a bowl game following that 10-2 season, Cerrone was among those upset.

"I was devastated," he said.

Cerrone also recalled coming back to DeKalb a year earlier to see NIU host MAC rival Bowling Green, then coached by Urban Meyer. The excitement of the game overwhelmed him.

"It was something I had never experienced," Cerrone said. "It was the first game I saw live with the student section (filled and rocking). It was unbelievable. You know how they say this isn't your father's whatever anymore. Well, this wasn't the Northern Illinois I remember. (Former NIU athletic director) Cary Groth had tears in her eyes."

The Huskies defeated Bowling Green 26-17 that November day. NIU finished the season 8-4 overall and 7-1 in the MAC.

So, just how big of a Huskie fan is the man who saw the Yankees win four World Series titles firsthand?

"One of my favorite pictures that I have is of an early Northern team, from around 1899 or 1900, that has the castle (Altgeld Hall) in the background," Cerrone said. "That's the one thing I always want the administration to remember. Don't lose sight of our history."

RANDY CLARK

Randy Clark vividly remembers his first National Football League huddle as a member of the St. Louis Cardinals.

"They had just signed me and I'd been practicing on the scout team," Clark said. "I didn't even have a playbook. One of the starters (in the offensive line) got hurt and I was sent in. I look around the huddle and there's (veteran quarterback) Jim Hart and (future Pro Football Hall of Fame lineman) Dan Dierdorf. Hart calls the play and starts to break the huddle. So I speak up and said, 'Wait, is that a run or a pass?' The guys in the huddle are all looking at me because they can't believe it. Dierdorf just glares at me and barks, 'Just block the bleeping guy in front of you.'"

Call it Clark's "Welcome to the NFL" moment. Call it learning on the job. Call it whatever you want, but those St. Louis Cardinals sharing that huddle might have been surprised that Clark's pro career would last eight seasons.

Born in Chicago, Clark moved with his family to Mt. Prospect at a young age. Upon entering Prospect High School, Clark played on the football and baseball teams.

"I played basketball in junior high," he said. "When I entered high school as a freshman I was 6 (foot) 3. I had always played in the post. There were four guys on the basketball team 6 (foot) 8 or taller. I saw the handwriting on the wall."

Clark saw time in both the offensive and defensive lines. Future Chicago Cubs' manager Mike Quade was the team's quarterback.

"It was good to see him get that job," Clark said.

Former NIU star quarterback George Bork taught and coached at Prospect High in those days.

"I didn't even know he played for Northern," Clark said. "He never talked about it."

Clark began to draw interest from recruiters as his 1975 graduation day approached.

"I never thought I'd wind up so close to home," Clark said. "I had an offer from Colgate (in Hamilton, New York). For awhile it looked like I'd go to the East Coast. Northwestern and Illinois showed interest. Every Big Ten team showed interest except Michigan and Ohio State."

However, NIU head coach Jerry Ippoliti and his staff won Clark over.

"It just happened that way," Clark said. "I really enjoyed the coaches. I was 6-4-ish and only about 200 pounds, which was small for a lineman. You couldn't redshirt freshmen back then so I was redshirted as a sophomore."

Meanwhile, Ippoliti was fired and replaced by former assistant Pat Culpepper.

"He was known for the flexibility he gave us, you could say," Clark said. "He had us in areas that we really weren't supposed to be. We would go into the racquetball courts and scrimmage, things like that.

"Pat was a real good recruiter. He was one of those convincing guys."

Clark credited offensive line coaches Todd Klein and Harry Van Arsdale with his development.

"Klein was pretty reputable," Clark said. "Culpepper got mad at a bunch of varsity linemen my redshirt year. It was the last game and he was thinking about playing me just to get back at those guys. That would have cost me the entire year (in terms of eligibility). Todd Klein stepped in and told Pat he couldn't do that. Both Todd and Harry were good line coaches. Their integrity was pretty good."

Clark came of age during Northern's early days in the Mid-American Conference.

"I remember a lot of our conference games were really intense," he said. "Central Michigan, Western Michigan and Ohio were always tough games for us."

Clark also enjoyed playing against in-state foes Western Illinois, Southern Illinois and Illinois State.

"I also remember playing Wisconsin (in 1977)," Clark said. "That marked the time when Northern was getting into playing the bigger schools."

Clark was also getting bigger.

"By my junior year I was playing center and around 240–245 pounds," he said.

Clark recalled going head-to-head against an All-MAC nose guard from Western Michigan.

"I can't remember his name, but I played fairly good against him," Clark said. "He was somewhere in the 205-pound range. He couldn't move me around the way he had other centers in the league. I don't know if the story is true or not, but someone told me later that he quit playing football because of that game."

By Clark's senior year he was also seeing time at offensive tackle on a solid run-blocking line.

"We could really pound the ball," Clark said. "I remember coming off for the punt team and having some banter with the offensive coaches about throwing too many passes. We weren't yelling or anything like that. We were just pleading our case to keep running the ball."

Like most former players, Clark remembers the unusual events that make college football unique.

"We were playing up at Wisconsin," he said. "I wasn't one of those guys who got too worked up for a game. I tried to keep calm before a game so I would usually hang back and let other guys rush out of the tunnel and onto the field.

"By the time I came out I saw (Wisconsin mascot) Bucky Badger lying there and his head was separated from the rest of his body. Somebody said later that Culpepper clocked him. Some said he ran into him on accident...I don't know what happened, but there was Bucky and there was his head just lying there."

Clark earned All-MAC honors. He was also an Associated Press All-America honorable mention selection.

When pro scouts began to show up at NIU practices and games his junior season, Clark began to consider the possibilities of the NFL.

"It's so hard to judge yourself in one conference," he said. "You wonder how you measure up against guys from the Big Ten or the Pac-10 or the other major conferences. Then you go against them and you realize they are not all supermen. You build more confidence as a player against those teams."

With the 1980 NFL Draft fast approaching, Clark began working out with one of the Northern track coaches.

"I was trying to increase my speed," he said. "There were no camps or combine in those days. There was the Blue-Gray Game and one or two more All-Star games. I was 6 (foot) 3 and about 255 (pounds). The average NFL center was about 253 at the time. I had pretty

good speed and footwork so I thought I had a pretty good shot (at being drafted) at the fifth or sixth round."

The Chicago Bears selected Clark in the eighth round as the 215th overall pick.

"They drafted me as a guard," he said. "That surprised me. I knew I didn't have the size to play tackle (at the pro level). I had never really played guard, just center and tackle."

Before getting cut by the Bears, Clark got plenty of snaps in training camp against future Pro Football Hall of Fame defensive lineman Dan Hampton.

"He just got me better and better," Clark said. "Dan Hampton wasn't weight-lifting strong, but he was leverage strong. He had those long arms that he would use against

Randy Clark was an NFL draft pick and All-Pro.

you. You couldn't get a hand on him. He really used those arms to his advantage. After going against him in practice, the preseason games seemed easy."

In addition, Clark worked out running stairs along Lake Michigan with Bears' legend Walter Payton.

"Of course I couldn't keep up with him," Clark said. "But that workout really helped."

Clark also learned to long snap for special teams.

"No one really wanted to do that back in those days," he said. "It was a job that was an afterthought. Today guys are getting scholarships and earning great contracts in the NFL for snapping."

Three weeks after being released by the Bears, Clark landed in St. Louis with the Cardinals.

"The New York Giants called right after that," Clark said. "That was about the time Bill Parcells was taking over as their coach. It would have been interesting to have gone to New York since they wound up winning those (two) Super Bowls with Parcells."

Still, Clark has no regrets for signing with St. Louis.

"Things worked out well," he said. "Larry Wilson was their GM at the time. He told me to report to the team at Busch Stadium. I got there and no one was around to meet me so I made my way into the locker room. The equipment guy was cussing up a storm because no one had told him about me."

Clark dressed for practice and sat around the locker room for an hour or so before other members of the team showed up. The Cardinals then boarded a bus and traveled to a nearby field for practice.

"I'm wondering what the heck is going on, but it turned out that they needed to practice on grass (rather than the artificial turf at Busch Stadium) because they were playing the Baltimore Colts the next game," Clark said.

"I followed Dierdorf the whole practice and tried to fit in," he said. "No one knew who I was or what I was doing there. The coaches asked me what position I played so I asked what they needed. 'We need a guard,' they said. So I told them that's what I was."

St. Louis kept Clark and by the 1983 season he was a starter on the Cardinal offensive line. In 1984, he had been named second team All-NFL by the Newspaper Enterprise Association.

Clark's career coincided with the end of Jim Hart's long NFL career and the emergence of Neil Lomax.

"I had come from the Bears where Vince Evans and Bob Avellini had been quarterbacks," Clark said. "I get to St. Louis and Jim Hart is unbelievable. He never overthrew a receiver. Well, maybe once every 50 or 60 passes he did. In Chicago it was two out of every three passes were bad.

"Jim had a quick release. He would read the defense and throw the ball away when nothing was there. Lomax had a strong arm, but he would hold on to the ball and take a sack instead of throwing it away. It was almost as if he didn't want the incompletion. But, let's face it, there's a big difference between second down-and-10 and second-and-20."

While his playing days were coming to an end in 1987, Clark was inducted into the NIU Athletics Hall of Fame. In 1999, Clark was named to the Huskie All-Century Team.

Following his career in pro football, Clark went to work for a telecommunications company. A decade later, he moved into the medical field and ICU Medical, Inc.

"I moved into the regional manager's job a few years ago," Clark said. "It's the type of promotion that you have to take when it comes along."

Clark spends about 150 days per year on the

road. Still, he found time to help coach his two daughters' basketball and softball teams as well as his son's sports.

"It's rewarding," he said. "I have really enjoyed it over the years."

And, no doubt, Huskie fans enjoyed watching Clark's career unfold over the years as well.

FOUR-DOWN TERRITORY

Favorite Football Movie—"Rudy" (because of) the fact the kid has a dream and is able to fulfill it when so many people are telling him it will never happen. He was told he was too small and wasn't good enough. He used it as motivation and ended up getting on the field. Too many people allow others to dictate their lives in what they can and can't do.

First Car—It was a '72 Dodge Charger. It was red. I worked at my dad's gas stations a long time to earn the money for it. My dad got a loan. Looking back, he probably worked out some deal and helped me more than I thought. I paid something like $180 a month for two or three years. I was really into cars. Friends of mine were always working on their cars, making them go faster. They would take them and run them at drag strips. I always wanted to do that too. My dad was a mechanic, but he never let me do anything to make my car run faster. I had a great-looking car, but it didn't run like my friends' cars.

Worst Summer Job—Working for the railroad. You would get creosote all over you. It would stick to your skin and your clothes while you were putting in rails and ties.

Favorite Subject in School—I got a business marketing degree from Northern. I really benefited from that, but one of the trainers at Northern taught a class that I took. I wrote a paper on the physical body improving power. I went to the library and researched it. I decided to look at the broad jump and the vertical jump. I talked the basketball coach into letting me test it out on his players. This was back in the '70s when that sort of thing wasn't really going on, especially with basketball. Anyway, I took measurements and the players were improving their vertical leaps by 10–14 inches. I realized that power really comes from your legs. I then applied it to football. It's something that really helped me in the offensive line.

DAVE PETZKE

It's better to give than receive. But, if it's 1978, and your name is Dave Petzke, it's most likely the other way around.

Petzke led the nation that year with 91 receptions for 1,215 yards. Northern quarterback Pete Kraker threw 11 touchdown passes. Every single one went to Petzke. He won the '78 Division I receiving title by an incredible 29 catches.

"Pete and I planned that," said Petzke from his home in Boulder, Colorado in late summer of 2009. "It was one of our goals. We had come within striking distance the year before."

Indeed they had. As a junior, Petzke finished seventh nationally with 57 catches for 743 yards in 1977.

"Pete and I worked that summer (of '78) on grain dryers out around Kirkland," Petzke recalled. "We'd work out in the hot sun all day. Then, we'd go back to the stadium and work out. We'd run. We'd lift weights. We'd run routes. We were so focused. (Looking back), it was so much fun."

The pair's hard work paid off as the Huskie passing game flourished.

"I had mixed emotions about it," Petzke said. "Our team was average at best (with a 5-6 record). (Leading the nation in receiving) was more important at the time because we needed to get a win some way. It was a bright spot for all of us.

"But, now after having coached, I'd trade all those catches for more wins."

Not many games stand out in Petzke's memory.

"Some guys can tell you everything—the score, who scored, all that stuff," he said. "I remember more of the strange stuff. Things like the time when some players and coaches gutted a pig in the shower."

Petzke does, however, recall his final game on the road against Ohio University.

"It was a long bus trip," Petzke said. "Everybody was focused on this Kraker-to-Petzke combination trying to set a record (of touchdown passes in one season).

"We're up on them and our coach sent in word for Pete to just kneel down. If you know Pete, he's the most straight guy you'd ever meet. He's into the Fellowship of Christian Athletes and all that sort of thing. But, he decides we're going for it. Pete calls for an out-and-up route. It worked, of course (since the defense wasn't expecting a pass). The ball was in the air, and the Ohio coaches are cussing."

Petzke hauled in the pass for his 11th touchdown of the season, thus etching his name into the NIU record book.

In December 1978, Petzke shared Mid-American Conference Offensive Player of the Year honors with Western Michigan tailback Jerome Persell. Petzke was the first NIU player to earn that honor.

The 6 foot 1, 180-pounder was a master of the sideline curl pattern. His disciplined pass routes drew comparisons to NFL legend Raymond Berry.

"He was so much better than me," Petzke said. "He was an athlete. People don't understand how good people like Raymond Berry or Steve Largent or Fred Biletnikoff are. It's a whole different world."

All of Petzke's success may have seemed highly improbable during Petzke's freshman year at Waldorf Junior College in Iowa.

"I'd never heard of Northern Illinois University in my life," said Petzke, who grew up in a family that moved frequently. "I went to my last year in high school in Minnesota. I lived in Kansas, Springfield (Illinois) and Idaho.

"I was a slow receiver in a wishbone offense. But, I could punt the ball. The Northern recruiter, I think it was Doug Klein, offered three of my teammates a visit. Three days before they were to go there, Northern invited me. They signed me as a punter."

As things turned out, Petzke never punted for the Huskies.

Northern's offer also turned out to be the only one Petzke got.

"I was hoping to go back west and play somewhere like Idaho State," he said. "But there's an interesting story. I met a girl who I became interested in. We were talking about doing the whole long-distance relationship thing and all. Well, her hometown turned out to be Malta (which is just west of NIU)."

Petzke wound up marrying the girl, whose maiden name was Rebecca Olson.

"It was fate," he said.

When his NIU playing days were over, Petzke spent the 1979 training camp with the Chicago Bears.

"I learned how to play receiver in Bears' camp," Petzke said. "You always hear how important footwork is for linemen. Well, it's just as important for receivers. I studied Steve Largent. His footwork was perfect."

Petzke was released by the Bears and later headed off to camp with Saskatchewan of the Canadian Football League.

"I started all four exhibition games," Petzke said. "In the last game, I got pulled for a Canadian player. I knew that was a bad sign."

At the time, the CFL allowed only 15 Americans on each team's roster.

"The Canadian player had my same skill set," he said. "Cut day was Thursday at 11 in the morning. The first game was Sunday."

On that Thursday morning, Petzke was in the locker room getting ready for practice.

"The teams checked the waiver wires and then made personnel decisions based on who was available to fill their holes," Petzke explained. "I was reaching for my playbook when there was a pat on my shoulder and I was told to go see the coach."

With his playing career over, Petzke took a part-time assistant coaching job under Bill Mallory at Northern.

"It was minimum pay with full-time work," said Petzke. "But it was unbelievable."

The following year Petzke was added as a full-time assistant to Mallory's staff. When Northern won the Mid-American Conference title and California Bowl in 1983, Petzke was hooked.

"Winning the MAC was so much fun," Petzke said.

Petzke spent three seasons at Northern and then moved to Indiana University when Mallory took the Hoosiers' head coaching job.

"Bill Mallory is the greatest leader you will ever meet," Petzke said. "He was tough, fair, honest and loyal."

Petzke spent eight years with Mallory at Indiana. They went to five bowl games during that stretch.

"When Bill took over, Indiana was nothing," Petzke said. "They were really down. But he turned it around. One year we beat both Michigan and Ohio State. There was still a gap (between Indiana and the Big Ten elite), but we were competitive."

Following 11 years of coaching, Petzke was ready for a new chapter in his life. Wanting to move back west, he took a job as a financial advisor with Edward Jones, first in Oregon, and then moved to Carson City, Nevada.

Today, Petzke is a wholesaler for American Funds.

"I call on financial advisors," he explained. "Every Monday morning I'm on a plane somewhere. It's kind of like recruiting."

One of his proudest moments came in 1987 when Petzke was inducted into the NIU Athletics Hall of Fame. His uniform No. 6 was also retired.

"It's an honor very few people get," he said. "I'm grateful for all the friends who made it happen."

Yes, sometimes it is better to receive.

Dave Petzke led the NCAA in receiving in 1978. He later coached for the Huskies under Bill Mallory.

FOUR-DOWN TERRITORY

Favorite Football Movie—"Rudy."

First Car—Dodge Dart with push-button shifting.

Worst Summer Job—I worked at a pea factory in Minnesota. To this day, I can't eat peas.

Favorite Subject in School—Football, and I'm not kidding.

THE 1980s

NIU FOOTBALL BY THE DECADE: 1980s

NIU ENROLLMENT—22,506 (1980)

IN-STATE TUITION PER SEMESTER—$447.25 (1980)

ROOM AND BOARD RATES PER SEMESTER—$885 to $1,195 (1980)

NIU PRESIDENTS—William Robert Monat (1978–1984); Clyde J. Wingfield (1985–1986); John E. LaTourette (1986–2000)

CONFERENCE—Independent, Mid-American Conference

NEWS OF THE DECADE—Reaganomics established; tainted Tylenol grips nation; Sandra Day O'Connor appointed to Supreme Court; Exxon "Valdez" crashes; U.S. invades Grenada and Panama; Challenger explodes; Iran-Contra debated; AIDS becomes mainstream story; Chernobyl disaster; insider trading grabs headlines; human rights groups target Tiananmen Square; Soviet bloc collapses

NOTABLE MOVIES OF THE DECADE—"Ordinary People," "Raging Bull," "Raiders of the Lost Ark," "Caddyshack," "Gandhi," "Chariots of Fire," "This Is Spinal Tap," "Risky Business," "Ghostbusters," "Back to the Future," "Out of Africa," "Platoon," "Top Gun," "Lethal Weapon," "Rain Man," "Field of Dreams," "Bull Durham," "Major League," "Driving Miss Daisy"

NOTABLE BOOKS OF THE DECADE—"Cosmos," "The Bonfire of the Vanities," "Ironweed," "Cultural Literacy," "Pet Sematary," "Patriot Games"

NOTABLE MUSICAL ACTS OF THE DECADE—Madonna, Michael Jackson, Prince, The Police, Bruce Springsteen, U2, REM, The Pretenders, Van Halen, Metallica, Talking Heads

1983 CALIFORNIA BOWL

Head coach Bill Mallory and his 1983 Huskies put Northern Illinois on the national college football map.

Picked to finish in the middle of the Mid-American Conference pack, the Huskies grabbed bowl game fans' attention in galvanizing style. NIU captured its first MAC championship and earned a berth in its first "major" bowl game.

Though Mallory had been to bowl games in his previous head coaching stints at Miami (Ohio) and Colorado, he recognized what it meant to NIU.

"I've never gone to a bad bowl," Mallory said. "There was great excitement for the fans, for the players and for the coaches."

The Huskies left the cold weather of DeKalb behind and headed to the California Bowl to face Cal State-Fullerton.

"The temperature was only in the 50s there, but it seemed warm to us," said defensive lineman Sheldon Sobol. "We were running around in shorts and T-shirts."

NIU faced a talented Titan team led by quarterback Damon Allen, the brother of 1981 Heisman Trophy winner and eventual Pro Football Hall of Fame running back Marcus Allen.

Damon Allen went on to become the most prolific passer in Canadian Football League history. Allen won four Grey Cups. In addition, he was a draft pick of baseball's Detroit Tigers.

But the December 17 bowl game belonged to the Huskies. NIU won a 20-13 thriller that provided its faithful with an early Christmas present.

"They probably underestimated us," said Sobol, who today serves as the state's attorney for Grundy County in his hometown of Morris.

The 1983 NIU Huskies were inducted into the university's Athletic Hall of Fame in 1995.

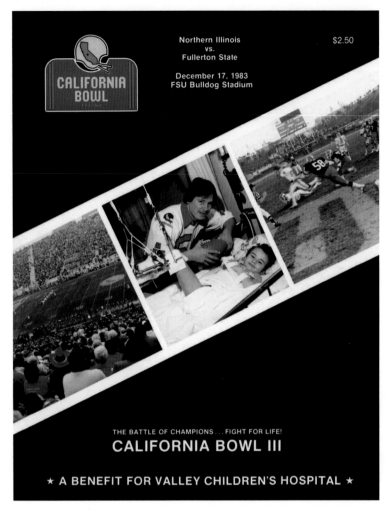

Northern Illinois
vs.
Fullerton State

$2.50

December 17, 1983
FSU Bulldog Stadium

CALIFORNIA BOWL

THE BATTLE OF CHAMPIONS...FIGHT FOR LIFE!

CALIFORNIA BOWL III

★ A BENEFIT FOR VALLEY CHILDREN'S HOSPITAL ★

Fullback Lou Wicks led the way with a career-high 119 yards on 14 carries.

"Lou saved the best game of his career for the last game of his career," Sobol said.

Tailback Darryl Richardson scored twice for the Huskies.

"They were both simple dive plays that ended up not being so simple," said Richardson in an e-mail. "I tried to jump over the pile on one, got pushed back and then bounced it to the outside to score. The other one I just tried to follow Lou and find a little crease."

NIU sealed the victory when its defense stopped Fullerton on a fourth-and-one play with 35 seconds left. Defensive back Jeff Sanders made the final play to preserve the win.

All the players interviewed were quick to credit Mallory and his staff for their game preparation.

"Watching the hard work and a great coach put that thing together was unbelievable," said quarterback Tim Tyrrell, the 1983 MAC Most Valuable Player. "You didn't want to let Coach Mallory down."

Defensive coordinator Joe Novak also praised Mallory. But he also pointed out that the Huskie head coach knew how to walk the fine line of bowl game preparation.

"Bill was great about letting the kids experience it. Don't get me wrong, we worked hard at practice in the morning, but we had fun as a group after that," Novak said.

Sobol noted that Novak also played a key role in the magical NIU season.

"He was extremely thorough in what we went through week after week," Sobol said. "We always had a pretty good handle on what the opposition was going to do."

Asked to pick out a play to illustrate his point, Sobol easily recalled a play from the fourth quarter.

"It was rather an insignificant play, but it really illustrates how well the coaches had us prepared," he said.

During the practices leading up to the bowl game, the coaching staff had drilled into the defense that CSF liked to run Allen on a naked bootleg in second-and-long or third-and-long situations.

With the score 17-10, Sobol realized that the Titans had yet to run the play in the game.

"In my head, I thought, 'This has to be it,'" Sobol said.

Sure enough, Allen took the snap and began to roll out.

"I hit the tight end or tackle, I can't remember which," Sobol said. "I got into the backfield and saw Allen's back and recognized the play.

"Instead of going for him, I got upfield another step. His eyes got really big when he realized what was happening. (Defensive lineman) Steve O'Malley smashed him."

While the game was going NIU's way, television viewers back in Illinois were left wondering what was going on in California. With temperatures below zero, the local TV station carrying the game lost its signal when the transmitter on top of the John Hancock Center froze in the third quarter. Thousands of complaints flooded the station's switchboard.

On the game's final play, Sanders brought down Allen to kill CSF's final drive and seal the victory.

"He was scrambling, trying to make a play," Sanders said from his home in Kansas. "I had contain on the play, meaning I couldn't let him get outside. He came over in my direction, and I ended up making a play and kept him in bounds."

When the game ended, Wicks was awarded the game's Most Valuable Player Award. For years, Wicks was under the impression that both he and Richardson were supposed to be co-MVPs. In fact, Wicks thought that since there was just one award to be handed out, Richardson had told the bowl officials to give it to the fullback.

"I think there was a little confusion there," said Richardson, today a mortgage banker and assistant junior college football coach. "I'm not sure who voted, but supposedly someone wanted to give it to me and then someone else wanted to give it to Lou. I thought Lou deserved it, as he played a great all-around game and he was a senior. What a way to go out."

While Wicks and Richardson starred in the California Bowl, Tyrrell has often been called the heart and soul of those '83 Huskies.

"Tim Tyrrell was a fiery type of a leader," said Novak. "I remember when we played undefeated Toledo. It was the eighth or ninth week of the season. *Sports Illustrated* was traveling with them. We always had meetings before each game in the student center. We always met by offense and defense. Well,

when the meetings wrapped up, all the players on offense shook hands with all the players on defense. It was a moving thing to see. It was almost a religious experience."

That "all-for-one" attitude still resonates with the team 30 years later.

"We were a team, plain and simple," Mallory said. "We didn't have any egos on that team."

Chicago radio and TV personality David Kaplan was a Huskie assistant basketball coach at the time.

"The whole town got caught up in it," Kaplan said.

Former NIU sports information director Mike Korcek pointed out that the '83 team produced seven NFL Draft picks and 19 professional players who saw action not only in the NFL, but also in the USFL, CFL and Arena football.

"Quite a tribute to Mallory and his staff," Korcek noted.

The university bestowed the ultimate honor when it inducted the entire team into the NIU Hall of Fame in 1995.

"The game was well played on both sides," said Tyrrell, who was inducted individually in 1992. "Winning the bowl was the icing on the cake."

BILL MALLORY

It seems appropriate that Bill Mallory belongs to a group called the Legends.

"We're a group of 17 retired coaches who watch DVDs of the most recent college football games and then cast a ballot," said Mallory, who coached Northern to its first Mid-American Conference title and a California Bowl victory in 1983.

The Legends includes 14 College Football Hall of Fame members—the likes of Frank Broyles, Vince Dooley, John Robinson and Gene Stallings. The group represents ten national championships and over 3,500 victories combined.

Bill Mallory coached the Huskies to their first major bowl victory. His 1983 team won the Mid-American Conference title and the California Bowl.

"We evaluate the teams of a given conference and then present our information in a weekly conference call," Mallory explained.

"I work with (former Ohio State coach) John Cooper on the Big Ten," said Mallory, who left NIU after the '83 season and spent the next 13 years coaching Indiana University.

"Everyone is open and honest," Mallory said. "There aren't any biases. We tell about the teams' strengths and weaknesses."

While the Legends' poll has no impact on the Bowl Championship Series (BCS), it may in the near future.

"The BCS listens in on our conference calls each week," Mallory said.

The BCS would do well to lend an ear. Forrest Gump has nothing on Bill Mallory. Sure, Forrest rubbed elbows with Elvis Presley, Bear Bryant and John F. Kennedy. But, Mallory's life reads like a Who's Who of college football royalty.

After starring at Sandusky High School under coach Jeff DeHaven, Mallory accepted an offer to play for the legendary Ara Parseghian at Miami University.

"Back then you tried out," Mallory recalled. "There were 30 or 40 of us that worked out. When it was over, Ara said he'd like to have me on his team."

Mallory's father, a high school basketball coach, was very impressed with Parseghian.

"Ara was a man of his word," Mallory said. "He told my dad, 'You're bringing me a boy. In four years I'll return him as a man.'"

Parseghian coached Miami for Mallory's first three years at Miami. When Ara left to coach at Northwestern, John Pont coached Mallory and the Redskins his senior season.

"John had been my freshman coach at Miami," Mallory said.

Following his graduation, Mallory accepted an assistant coaching position at MAC rival Bowling Green under Doyt Perry.

"He was unique," Mallory said. "He was a matter of fact guy. (Since I was from Bowling Green's rival school) he kept asking me, 'Can I trust you?'"

It took three Mallory phone calls and recommendations from Bo Schembechler and Bill Gunlock, but Perry finally hired the Miami graduate.

"As I said before, my father was a basketball coach," Mallory said. "He didn't know if a football was pumped or stuffed. But he knew I wanted to coach and teach. In those days there was never a graduate assistant program. But he told me to get a master's and get a good foundation in coaching."

Mallory got his master's in just one year and then coached East Palestine (Ohio) High School to an undefeated season.

"Then I got a call from Doyt," Mallory said. "I got to be a defensive coordinator at a young age. It was a tremendous break."

Mallory parlayed the opportunity into assistant coaching positions under Carm Cozza at Yale and Woody Hayes at Ohio State.

"Woody was a real history buff," Mallory noted. "His outlet was reading. He wouldn't go home. His wife was a saint. After we were done with football, Woody would stay in his office reading a history book. We always got a book review the next morning."

Following the Buckeyes' 1968 national championship, Mallory was offered the head coaching position at Miami, which had become open when Schembechler took the Michigan job.

"I'm so grateful to Woody," Mallory said. "When I went to him for advice (about being a head coach), he didn't talk about X and O's. Woody told me to make sure my players were well prepared for their futures. He told me to stress the importance of graduation. He taught me that winning would take care of itself."

Hayes' words became reality as Mallory rolled up 39 wins in five seasons at Miami. His final Redskins' team posted an 11-0 record and a Tangerine Bowl title in 1973.

Colorado was Mallory's next stop. He spent five years as the Buffaloes' head coach. He managed to win 35 games and earn berths in the Astro-Bluebonnet and Orange Bowls in that time.

Mallory left Colorado when he could no longer agree with his athletic director. After he was away from the game for a year, Northern came calling in 1980.

"They contacted me about the job when I was in Colorado," Mallory said. "I knew I was going to come back to the Midwest."

NIU's first contact came from assistant athletic director Jerry Ippoliti, who had coached the Huskies from 1971 to 1975.

"I knew Jerry from our days at Miami," said Mallory.

NIU athletic director Deacon Davis then interviewed and hired Mallory.

"(Northern) had not had the greatest amount of success at that point in time," Mallory remembered. "They had gone through struggling times in the MAC. I wanted to make sure there was a commitment to get things going.

"We wanted to set a vision and a tradition. There wasn't a whole lot of respect for Northern in the MAC. Many people asked me, 'Can you ever win there?'"

Northern did win. The Huskies finished with a 7-4 record in Mallory's first season. The next season, 1981, saw NIU dip to just 3-8.

"We had to bear down on recruiting, upgrade our talent level and get balance on both sides of the ball," Mallory noted.

After improving to 5-5 in 1982, Mallory's Huskies took the MAC by storm in '83.

"We opened at Kansas and won (37-34). Then we went to Wisconsin and played them tough the first half before it got away from us (in a 37-9 loss)," said Mallory.

"After that, we were pretty consistent in our play," he said.

Northern's lone conference loss came against Central Michigan as the Huskies rolled to their first MAC championship. That led to an invitation to the California Bowl.

"There was great excitement from the fans, players and coaches," said Mallory. "The defense was very stable throughout the year. But don't sell our offense short. We were a good-possession, sound offense that put points on the board."

Led by game Most Valuable Player Tim Tyrrell, NIU defeated Cal State-Fullerton 20-13 to win the California Bowl.

"(Bill Mallory) is by far the biggest influence in my life as a coach," Tyrrell said. "He carried the message. He walked the walk."

That '83 team was inducted into the NIU Hall of Fame in 1995.

"It's a great honor and very deserving," Mallory said.

With success came an offer from a Big Ten university.

"I can say with all honesty that I never pursued a job," Mallory said. "My focus was making the job at hand successful."

But, a telephone call from Bob Knight of Indiana changed things.

"He was close to Bo and Woody," Mallory said. "I asked what had happened to (IU football coach) Sam Wyche. Coach Knight told me he had taken the Cincinnati Bengals' job."

Thus, Mallory and his staff arrived in Bloomington, Indiana to start a new era for the Hoosiers.

Overcoming an 0-11 start in 1984, Mallory went on to become the winningest coach in Indiana history. In his 13 seasons with the Hoosiers, Mallory won 69 games and earned six bowl appearances. He also won back-to-back Big Ten Coach of the Year awards. His 1988 Indiana team earned a Top 20 ranking.

Mallory also won respect throughout the land. After his Hoosiers lost a showdown with Michigan State for the Big Ten title in 1987, Mallory visited the Spartan locker room to congratulate the MSU players and coaches. The video clip has become a favorite on YouTube.

"Bill was tough, fair, honest and loyal," said Dave Petzke, the NIU Hall of Fame receiver who served as an assistant coach to Mallory at both Northern and Indiana. "If he called tomorrow and needed me, I'd drop everything and go."

Former Big Ten official Roger Haberer recalled a time he blew a call while working an Indiana game as the umpire.

"I made a heck of a mistake (against Mallory's Hoosiers)," Haberer recalled. "He didn't like it, but he just went on with the game."

David Kaplan has worked in Chicago radio and TV since the mid-1990s. Prior to that he worked as an assistant basketball coach at NIU from 1982 to 1986.

"I was a young part-time assistant," Kaplan said in the summer of 2010. "One of my duties was to run the study hall for the athletes. There were three different rooms to monitor. Just as soon as I'd get one room quiet and working and move on to the next, they'd start up again, doing everything but studying.

"All of a sudden Bill Mallory walks in and he goes nuts. The way he took control of those rooms you could tell he was the man in charge."

Though it's been over a decade since Mallory last coached, he still adheres to the principles that outlined his philosophy on the profession.

"Coaching is teaching and parenting," Mallory said. "I was blessed as a young man to be around a lot of great coaches. It's about the player. He has to become a total individual. His experiences from football must also be those of the real world.

"He has to have a strong focus. He must have academic support. I didn't want what I called athletic bums who only wanted to play football and not get an education. You do things the right way. You conduct yourself in a class fashion on and off the field."

During his coaching days, Mallory required his players to dress appropriately.

"Their shoes had to be polished and they wore ties," he said.

Mallory stressed being on time.

"If you weren't there five minutes before things started, the doors were locked and I'd see you at six the next morning," he noted.

He even brought in professionals to teach his players etiquette.

"You had to realize that your present leads to your future," Mallory said.

His rules applied to all.

"It doesn't matter if you're on the first team or the fifth team," he said.

On the field, Mallory was a strong believer in defense. He wanted a sound possession-oriented offense that didn't turn the ball over inside the 50. Mallory also stressed the kicking game.

"It wins a lot of games for you," he said.

Mallory's legacy thrives with his three sons, all of whom played at Michigan and now coach.

"Mike was with the (New Orleans) Saints and also coached in college. Curt is at Illinois (and later Indiana) and Doug coaches at New Mexico," the boys' proud father said.

Mallory spends time every season with each of his sons. He was even asked to address the Saints in training camp by head coach Sean Payton, a player Mallory had recruited while at Northern.

"I've talked to college teams most of my life, but I wasn't sure it would work with a pro team," Mallory said.

Payton said, "He not only spoke to our team, Bill did a really good job."

Now in his seventies, Mallory spends his retirement years with his wife Ellie. The couple still lives in Bloomington eight months of the year. Winters are spent in Florida.

"We do things we never got to do when I coached," he said. "There's the family and grandchildren."

There was also time spent with his former assistant Bill Lynch, who served as the Hoosiers' head coach for four seasons.

"I'd bounce ideas off him and he could take them or throw them aside," Mallory said.

There's also all that time spent with those DVDs.

"Football is still with me," Mallory said. "I enjoy watching those games and breaking down a team."

Spoken like a true legend.

FOUR-DOWN TERRITORY

Favorite Football Movie—I don't really have one. I really enjoy watching games.

First Car—It was a 1956 or '57 Chrysler my dad gave me when I graduated college and took my first job at Bowling Green.

Worst Summer Job—None of the jobs drove me nuts. My brothers and I always worked in the summer. It gave us spending money.

Favorite Subject in School—History, especially American history.

TIM TYRRELL

If you've seen the movie "Invincible" then you've had a glimpse into the career of Tim Tyrrell.

"That was me, that was my story," said Tyrrell of the film that was based on Vince Papale, a 30-year-old bartender from South Philadelphia who overcame long odds to play for the NFL's Philadelphia Eagles in 1976.

"(Like Papale) I was an undrafted free agent who worked his butt off to make it in the NFL. That movie is the most realistic I've seen, especially in the way it showed how rookies are treated."

Tyrrell quarterbacked the 1983 Northern Illinois Huskies to the program's first regular season Mid-American Conference title and a victory in the California Bowl.

Along the way Tyrrell was the first NIU player to win the MAC Most Valuable Player Award (then called the Jefferson Award). After graduation, Tyrrell found himself in pro football.

"I did whatever I had to do to stay in the league," Tyrrell said. "I was a high intensity guy. I just didn't quit. You had to be that way to stick around.

"I was always in fights (in training camp). I must have fought half the team."

Playing primarily special teams, Tyrrell spent six seasons in the NFL with the Atlanta Falcons, Los Angeles Rams and Pittsburgh Steelers.

"It was so great, so satisfying," Tyrrell said. "I'm so grateful to have had the opportunity to play in the league. They don't call it the NFL—Not for Long—for nothing.

"It was such a rush. I can't tell you how tired I was and how beat up I got. It was like being in an accident every day, but I hardly ever went into the training room. I didn't want to risk it."

Just how much did playing in the NFL mean to Tyrrell?

"I've never done drugs, but I've been told that people who do crack are always trying to recapture the first of the first time. It's something that was so unbelievable for them, they just have to keep going," he explained. "That's the way the NFL was for me."

Tyrrell remembers waking up several times and thinking just how fortunate he was.

"I would have played for free," Tyrrell said. "I only hired an agent to get me a league minimum contract."

But, Tyrrell was hardly an overnight success story. Instead, it's one filled with grit and determination.

Tyrrell was a running back at Conant High School in Hoffman Estates.

"My junior year I started getting letters from schools," he recalled. "But, in my senior year the very first day of camp I tore cartilage in my knee. I tried to come back and play, but it just wasn't there."

Following graduation, Tyrrell spent a year working at a local Dominick's grocery store. Then, he walked on at Harper Junior College in Palatine.

"I missed football," he said. "I really wanted to play."

Three games into the season, the Harper coaches moved Tyrrell from running back to quarterback.

"I loved it," Tyrrell said. "I loved having my hands on the ball every play."

He also loved contact.

"If I threw an interception, I couldn't wait to run down and hit the defensive player as hard as I could," Tyrrell said. "That was my aggressive style."

That style caught the attention of four-year colleges around the Midwest.

"I have 12 offers," Tyrrell said. "Nine of them wanted me as a defensive back. Three of them wanted me as a quarterback."

The three schools were Murray State, Southeast Missouri and Northern.

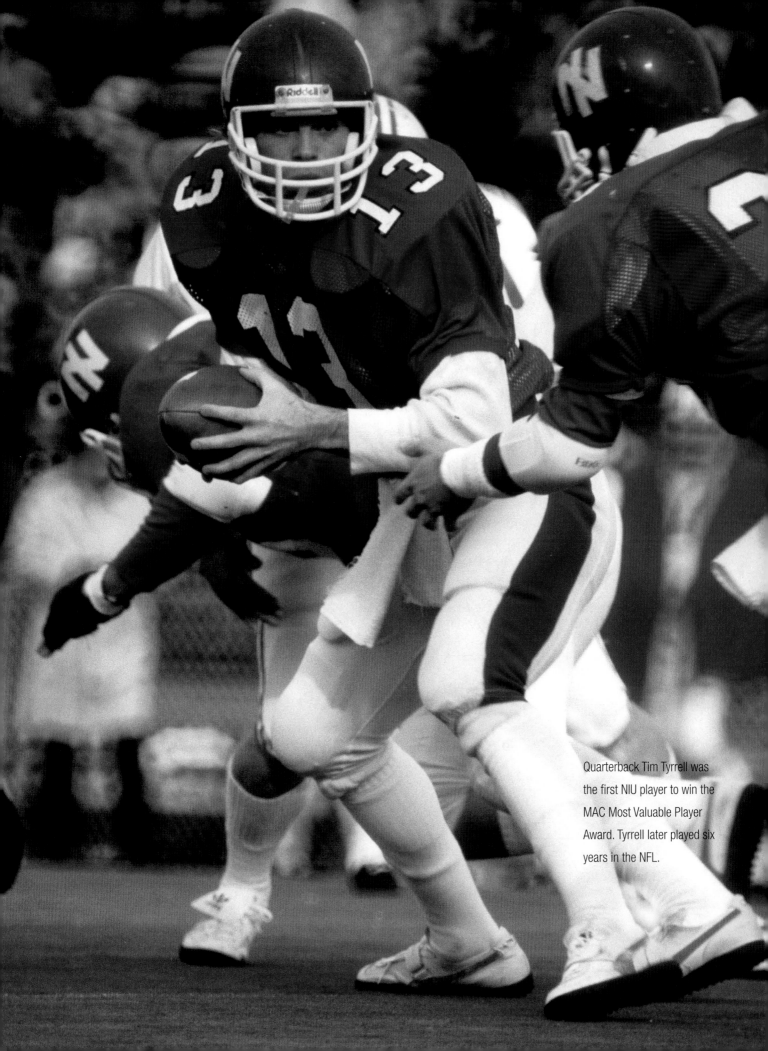

Quarterback Tim Tyrrell was the first NIU player to win the MAC Most Valuable Player Award. Tyrrell later played six years in the NFL.

"There seemed to be a certain mold that Coach Mallory recruited," Tyrrell said. "He didn't just want talented guys. You had to be his type of player."

That type of player was one who would prepare himself for any situation and fit into the team concept.

"I'd say it worked," Tyrrell said. "There are probably 50 guys from those days that I'm still close with. That's a great way to go through life."

It was also a great way to go through the 1983 season. NIU tied a school record with 10 wins in 12 games. It also marked the first Huskie appearance in a "major" bowl.

"That whole season was a dream season," Tyrrell said. "We were picked to finish sixth in the preseason conference poll. It turned out to be a storybook season."

The season began with an upset of Kansas from the Big 8 Conference. It ended with a thrilling victory over Cal State Fullerton in the California Bowl. And nearly everything in between was special.

Mallory viewed his quarterback as one of the keys to the team's success.

"Tim was the hub of our offense. He was an inspiration to those around him," Mallory said.

Mike Korcek, NIU's longtime sports information director, added, "What a great kid and all-purpose quarterback. (He was) great on play action passes. (He had a) linebacker mentality at QB."

That mentality was evident in his play. In one of the most memorable plays of the remarkable '83 season, Tyrrell ignited the team with a third quarter, 43-yard scamper down

the Huskie Stadium east sideline to rally NIU past Bowling Green State.

"We needed something to get life back in the team," said Mallory. "That first score was like giving someone who hasn't eaten in a while something to eat. I knew we were on our way."

"Like I said before, I loved playing quarterback," Tyrrell said. "We ran play action on every play. I loved to run the ball. I didn't go out of bounds very much. I liked to complete passes, but if I had to tuck it and run, that was fine with me."

That was also fine with his teammates and coaches.

"Tim Tyrrell was a fiery type of leader," said Joe Novak, then NIU's defensive coordinator. "He really played to win."

Today, Tyrrell is still playing to win. More than 20 years after last playing in the NFL, Tyrrell still uses the experiences he gained in football to guide his life.

"I'm in sales. I'm an individual rep for several companies," Tyrrell said. "Many of the lessons I learned in the game are still part of me today."

Many of those lessons came from Mallory.

"People say I'm intense," Tyrrell said. "Well, that came from Coach Mallory. With him it was no excuses, get it done and give yourself a chance to succeed."

Sounds like a line from "Invincible," doesn't it?

FOUR-DOWN TERRITORY

Favorite Football Movie—I loved "Brian's Song" and had the chance to meet Gale Sayers, but it's "Invincible."

First Car—1972 Vega hatchback that was half orange and half rust. I loved it.

Worst Summer Job—Making rain buoys or lifesavers at a factory in Wheeling. We hand-dripped them in glue. They were on a rack. It was liquid rubber, and we did it without a mask. It really got to you after a while.

Favorite Subject in School—Horticulture. Believe it or not, Mr. Don Fletcher, my high school teacher, was such a great guy. I actually had his class put together a plan for my house.

LOU WICKS

The ripple effects of a coaching change are far-reaching. Lou Wicks is a prime example.

Growing up in Champaign, Wicks became a star running back at Central High School in the late 1970s. In fact, Wicks was later inducted into the school's Hall of Fame.

In the final game of his senior season, Wicks rushed for 123 yards in a loss to the No. 1–ranked Peoria Richwoods in the state playoffs. Richwoods' coach Tom Peeler noted, "He's an extremely hard runner to bring down, and I think Central is as good as any team we've faced all year."

Upon graduation, Wicks seemed destined to have "local boy makes good" headlines written about him at the University of Illinois.

"I was actually verbally committed to Gary Moeller and the University of Illinois," Wicks said in an e-mail.

However, Moeller was fired after the 1979 season and replaced by Mike White.

White pulled the scholarship offer that had been made to Wicks.

"Mike White wanted me to walk on," Wicks said. "Gary Durchick and Joe Novak were both on Moeller's staff and were picked up by Coach (Bill) Mallory."

Mallory had recently been named as the new head coach at Northern.

"Both (Durchick and Novak) proceeded to recruit me to NIU," Wicks said. "I remember the first time I met Coach Novak and asked him about NIU, he responded that he knew nothing about NIU, but Coach Mallory would make it a positive experience for me."

Fullback Lou Wicks was selected as the 1983 California
Bowl Most Valuable Player.

According to Mallory, Wicks was a true competitor.

"Lou was tough," said Mallory. "He had a great attitude. He fit well into our system. He was more than just a blocker from his fullback spot. We'd run him on quick traps, dives and belly plays. Our system also put him in the passing game. Lou really kept defenses honest."

While the magic of the 1983 Mid-American Conference championship season remains special to him, most of Wicks' memories center on the momentum gained during the second half of the '82 season.

"I believe we finished 4-1 in the last five games," he said. "I also remember how disappointed we were in how we played in the Central Michigan game."

The Huskies lost that game to the Chippewas 30-14, yet were still able to win the school's first MAC title.

The conference title sent NIU into the California Bowl, marking the first time in school history that the Huskies had earned a berth in a major post-season game.

NIU took things a step further, defeating Cal State-Fullerton 20-13, and was crowned California Bowl champion. For his part, Wicks rushed for 119 yards out of his fullback position. Tailback Darryl Richardson scored twice for the Huskies.

"After the game I thought Darryl and I were going to be co-MVPs, but at the presentation he was not there and they said I was the MVP," Wicks said. "I believe they just wanted one MVP and Darryl told them to give it to me.

"That is the kind of a guy he is and was most of our team."

Longtime NIU play-by-play man Bill Baker fondly recalls 1983 and the California Bowl victory.

"We didn't have any superstars, but we had good solid football players," Baker said. "When

was the last time a fullback was the MVP of anything? Probably 1983."

The same season NIU won the California Bowl, the University of Illinois captured the Big Ten and played in the Rose Bowl. Does Wicks ever regret his decision to pass on White's offer to walk on for the Illini?

"No, not really," he said. "I was pretty content at NIU. I have a brother who is a year behind me and attended the U of I, and my dad was a professor there. They both went to the California Bowl over the Rose Bowl."

Wicks further noted that 1983 was a successful season for numerous programs in the state. He cited the national championships won by Southern (I-AA) and Augustana

(Division III). In addition, Eastern made the playoffs.

After graduation from NIU, Wicks became a graduate assistant under Mallory at Indiana University. Wicks spent two years with the Hoosiers and earned a master's degree in sports fitness.

From there, he served as an assistant coach at Elmhurst College for three years. Wicks then moved to the high school ranks where he was the head football coach and athletic director at Carmi-White County.

"After seven years (we) moved back north," Wick said.

He was hired as the head football coach at Tremont High School in 1997. His Tremont teams have qualified for the state playoffs six times, including an 11-1 season in 2002.

"That was an exciting year, both my sons played on that team," Wicks said. "They are both serving in the United States Marines."

As for his NIU days, Wicks said, "I truly loved my experience."

Today, his daughter attends Northern and does video work for the football team.

The ripple effects continue to be far-reaching, even four decades later.

FOUR-DOWN TERRITORY

Favorite Football Movie—"Brian's Song."

First Car—A 1971 Olds 98.

Worst Summer Job—Loved them all.

Favorite Subject in School—Math.

DARRYL RICHARDSON

Darryl Richardson didn't picture himself as a Northern Illinois Huskie.

"I was not recruited by NIU to start with and NIU was not a place I thought I would end up," the former Huskie tailback said in an e-mail. "I was being, I guess what you call, heavily recruited by many schools. (It) started my junior year (of high school)."

Richardson, the star of Wheaton North High School, played on two state championship teams.

As a result, Richardson received weekly recruiting attention from the likes of Penn State, Iowa, Nebraska, Illinois, Purdue, Michigan State, Ohio State and Iowa State.

"The mailman had to bring the mail to my mom half the time because it wouldn't fit in the box," he said.

Richardson's recruitment wasn't just limited to letters, game programs and posters.

"One Big Ten school even got me a summer job, but we'll keep them anonymous," Richardson said.

Yet, the high school standout heard virtually nothing from NIU.

"Before the state (title) game my senior year I spoke with coaches from Iowa, Penn State and Illinois and received good-luck grams from them as well through the mail," Richardson said. "(However), that was the last I heard from them."

That made it possible for schools like Northern, Southwest Missouri State and Indiana State to get their foot in the door.

"Things may have been different, but Coach (Jim) Rexilius, a longtime coach and legend at Wheaton North High School, left to take a college job," Richardson said.

Thus, the new coaching staff may have sold Richardson short.

"I'm not sure they did a great job of selling me, and with a father who was never home, I was pretty much on my own," Richardson said. "I guess I didn't do a good job."

That being said, things worked out pretty well, however, when NIU head coach Bill Mallory's staff got Richardson to commit to the Huskies.

Darryl Richardson was a highly recruited tailback from Wheaton North High School.

Richardson was a key component to the offense during NIU's run to the Mid-American Conference title and California Bowl championship in 1983. Richardson led the Huskies in rushing with 1,204 yards. He averaged 5.1 yards per carry.

Moreover, his 187-yard, two-touchdown performance against Ohio University at Huskie Stadium helped NIU clinch the MAC crown.

"The electricity at the games as the season progressed and how we became closer to our goal (is something I'll always remember)," Richardson said.

He also cited the "fun and camaraderie I had with the guys" as a huge part of the experience.

"A lot of my good friends and I were underclassmen so we stayed in the dorms," he said.

Richardson scored a pair of touchdowns for the Huskies in the California Bowl. Though he was under strong consideration for the bowl's Most Valuable Player Award, teammate Lou Wicks received the honor.

Following the remarkable season, Mallory left DeKalb to accept the head coaching position at Indiana University. Little did Richardson realize, but his best collegiate days were behind him.

"Part of me wanted to leave and go to Indiana with Bill Mallory and his staff, especially after they gave the job to Lee Corso instead of Gary Durchik, the lone holdover who stayed to try to get the job," Richardson said.

However, he decided to remain at NIU.

"I knew I could graduate in four years," he said. "If I transferred then I would have had to sit out a year and go at least four-and-a-half to five years. You can also throw in my girlfriend at the time, Kelli. She happened to be a cheerleader at Northern. I guess I didn't want to leave her either and today we remain very good friends."

Though Richardson stayed a Huskie, the happiest part of his collegiate career left with Mallory.

"It was a little tough for me," Richardson said. "Offensively we went from the I-formation to the wishbone, to split backs, to the veer and whatever else you want to throw in there.

"Not that I couldn't adapt, but those offenses call for totally different line personnel. That's why they give new coaches three to four years to recruit the types of players they need to make their system work."

Injuries also began to take their toll on Richardson.

"Being the focal part of the offense, I took the most abuse," he said. "My junior year was a struggle as I tried to play all year with an Achilles' problem that I got in pre-camp."

Tim Weigel from Chicago's ABC affiliate came to DeKalb to film a feature on Richardson to run at halftime of the Huskies' season opener.

"That didn't happen much back in those days," Richardson said.

However, the mounting physical ailments derailed Richardson's junior season.

"I'm not sure I was ever even 75 percent healthy the entire year," he said.

Richardson's final season was a roller coaster under first-year Huskie head coach Jerry Pettibone.

"What also made it a tough year was listening to the paper take shots at me about which player will we see this year?" Richardson said.

However, Richardson did manage to string together consecutive 100-yard games to finish out his career. He managed to again lead NIU in rushing (585 yards, 4.8 average) but carried the ball only about half of his 1983 total.

Richardson did draw interest from pro football when his college days were over.

"The Washington Redskins did contact me before the draft and asked me a bunch of questions," he said. "(They) took my number and asked where they could fly me out of, but I never heard from them on draft day."

Thus, Richardson signed with Green Bay as a free agent. However, his pro career was short-lived. Yet, football remains a part of Richardson's life.

"I broke into coaching at the College of Du-Page in 1993," he said. "Another former Huskie, Scott Kellar, was on that same staff. My first three years there, we broke the national junior college record for consecutive wins. We won 35 games in a row, which included three undefeated seasons.

"The head coach stepped down (he had been there over 20 years) a couple years later and the president dropped football. They only dropped it for one year, however, after a lot of flack from the community and alumni."

After a year away from coaching, Richardson joined the staff at Joliet Junior College.

"We have won two non-scholarship national championships and one outright national championship," he said. "I also coached in the Arena League for one year in Tulsa, Oklahoma."

Richardson's day job is as a mortgage banker.

"(I work) at Compass Mortgage in Warrenville," he said. "The owner is a former Huskie as well, and I also played high school football with him."

All this for a guy who nearly didn't end up at NIU.

FOUR-DOWN TERRITORY

Favorite Football Movies—"Remember the Titans" and "Jerry Maguire"—the true symbolism behind both movies.

First Car— Ford Mustang.

Worst Summer Job—Scraping and painting.

Favorite Subject in School—English.

TODD PEAT

Though it's been nearly three decades since Todd Peat played at Northern Illinois, his former coaches and teammates still marvel at his athleticism.

"I'd put him right up there with any of the outstanding linemen I had," said Bill Mallory, who coached Peat as a freshman before moving on to Indiana University. "He takes a backseat to no one. He certainly could have played for me at IU or a number of other places in the Big Ten."

Peat came to NIU despite playing in the University of Illinois' backyard at Champaign Central High School.

"I think the University of Illinois had him on the back burner, which was a mistake. It worked out well for us at Northern though," said Mallory.

"I was a ball boy for Illinois. I really wanted to go there," Peat told Bob Asmussen of the *Champaign News-Gazette*. "I used to sneak into the weight room and lift with the guys. I'd ride my bike to the University of Illinois."

Mike White was the Illini head coach at the time. Years later, Peat played for White on the Los Angeles Raiders.

"We used to get a big laugh out of it because he told me he fired the recruiting coordinator," Peat told Asmussen.

Former Huskie running back Lou Wicks knew Peat's talents firsthand.

"Todd and I actually went to high school together, but never played on the varsity together," Wicks said in an e-mail. "I was a couple of years ahead. He is today the most athletic big man I have ever seen. In his first college game ever, Kansas used every defensive tackle they had (against Peat). Todd just dominated them. I have too many incredible stories about Todd. Most you would not believe."

Todd Peat was an NFL All-Rookie team member who played six pro seasons. He was a pivotal member of the 1983 MAC and California Bowl champions.

Perhaps his teammates would, however.

"(Todd) was a tremendous athlete," said former NIU quarterback Tim Tyrrell.

Darryl Richardson, the backfield mate of Wicks and Tyrrell, went even further.

"Todd Peat was an awesome presence on the field," Richardson said in an e-mail. "He could blow you up on a one-on-one block, he was quick enough to trap as well as pull and lead (block). Then throw in that he was technically sound.

"Todd had all the tools. I still remember him as a freshman, as they redshirted him because he was, of course, overweight, but he had a knee injury in high school as well. That gave the staff a chance to put him on a so-called diet, as he came in over 400 pounds. They told him he had to get down to a certain weight and I'm not sure if he actually made it, but they gave him the benefit of the doubt and his play on the field didn't make them regret it. Great player."

Listed at 6 foot 2, 294 pounds, Peat landed a spot on the Best of NIU Football Team selected by a committee in 1998. Peat is also a member of the NIU Hall of Fame.

"Todd was an excellent lineman for us. He was also a quality individual of strong character and great attitude. He was focused," Mallory said.

Peat played a pivotal role in NIU's 1983 California Bowl victory. With 5:25 remaining, the Huskies had the ball on their own 20-yard line. Facing a fourth-and-one to go and clinging to a 20-13 lead, Mallory sent Tyrrell on a quarterback sneak behind Peat. The freshman guard led the way as Tyrrell picked up the critical first down. NIU then bled nearly four additional minutes off the game clock en route to the win.

"How many freshmen are there that you'd run behind?" Tyrrell said.

"Todd Peat for one," said Mallory.

The St. Louis Cardinals selected Peat in the 11th round of the 1987 National Football League Draft. Peat played six pro seasons, spending time at guard and tackle. He was traded to the Raiders in 1990 and retired following the '93 season.

Since retiring from the NFL, Peat remained in Arizona, where he played with the Cardinals. A father of seven children, Peat now sees the recruiting game as a parent. Todd Jr., his oldest, signed with Nebraska in 2011. His second son, Andrus, had offers as a sophomore.

"They both are doing extremely well," Peat said of his sons. "Every parent thinks their kid is the greatest. But what I can tell you is that we work hard. We're preparing for the next football season. Football and their academics are the two most important things, and academics are first."

One only wonders if Huskie fans may again see a Peat in their lineup.

THE WILD (AND CRAZY) TIMES OF LEE CORSO

Nearly anyone who follows college football knows Lee Corso, analyst for ESPN's "Game Day."

NIU faithful will no doubt remember the very brief tenure of Corso as the Huskies' 16th head football coach.

Corso was hired when Bill Mallory left NIU to accept the head coaching position at Indiana University following the 1983 California Bowl. Ironically, Corso was a former IU head coach himself.

"I thought there is no way this guy would be here a year from now," said David Kaplan, the well-known Chicago radio and TV broadcaster who was an NIU assistant basketball coach at the time.

NIU play-by-play man Bill Baker began his Huskie broadcast career in 1980. He remembers the Corso "nine-game experiment."

"I say this looking back with hindsight, it was a disaster," Baker said. "He came here from Indiana University where he had a TV show. He brought that with him. He did a coach's show on Channel 7 on Sunday mornings. I liked Lee. He was very personable, but I always saw him as more of an entertainer than a football coach. I don't recall seeing the 'real, get-down-after-it' football coaching from him."

Jack Pheanis arrived as a student-athlete in 1950. Following his playing days, Pheanis would spend nearly a half century as an NIU coach. His memories of Corso weren't positive ones.

"I always had the idea he was not happy at Northern, like he was looking to go somewhere else," said Pheanis. "The only good thing I can

Lee Corso of ESPN fame coached at NIU during the 1984 season before leaving for the United States Football League.

say about him was that he was a churchgoer. You would see him at Mass Saturday night or Sunday morning regularly."

Rumors began circulating that Corso was going to leave NIU for the United States Football League (USFL).

"The media tried to pin him down, but he was tightlipped," Baker said. "I remember after the win over Central Michigan, the team had given him the game ball. Our broadcast team was getting in the car after the game. It was me, Sid Simmons and Mark Lindo. The parking lot was empty and it was dark. Then we saw one lonely figure walking across the parking lot."

After turning on his headlights, Baker realized it was Corso.

"He was going back to a hotel. He had a briefcase in his hand but no game ball," Baker said.

Baker offered Corso a ride, which the coach accepted.

"It was a two-minute ride or so to the hotel where he was apparently living, at least for part of the time," Baker said. "There were two games left in the season and one of us asked Lee if we would see him next week in Ohio (for the Huskies' next game).

"He asked if this was off the record. Of course, we said yes. With that, Corso stuck out his hand and said, 'It was good working with all of you.' He jumped out of the car and headed for the hotel. I can still see him climbing the steps to the second floor. I didn't see him again until (ESPN) 'Game Day' was doing the Northern–Bowling Green game in 2004."

According to longtime NIU assistant coach Mike Sabock, Corso spent the season living at Huskie Stadium.

"There were rumors swirling about the USFL and the Orlando Renegades," Sabock said. "We were playing our ninth game of the season against Central Michigan. Lee always assigned us certain things to watch during warm-ups like if the other team was wearing the right shoes for our turf or whatever. Lee

always slapped the table and off we went. So we (coaches) went back inside to meet. After we all gave our reports, Lee said, 'One more thing, staff meeting tomorrow at eight o'clock.' He slaps the table and leaves. We're all sitting there wondering the worst.

"Well, Lee lived in the stadium. His wife never moved to DeKalb. She was still back in Bloomington (Indiana). So, Lee lives in the stadium. Actually it was the room that later became my office. He slept on a couch, used the bathroom down the hall and showered in the locker room.

"So the next morning we pull up to see his car packed with all his belongings. There's only enough room for the driver. The car is parked facing the exit. He gathers us together, tells us that he's leaving to coach Orlando in the USFL, slaps the table and leaves."

Just like that Corso was gone from DeKalb and into the USFL.

Like Sabock, Pheanis remembers Corso living in the stadium.

"One time I went up to wish him luck before a game," Pheanis said. "I was there early and (Corso) was in his underwear, just Jockey shorts. No shoes or shirt or anything. He was walking around the office like that. There weren't any women around, but I remember thinking, 'What the heck is he doing?'"

Numerous requests were made through ESPN to interview Corso for this book. However, no response ever came.

Corso did discuss the USFL in a 2010 cnnsi.com column.

"My involvement with the USFL began in the broadcast booth before I ever coached a game in the league," Corso wrote. "I teamed with play-by-play man Jim Lampley on the first ever USFL telecast, a 28-7 win for the Chicago Blitz over the Washington Federals, and a mere two years later I was coaching the Federals franchise, which had been relocated to Orlando and renamed the Renegades.

"We promptly lost our first six games of the season, not only coming out on the wrong end, but failing to even cover the spread. Talk about a bad situation. I made things pretty hard when I did my radio show live from a local bar and even harder when we went to live television. Those things are tough when your teams can't cover."

For Pheanis, seeing Corso on ESPN's "Game Day" is hard to stomach.

"His heart wasn't at Northern Illinois, which was what really bothered me the most," said Pheanis. "And where did he go? Some bandit outfit down in some pro football league that didn't last!"

Sort of like Lee Corso's brief tenure at NIU.

JERRY PETTIBONE

When Lee Corso bolted Northern for the United States Football League, the Huskies' best option proved to be a man **with** the option.

"Bob Brigham was the AD at the time and he hired me," said Jerry Pettibone.

The longtime collegiate assistant had cut his teeth with the likes of Bud Wilkinson, Barry Switzer, Jackie Sherrill and Tom Osborne. Pettibone brought the wishbone offense with him to DeKalb.

"It was something I knew well," Pettibone said.

He also knew something about winning football. Pettibone had earned Catholic All-State honors as a running back at Jesuit High School in Dallas. The school won Texas state championships his junior and senior seasons.

Pettibone then took his game to the University of Oklahoma, the school that had won national championships in 1956 and '57.

"J.D. Roberts, who had been an Outland Trophy winner at OU, recruited me," Pettibone said. "It was a tremendous honor to play at Oklahoma."

Pettibone played both running back and defensive back for Wilkinson from 1959 to 1961.

"Coach Wilkinson is one of the classiest and best coaches in the history of college football," Pettibone said. "What I learned under him I carried with me into my own coaching career."

The list Pettibone got from Wilkinson is long: surround yourself with quality people, do things for the right reasons, value the college education, encourage teamwork and a genuine love for the game.

Pettibone's coaching career began in 1966 with Jim MacKenzie at Oklahoma.

"Jim came over from Arkansas," Pettibone said. "He came after Gomer Jones, who had followed Wilkinson. Jim gave me the opportunity to coach."

MacKenzie, however, lasted just one season.

"He died of a massive heart attack," Pettibone said. "He was only 31."

Chuck Fairbanks succeeded MacKenzie. Pettibone remained on the Sooner staff for nearly all of the next decade.

"I spent about eight months at SMU with Hayden Fry," Pettibone recalled. "That was 1970, and I was his recruiting coordinator and freshman coach."

Pettibone returned to Oklahoma for the 1971 season. For the next three seasons, his job was clearly laid out for him.

"I believe that I was the first full-time recruiting coordinator in college football," Pettibone said. "That's all I did, recruit."

And recruit, did he ever. The Sooners posted an unbelievable 73-7 record from 1971 to 1977. When Fairbanks left for the NFL after the '72 season, Barry Switzer took the Sooner helm.

"The lowest we finished was fifth in the nation from 1973 to 1977," Pettibone pointed out. "We had a 31-game winning streak."

Oklahoma won back-to-back national championships in 1974 and '75. Pettibone recruited an amazing array of talent during those years, including future Heisman Trophy

winner Billy Sims and Outland Trophy recipients Lee Roy Selmon and Greg Roberts.

One of Pettibone's early Oklahoma recruiting classes sent 17 of 25 players into the NFL. In addition to the national championships, he was part of seven Big 8 Conference titles for the Sooners.

"That was a tremendous coaching staff," Pettibone said. "Of course you had Barry, but the assistants included Galen Hall, Larry Lacewell and Jimmy Johnson."

It also included a volunteer named Mike Shanahan from Eastern Illinois who would go on to win a pair of Super Bowls with the Denver Broncos.

Following an Orange Bowl victory over conference rival Nebraska, Pettibone left Oklahoma. Ironically, his next coaching destination was Lincoln, Nebraska.

"You just didn't do that back then," Pettibone said. "It would be like playing for Texas and then winding up at Texas A&M."

So why did he do it then?

"All I knew was the Oklahoma way," he explained. "This gave me another way of doing things. See, there are many ways to do things."

It also gave him the opportunity to coach under another legend, Cornhusker coach Tom Osborne. Pettibone served as split ends coach and recruiting coordinator, a title that he was gaining quite a reputation for.

Pettibone helped land prized recruits Irving Fryer, Mark Traynowicz and Mike Rozier, winner of the 1983 Heisman.

After three years at Nebraska, Pettibone experienced yet another way to do things. Jackie Sherrill left Pittsburgh and became the head coach at Texas A&M.

"Jackie called and offered me a job," Pettibone said. "I was at A&M from 1982 to '84. I coached wide receivers and was the recruiting coordinator. The last two years, I was also assistant head coach."

Jerry Pettibone played at Oklahoma for famed coach Bud Wilkinson prior to a successful coaching career.

Pettibone's reputation was then firmly established. No less than *Sports Illustrated* named him as the No.1 recruiter in America. His first A&M class ranked tops in the Southwest Conference and fifth nationally. That class produced six Aggie starters the very first year in College Station.

It was time for Pettibone to become a collegiate head coach.

"I spent 19 years around the staff room as an assistant," he said. "In this line of work where you sit says a lot. Everybody has a place. The head coach sits at the head of the table. The defensive and offensive coordinators are on each side of the head coach. When I was a graduate assistant under Bud Wikinson I didn't even sit at the table. I was on a folding chair away from the table."

Pettibone's head coaching opportunity came from NIU. When Corso left the Huskies with two games remaining in the 1984 season, Ted Huebber took over as interim coach but was never really considered for the job permanently.

"I was recommended by a former Nebraska lineman named Lawrence Cooley who was on the Northern staff," Pettibone said.

NIU athletic director Bob Brigham hired Pettibone over finalists Joe Novak, then an assistant under Bill Mallory at Indiana, and Glen Mason of Kent State. Novak finally became the Huskies' head coach in 1996.

"Joe did one heckuva job at Northern," Pettibone said.

Finally given the chance to run a team as the head coach, Pettibone thought back to that table in staff meetings.

"It's human nature to scrutinize the head coach's decisions," Pettibone said. "But, when you sit at the end of the table and feel the responsibilities of being in charge, it's overwhelming."

Pettibone also soon realized what the Huskie players had gone through.

"Counting Ted Huebber, those players had four coaches in a little over a year," Pettibone said. "Tim Griffin, a kid from St. Lawrence High School, came to me and asked if it were true that my wife and I had bought a house in Sycamore. I told him it was true. He jumped for joy and let out a yell that 'Coach is staying!'"

Knowing full well that recruiting is the lifeblood of any program, Pettibone and his staff beat the bushes for talent.

"We recruited from day one. Most of our players came from a 50-mile radius of DeKalb," Pettibone said. "They came from the Catholic League, the Public League and small towns. They came with a blue collar attitude and were ready to work."

Pettibone's staff also hit the ground running in another way—literally.

"We ran the wishbone that Jerry brought with him," said assistant coach Mike Sabock.

However, NIU fans didn't really take a liking to Pettibone's offense.

"For whatever reason, the fans never really bought into it," Sabock noted.

Perhaps one of the reasons was that Pettibone's first two Huskie teams struggled.

"The first year we were still in the Mid-American Conference," Pettibone said. "We went 4-7."

Then came a decision that hurt the program. NIU left the MAC and became an independent.

"We played the toughest schedule in the NCAA," Pettibone said. "It was brutal."

Northern won just two games against the likes of West Virginia, Wisconsin, Iowa and No. 1–ranked Miami.

"But, we came through it," Pettibone said.

By 1987, Pettibone's Huskies began to turn things around. That season NIU went 5-5 with a tie against Northwestern. In 1988, the Huskies posted a 7-4 record. The following year, 1989, brought a nine-victory season.

Led by quarterback Stacey Robinson, a recruit from downstate Danville, the Huskies broke opponents with the wishbone.

Robinson's finest day came a season later in an October 6 matchup with 24th-ranked Fresno State in DeKalb. The Huskies rolled up 733 yards in a 73-18 rout of the Bulldogs.

"I thought I was in Norman, Oklahoma," said Fresno State coach Jim Sweeney after the pasting.

"It was a magic day," Pettibone said. "(Fresno State) had not seen option football before. They weren't prepared for it."

Sports information director Mike Korcek remembered, "In the press box, I was on the phone the entire game. No one would believe the score and yardage."

Korcek further noted that Pettibone kept the score down considerably.

"Anyone with less ethics could've made it 95-18 easily," Korcek said.

After the season, Pettibone left DeKalb to take the head coaching position at Oregon State.

"When I look back on the six years I was at Northern Illinois, I feel good about it," Pettibone said. "We had winning seasons four of those six years."

Under Pettibone, NIU defeated its first Big Ten team in school history (Wisconsin by a 19-17 score in 1988). The Huskies established 51 school and seven NCAA records during his final three years.

Today, Pettibone works for a window and door manufacturer based in Oregon. In addition, he moonlights by evaluating potential recruits for colleges from his home in Colorado.

"I talk to him a few times a week," said Sabock, recently retired from Western Michigan University.

Most likely, some of those conversations stray from recruits and relive wishbone days gone by.

FOUR-DOWN TERRITORY

Favorite Football Movie—"Remember the Titans," but the movie I showed my teams at Northern and Oregon State to stress teamwork and getting ready to play was "Hoosiers."

First Car—A 1957 Chevy with a vacuum shift. When I was a senior in high school I had a *Dallas Morning News* paper route. I used that car for the job. I ran that thing into the ground.

Worst Summer Job—Between my sophomore and junior years at Oklahoma I was a bricklayer's helper. We worked building a new Blue Cross Blue Shield building in downtown Dallas. I'd stack bricks on pallets and carry them over to the bricklayer. I'd also mix up cement. It was a backbreaking job.

Favorite Subject in School—I was a business major at Oklahoma. I really enjoyed a business law class that I had as a junior. In fact, it inspired me to attend half a year of law school on the GI Bill. It was one of those classes that the teacher made all the difference.

STACEY ROBINSON

While George Bork moved the football through the air in the early 1960s, Stacey Robinson chewed up yardage with his legs nearly three decades later.

Robinson, from downstate Danville, thrived in head coach Jerry Pettibone's wishbone offense.

"Stacey Robinson had a real feel for the wishbone," Pettibone said. "He played behind a really good offensive line and he understood the offense. Stacey knew how to read it and made split-second decisions under pressure."

Robinson never made better reads and decisions than October 6, 1990 when he rushed for 308 yards and five touchdowns as NIU stunned 24th-ranked Fresno State 73-18. In all, the Huskies rolled up 806 total yards, 733 coming on the ground.

"We terribly underestimated the speed of their attack," Fresno State head coach Jim Sweeney said afterward. "We were outcoached in that area. Stacey did a tremendous job of carrying the football outside. He showed more running ability than we estimated he had.

"The teams that we play are downfield passing teams. Even if they run the option, they wouldn't run it the way (Robinson) does. He owns it."

Robinson set a Huskie single-game rushing record and tied the school mark for touch-

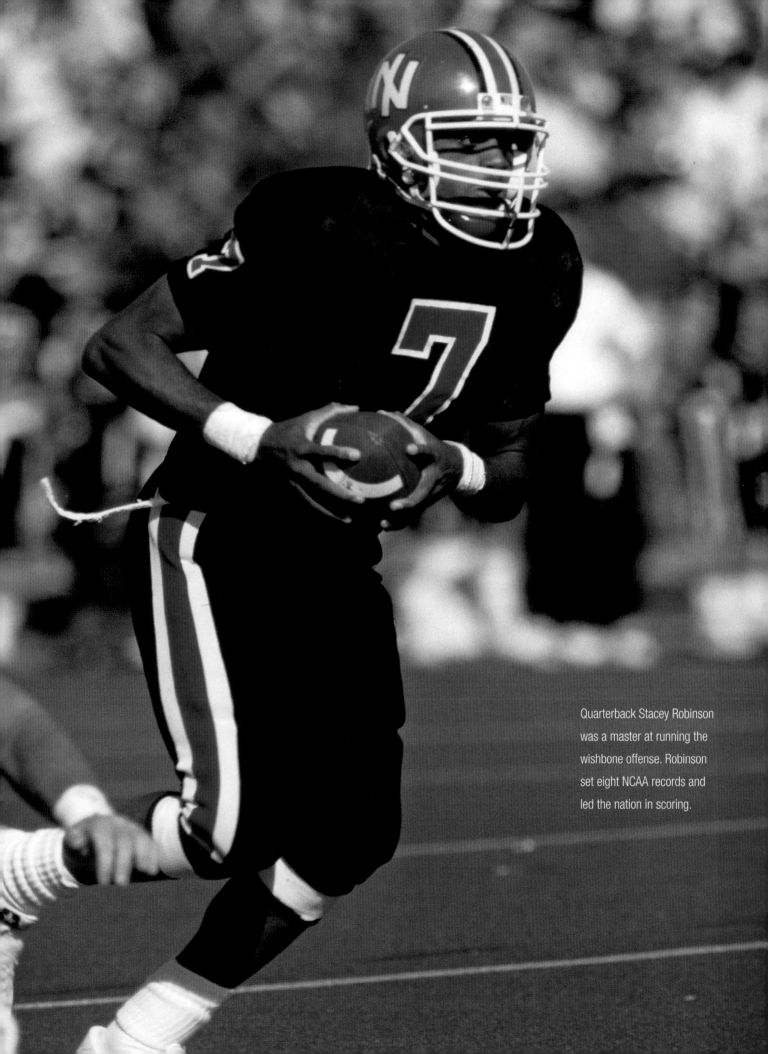

Quarterback Stacey Robinson was a master at running the wishbone offense. Robinson set eight NCAA records and led the nation in scoring.

downs in a game that day. Amazingly, he ran for 287 yards and all five of his touchdowns in the first half.

Ironically, Fresno State entered the game with the nation's second-ranked scoring defense, yielding just eight points a game. Moreover, the Bulldogs had not given up a touchdown in their previous two games. Fresno State, 5-0 entering the game, had only lost once in its last 24 games.

"I knew on the first series that this was going to be a good day," Robinson said afterward. "I thought (Fresno State) was going to make me pitch the ball. But when they didn't, I was shocked."

Robinson broke the collegiate quarterback record held by Nolan Cromwell of the University of Kansas. Cromwell, who later played safety for the Los Angeles Rams, rushed for 294 yards in a 1975 game.

"Records and stats are great, but my main goal was staying focused and not losing the football game," said Robinson.

The victory evened NIU's record at three wins and three losses on the season.

The 73 points were the most the Huskies had scored since 1921. NIU set school records for total offense (806) and first downs (36) that day.

The rousing NIU victory was chosen as "The Greatest Game" in "The Best of the First Century." The 2004 NIU Media Guide called it "the ultimate Fantasy Island Huskie triumph."

Robinson's performance was highlighted as the No. 2 college football story on ESPN's "Sports Center" that evening. In addition, Robinson earned the cable network's national player of the week honors. *Football News*, *Sports Illustrated* and the *Chicago Tribune* all followed suit.

"That was an All-America performance," said Pettibone. "Unbelievable. I saw Mike Rozier and Roger Craig at Nebraska and Billy Sims at Oklahoma. I've seen a lot of great individual games. I thought that was the best."

Interestingly, Fresno State held a brief 7-0 lead early in the game. Then the NIU onslaught began.

On the first possession following the Bulldog score, Robinson found the end zone on a 39-yard run. The Huskies then reeled off five more touchdowns to take a 42-7 lead. With the game safely in hand and with sportsmanship in mind, Pettibone removed Robinson from the game early in the third quarter.

As of 2011, Robinson's 308-yard performance ranks as the third-best day by an NIU rusher. Only Garrett Wolfe (325) and LeShon Johnson (322) ever enjoyed higher rushing totals.

Robinson, a 2001 NIU Athletic Hall of Fame inductee, scored 19 touchdowns in back-to-back seasons (1989 and '90).

Robinson's big-play ability was highlighted in Ted Mandell's "Heart Stoppers and Hail Marys: 100 of the Greatest College Football Finishes." In a battle of what Mandell called "two of the all-time great option quarterbacks," Robinson squared off with Brian Mitchell of Southwest Louisiana in 1989.

With NIU trailing by three points late in the game, the Huskies took over on their own 23-yard line. Twelve plays and two fourth-down conversions later, NIU had the ball on the Southwest seven with just three seconds remaining.

The Huskie coaching staff called for Robinson to run an option play to the left. The elusive quarterback weaved his way into the end zone to give NIU a 23-20 victory on the game's final play.

A year later, the Huskies were in a similar situation. This time around, NIU held a 17-13 lead over East Carolina with two minutes to go. ECU quarterback Jeff Blake, a future Cincinnati Bengal, drove his team the length of the field for a touchdown that put the Pirates ahead 20-17 with 40 seconds left.

NIU's chances for victory appeared over when Robinson threw an incomplete pass on the right sideline. However, ECU was penalized for having too many men on the field. Thus, NIU had one last chance with no time on the clock.

From his own 35-yard line, Robinson fired a crossing route pass to Larry Wynn 18 yards down the field. Wynn ran to the ECU 35 and then lateraled to Kurt Cassity. Cassity nearly scored what would have been a miracle touchdown. However, he was driven out of bounds at the ECU one.

Longtime Huskie play-by-play broadcaster Bill Baker said that NIU's recent string of success running the football began with Robinson.

"I used to marvel at the way Stacey Robinson ran that offense," Baker said. "To this day, I just don't know how he knew to make his cuts. His decision making was incredible. He would know when to pitch the ball and when to hold on to it and run. Once his decision to keep the ball was made, that defense had better have been ready or it was off to the races."

And more often than not, it was a race that Stacey Robinson finished first.

THE 1990s

NIU FOOTBALL BY THE DECADE: 1990s

NIU ENROLLMENT—22,679 (1990)

IN-STATE TUITION PER SEMESTER—$1,278.19 (1990)

ROOM & BOARD RATES PER SEMESTER—$1,333 to 1,818 (1990)

NIU PRESIDENT—John E. LaTourette (1986–2000)

CONFERENCE—Independent, Big West Conference, Mid-American Conference

NEWS OF THE DECADE—Nelson Mandela elected; Hubble telescope provides new look at space; Dolly the cloned sheep born; the Internet goes public; Bill Clinton elected two terms; Rodney King beaten; O.J. Simpson acquitted; Columbine killings shock nation; Oklahoma City bombed

NOTABLE MOVIES OF THE DECADE— "Dances With Wolves," "The Silence of the Lambs," "Unforgiven," "Schindler's List", "The Fugitive," "Forrest Gump," "The Shawshank Redemption," "Wayne's World," "Braveheart," "Apollo 13," "Titanic," "L.A. Confidential," "Goodfellas," "Shakespeare in Love," "Pulp Fiction," "Saving Private Ryan," "American Beauty," "The Green Mile"

NOTABLE BOOKS OF THE DECADE— "The Firm," "Into Thin Air," "Angela's Ashes," "Men Are from Mars, Women Are from Venus," "Tuesdays with Morrie," "The Perfect Storm"

NOTABLE MUSICAL ACTS OF THE DECADE—Nirvana, Guns n' Roses, Green Day, Jay-Z, Dr. Dre, Pearl Jam, Dave Matthews Band, Garth Brooks, Billy Ray Cyrus, Puff Daddy, Tupac Shakur, Spice Girls, Dixie Chicks

LeSHON JOHNSON

LeShon Johnson hasn't forgotten what Northern Illinois University did for him.

"They were so good to me," recalled Johnson from his native Oklahoma. "(My career at NIU) was a blessing to me. It really makes me appreciate all that Northern Illinois did for me."

Johnson fondly recalls his breakout senior season of 1993. The numbers and accolades are mind-boggling. Johnson finished sixth in the Heisman Trophy race. He earned UPI National Back of the Year honors. Johnson was a top-three finisher for the Doak Walker Award. He was chosen as Big West Conference Co-Offensive Player of the Year.

Johnson compiled an NIU and Big West–record 1,976 yards and 12 touchdowns on 327 carries. At the time, he produced the fourth-best single season in NCAA Division I history (the top three were Barry Sanders, Marcus Allen and Mike Rozier, all Heisman winners).

Not only did Johnson lead the country in individual rushing and all-purpose yardage, he outrushed 65 of the nation's then 106 Division I-A teams. Moreover, Johnson's 179.6-yards-per-game rushing average outgained such postseason bowl entries as Alabama, California, Indiana, Miami (Florida), Texas and Utah.

T-shirts bearing a "LeShon for Heisman" banner sold all over campus. A full video crew, including ESPN College "Game Day" anchor Chris Fowler, spent a full day in DeKalb. *Sports Illustrated* featured him.

In short, LeShon Johnson was the biggest thing to hit DeKalb since Cindy Crawford.

"It was overwhelming. I worked hard, and it was nice to get noticed," Johnson said. "I wish I could have spent more time with my teammates. (But) I was just so focused on football. Looking back, so many people did so many things for me. My teammates, my friends, the coaches—they all were so important."

Johnson also recognized the efforts of NIU sports information director Mike Korcek .

"Mike did so much for me," Johnson said. "He pumped me up. He really got the word out."

With Korcek leading the campaign and Johnson piling up the yardage, the nation took note. Johnson was a unanimous choice on **13** first-team All-America teams.

"All the biggies," said Korcek. "AP, UPI, Football News, Sporting News, AFCA, Walter Camp . . . (It was) unprecedented. At the time only five or six players in the state had made first-team All-America (including the great Harold "Red" Grange of the University of Illinois)."

Remarkably, all of these accolades came Johnson's way while he played for a four-win NIU team that had no television appearances.

All this was a far cry from Johnson's upbringing in Haskell, Oklahoma.

As a child, Johnson dreamed of being a rodeo cowboy like his father, Luther, who spent 23 years as a professional bullrider. In fact, while starring for the Haskell High School football team, LeShon rode bulls in amateur rodeos.

Fearing injury, his coach at Northeastern Oklahoma Junior College forced Johnson to give up his hobby.

Johnson told *Sports Illustrated*'s William F. Reed that he missed bullriding.

"Even though you can get beat up just like you do in football," Johnson was quoted in *SI*. "I've had a bull step on me. That's scarier than getting tackled."

When his junior college career ended, football programs lined up to court Johnson.

"I was all set to sign with the University of Tennessee," said Johnson. "I always wanted to play in the SEC."

However, Johnson narrowly missed being accepted at Tennessee due to grades.

"Oklahoma State had also wanted me, so when things fell through at UT, I called up Coach (Pat) Jones," Johnson said. "He told me,

LeShon Johnson finished sixth in the 1993 Heisman Trophy balloting.

'You should have signed here when you had the chance' and then he hung up on me."

While Johnson was also looking at Tulsa, NIU called "out of nowhere."

Huskie head coach Charlie Sadler and his staff quickly went to work on Johnson.

"They brought me up and gave me a tour of the campus," Johnson said. "I felt really comfortable with everything. Being 19, I really didn't know what everything was about. I signed some papers. When I got home I told my mom that I wanted to go to Northern Illinois. I called them up and told them I was ready to sign. They said, 'You already did sign!'"

With Johnson in the fold, Sadler made "Cowboy" the focal point of the NIU offense.

"The coaching staff gave me the ball even when I didn't want it," recalled Johnson. "There were times I wanted them to throw the ball. Sometimes I was so tired from running, but they kept giving me the ball."

The college football world took notice. Not only did Johnson finish sixth in the Heisman balloting, he also got five first-place votes.

"When you think about all those great players that year, it was such an honor," Johnson said. "I never really thought about it until the end of the season."

Former Huskie teammate and Canadian Football League star Eddie Davis was often awed by Johnson's performances.

"He's the best running back I'd seen," Davis said. "LeShon was so fast. Normally a back lines up seven yards behind the line of scrimmage. We lined LeShon up ten yards deep because he hit the hole so fast."

Broadcaster David Kaplan said, "He was ridiculously good. Every week you thought LeShon might run for 300 (yards)."

Johnson was highlighted several times in "The Best of the First Century" NIU honors. His 306-yard performance against Iowa in 1993 ranked as "The Greatest Performance." His school-record 322-yard day on only 20 carries against Southern Illinois was selected 10th on the list.

In addition, Johnson's electrifying touchdown run against Southern Mississippi in 1992 was the runner-up as "The Greatest Play."

"Best run in traffic and longest by a Huskie on Homecoming," read the capsule in the 2004 NIU Media Guide. "Momentum-changing 85-yard TD run. . . . The 'Cowboy' took a pitchout, swept outside, cut back on a dime and broke an ankle tackle, accelerated through a group of would-be USM tacklers, and finished The Run with a 30-yard sprint down the west sideline. Vintage LeShon (188 yards) in a 23-10 Huskie upset."

Johnson ended the year just 24 yards away from the coveted 2,000-yard plateau.

"LeShon had a hip pointer or a muscle pull that last game," NIU play-by-play broadcaster Bill Baker said. "He was hobbled. He was hurt. But the coaching staff wanted LeShon to reach 2,000 yards. They just kept giving him the ball. He just came up whisper short."

The Green Bay Packers selected Johnson in the third round, 84th overall, of the 1994 NFL Draft.

"I had worked so hard to get there," Johnson said. "There wasn't a day anyone had to tell me to keep up the hard work. It's something I just always did."

But Johnson was about to learn a valuable life lesson.

"Once you get there, you can't relax," he said. "But, I got there and I relaxed. My career took a turn for the worse. I relaxed. I have no one to blame but myself."

Johnson's confidence also took a severe hit when the Packers tried to change his running style.

"I was always a north-south runner, you know, a guy who hit the hole and got upfield," Johnson said. "The Green Bay coaches were screaming at me. They didn't want that. I began to question myself."

After two years with the Packers, Johnson found himself playing for the Arizona Cardinals. He rushed for a career-high 634 yards and three touchdowns in 1996. He also turned in his career-best game with a 214-yard performance against New Orleans on September 22.

Johnson spent three seasons with Arizona before joining the New York Giants in 1998. It was then that life threw him for a loss. He was diagnosed with non-Hodgkins lymphoma after joining New York.

"I just felt like I was back to myself," Johnson said. "We were in a meeting room and the coaches reminded us to get our physicals. I almost didn't do it that day, but didn't want

to answer to my coach. He was a real straight shooter, so I thought I'd better do it."

A short time later, Johnson was sent a message to report back to the office.

"I thought, have I been traded? What's going on?" Johnson recounted. "That's when I got the word. LeShon, you have cancer and we need to take action."

Despite the bad news, Johnson went back to his old work habits.

"I just hung in there and did what the doctors told me to do," he said. "There's nothing you can do. That's life. It made me a stronger person."

Johnson did return to play for the Chicago Enforcers in the short-lived XFL in 2001. When the league folded during its inaugural season, Johnson's career also came to an end.

"God had a plan for me," Johnson said. "My guess is that pro football wasn't part of the plan."

Johnson spent time in Arizona building custom homes. However, like many Americans, business went south following the market crash and subsequent tough economic times.

"(Soon after) my mom had a stroke, and I missed the open country of Oklahoma," Johnson said. "So I packed up and moved back here."

Johnson started coaching his 11-year-old son's team.

"I want to get into coaching, it's something I really believe would be good," Johnson said. "I've got a few contacts from college and pro ball. That's something I want to pursue."

And as for his past success?

"It was really special to me," he said. "I really didn't appreciate it until this part of my life. But now when I run into old friends, I don't forget. So many of these people helped me. Many of them don't even realize it. If I can help someone, I'll try to do it."

And when LeShon Johnson puts his mind to something, look out.

Favorite Football Movie—"Any Given Sunday."

First Car—1977 Monte Carlo.

Worst Summer Job—Stomping Spinach.

Favorite Subject in School—P.E.

EDDIE DAVIS

It's a long way from the heat and humidity of a St. Louis summer to the cold winds of a Canadian winter. Yet, that distance just may be enough to land Eddie Davis in the Canadian Football Hall of Fame.

"I'd be very grateful (if that happened)," said Davis from his Calgary home during the 2009 season. "But, that's not up to me. It's up to the writers and the voters."

Davis, who lettered all four seasons at Northern under Charlie Sadler, certainly has a solid chance.

"Given the length, quality and the fact Eddie won two Grey Cup games in his career, I would say definitely," said Murray McCormick of the *Regina Leader-Post* in an e-mail. "But I never know when it comes to those kind of things. Still, he would get my vote for just being one of the nicest men I have ever dealt with in football. A class act who I think can still play another couple of years."

Over the course of his 15-year pro career, Davis played 236 CFL regular-season games and amassed 801 defensive tackles, 112 special team tackles, 111 pass knockdowns, 34 interceptions and 16 quarterback sacks. He was also named a CFL All-Star three times and a West Division All-Star five times. He captured two Grey Cups—one with the Calgary Stampeders in 1998 and the other with the Saskatchewan Roughriders in 2007.

When he retired in the summer of 2010, Davis ranked fourth on the all-time CFL list for tackles. What's remarkable is that he played a decade and a half at defensive back, a position that generally relies on speed and reaction.

"I have the Fountain of Youth in my basement," Davis joked. "Seriously though, it's hard work. I work my butt off every off-season. I have a personal trainer. Every year we start in January and work until camp starts at the end of May."

Fellow NIU alum and CFL defensive back Randee Drew is amazed by Davis' career.

"He has stood the test of time and played so well for so long up here in the CFL," Drew said. "I commend him because it's hard to play pro ball period and at least for so long. He's a great athlete, person and competitor. I have the utmost respect for him."

It's not just longevity that keeps Davis in the CFL. It's talent and performance.

"I always take the best wide receiver on the other team," Davis noted.

The highlights of Davis' Canadian career have been two Grey Cup titles. The first came in 1998 as a member of the Calgary Stampeders.

"That was the first championship I'd won at any level," Davis said. "Jeff Garcia was our quarterback. We won on a last-second field goal. It was everything you'd want."

The feeling returned in 2007 when Davis was a member of the Saskatchewan Roughriders.

"I've made my mark," he said.

Playing in the CFL for so many years wasn't on Davis' mind when he was recruited by Sadler in 1991.

"Charlie Sadler had recruited me when he was the defensive coordinator for Oklahoma," Davis recalled. "When he got the job at Northern, I decided to take a visit there. I liked it and made my decision to sign (with NIU)."

Playing for NIU at the time wasn't easy.

"We didn't win many games when I was there," Davis said. "We only won something like 15 games in four years."

Eddie Davis played at NIU in the early 1990s. Davis later enjoyed a stellar 15-year career in the Canadian Football League.

Still, he learned from Sadler and his staff.

"I've seen a lot of coaches in my time," Davis said. "(Sadler) was fair. He knew how to relate to his players. That's the biggest thing for a coach, especially with young guys."

Davis enjoyed his time as a teammate of NIU great LeShon Johnson.

"I remember playing against Iowa when he broke the record (for most yards in a single game by an NIU player at the time)," Davis said. "It was freezing cold, but LeShon ran that day. He got over 300 yards.

"He was the best running back I'd seen. He was so fast. Most teams line their backs up seven yards behind the ball. We lined LeShon ten yards deep. He'd hit that hole and just outrun people."

When his collegiate career ended, Davis hoped for a shot with an NFL team.

"I honestly didn't know (what would happen)," he said. "Being an American, I always looked up to guys like Walter Patyon, Barry Sanders, Deion Sanders. My first choice would have been the NFL."

There were indications that his hometown St. Louis Rams would draft Davis.

"That didn't happen, but I got invited to the Birmingham Barracudas' camp," he recalled. "At that time there were seven CFL teams that played in the U.S.

"Birmingham brought in something like 350 guys to camp. I was one of about 40 the team kept."

Davis spent his rookie season in the defensive backfield and on special teams in 1995.

However, the Barracudas folded. Davis was placed into the dispersal draft and was selected by Calgary. He started all 17 games the next season with the Stampeders. Davis tied for third on the team in tackles, registered two interceptions and scored his first CFL touchdown when he returned a fumble 37 yards against Hamilton.

Davis spent five years with Calgary, the place he now calls home.

"I've lived here since 1997," he said. "I met my wife and have two kids now. I'll probably never go back to the States. This is home now."

Following his time with the Stampeders, Davis signed with Saskatchewan as a free agent in 2001.

Davis has also contributed off the field. He has been a player representative with the union since 2002.

"We just signed a new collective bargaining agreement," he said. "We've made some major achievements with the best interests of the players in mind."

Davis is especially proud of the progress made in regard to player pensions.

"I'm always telling the younger guys they need to appreciate those who came before them," Davis said.

Following his retirement as an active player, Eddie Davis now qualifies as one of those.

"I want to thank everyone that's ever been involved in my football career, but football is over for me," Davis said at his farewell press conference. "Having time to think, think, and think some more, I'm happy to say that football needs me more than I need football, but nobody needs me more than my family."

Davis may have one final destination in Canada: Hamilton, Ontario—home of the Canadian Football Hall of Fame.

Maybe it's not so far from St. Louis after all.

FOUR-DOWN TERRITORY

Favorite Football Movie—"The Program," just about the whole NIU team went to see it when it came out.

First Car—1978 canary yellow Dodge Aspen station wagon.

Worst Summer Job—Worked for the parks department in St. Louis.

Favorite Subject in School—Math.

HOLLIS THOMAS

With 12 seasons under his massive belt, Hollis Thomas spent more time in the National Football League than any other NIU Huskie ever.

Thomas played for NIU from 1993 to 1995 under head coach Charlie Sadler. He emerged as a presence at nose guard on an inconsistent defense during a season that featured star running back LeShon Johnson on a four-win Huskie team.

"Hollis did the job up front for us," said former NIU teammate and fellow St. Louis product Eddie Davis. "He was difficult to move. Opponents didn't run on Hollis."

Even in those days, weight was an issue for Thomas.

"My strengths are my power and my quickness," the then 6 foot, 300-pounder told Rich Carlson of the *Northern Star* in 1993. "I could improve on my weight by losing five or ten pounds to get down to 290."

Thomas never saw the 290-pound neighborhood again. Nicknamed "Big Cat" by his teammates, Thomas tipped the scales at 319 as an NIU upperclassman.

"The funniest thing I remember about Hollis was the day he reported to Northern as a freshman," said former Huskie assistant Mike Sabock. "He, of course, had that short, stocky build. His mother was worried that he wouldn't get enough to eat at school. He showed up with this five-gallon bucket full of powdered Kool-Aid. Hollis loved his Kool-Aid."

Yet, Sabock recognized talent when he saw it. In 1995, Thomas earned First-Team All–Big West Conference honors.

"I knew he'd be an NFL player," Sabock said. "There was no question Hollis could make it. In the NFL, you play so many situational plays. He could play run-stopper on first down and then come out for a breather on second or third down.

"Unfortunately for us, he had to be an every-down player so he wore down as the game went on. He couldn't maintain it for 60 or 70 snaps, but when he was fresh he would kick everybody's butt. It didn't matter who was across from him. It could have been a player from Iowa or Nebraska. It didn't matter."

Undrafted out of NIU, Thomas signed as a free agent with the Philadelphia Eagles in 1996. He played well enough to be named to the All-Rookie Team by *Football News*.

Thomas played nine seasons with the Eagles, developing into one of the key pieces to their rugged defense.

After being cut by Philadelphia, Thomas signed with the New Orleans Saints in 2006. He was suspended by the NFL for violating the league's performance-enhancing drugs policy. Though he appealed the suspension on the grounds that the test results were a "false positive" because of his asthma medicine, Thomas lost his appeal.

Nonetheless, Thomas and the Saints enjoyed success under new head coach Sean Payton. New Orleans made it to the NFC Championship game for the first time in franchise history.

Thomas spent three seasons with the Saints. After being released by New Orleans, he split time with St. Louis and Carolina in his final NFL season.

Thomas finished his NFL career with 261 tackles, 17.5 sacks and a trip to the Super Bowl with Philadelphia.

"To last as long as Hollis did is a surprise," said Sabock. "That's no slap against Hollis. Playing as a defensive lineman, you get cut and you take a beating. It's phenomenal for Hollis Thomas to have lasted that many years in pro football."

In the summer of 2010, the 36-year-old Thomas earned an eight-game suspension for his second performance-enhancing drug violation.

Hollis Thomas played at NIU in the 1990s. Thomas remains the Huskie with the longest NFL tenure with 12 seasons as a pro player.

Hoping to still get back into the NFL, Thomas signed with the Omaha Nighthawks of the second-year United Football League.

"I'm a fat person, so if I sit still for a long period of time . . . nobody's going to want a fat, out-of-shape guy to come back," the 335-pound Thomas told Elizabeth Merrill of espn.com. "Coming out here (to Omaha) and getting the opportunity to play will get me in good shape. When the time comes, I'll be ready."

Unfortunately for Thomas, Omaha cut him prior to its first game.

Yet, while his career may have ended unceremoniously, Hollis Thomas holds the distinction of playing for the longest NFL tenure in NIU history.

THE JOE NOVAK ERA

(1996-2007)

JOE NOVAK

A new era of Northern Illinois football came with old rules.

When NIU hired Joe Novak as its 19th head coach in 1995, the Huskies were getting more than just a football man.

"It was something personally that meant a lot," said Novak from his retirement home in North Carolina.

"I was 51 years old when it happened. I was beginning to wonder if it would happen."

Novak had certainly earned his opportunity. He had spent 22 years as a collegiate assistant coach.

"Ninety percent, if not 100%, of assistants want to be a head coach," Novak said.

Given the fact he had to wait so long to become a head coach, Novak saw only one way to run a program.

"At my age, Northern was the last stop. I knew that I'd run things the right way, or I wouldn't have been able to live with myself," Novak explained.

That path had already been paved for Novak. He saw it firsthand in the 16 years he spent working as an assistant under Bill Mallory, first at Northern and later at Indiana University.

Novak said, "When I got the (NIU) job, I followed Bill Mallory's program.

"We recruited Chicago heavily. We also established a three-to-four-hour radius for recruiting. If we could get those kids, we'd be successful."

But the program was about more than just getting good players. It meant players would go to class and earn degrees. It meant honesty, integrity and respect. It meant toughness, hard work and accountability.

Initially, those tasks facing Novak and his staff were difficult.

"Nothing against the previous coaches because they were good football coaches, but it was a situation where they had gotten a bit desperate," Novak said.

Longtime NIU play-by-play broadcaster Bill Baker put Novak's task in stronger terms.

"There was so much damage to repair," Baker said. "It was like tearing down a house and building a new foundation in a new location. Joe Novak and his staff faced a great challenge head on."

Out of that desperation, NIU's roster was stocked with players who weren't interested in Novak's plan.

"We had some cleaning out to do," Novak said. "When I met with (athletic director) Cary Groth I told her that we'd need to tear this down to build it up."

With the support of Groth and the NIU administration, Novak did just that.

"We had 25 or 30 kids leave the program," he said.

Former Huskie All-American wide receiver Dave Petzke had served as an assistant coach with Novak under Mallory.

"What Joe accomplished is quite incredible," said Petzke. "He took a program not built on a solid foundation and got it going again. He did it the hard way, the right way. He wasn't going to cut corners either."

Yet, the final component of Novak's plan took more time—winning. In his first season at the NIU helm, the Huskies won just one game. The next season, 1997, marked Northern's return to the Mid-American Conference. The Huskies went winless in 11 games.

By the end of the '98 season, Novak's NIU record stood at 3-30 in three seasons. While the administration stayed with him, Novak said "it got close" to his termination.

Yet, fans and players also saw Novak's vision.

"Joe Novak is a kind, caring football professional who will elevate you as a person and a player if you allow him to," said guard Ryan Diem, who later played for the Indianapolis Colts. "I left his program with the regrets of a senior, but I would also recommend it in a second to anyone who asked. You can't say enough good about him."

It wasn't just his players who were touched by Novak.

"I'd left my job at Northern," said former Huskie assistant basketball coach Jeff Strohm. "The next year, we (the University of Utah) played in the national championship game. Coach Novak sent me the nicest congratulations note afterward. It certainly wasn't something he had to do."

When Novak's fourth season at NIU rolled around, the good began to translate into victories. Northern finished 5-6 and tied for second in the MAC West. After consecutive 6-5 seasons, the Huskies were on the verge of a return to glory.

In 2002, Northern posted an 8-4 record. The Huskies tied for the MAC West flag for the second straight season. They knocked off 20th-ranked Bowling Green, and Novak earned MAC Coach of the Year honors.

Then, the Huskies enjoyed the season that remains most vivid in Novak's memory.

"Of course, it's the 2003 season," Novak said.

NIU finished the year with a 10-2 record that opened with an upset of 15th-rated Maryland.

"That game was unique," Novak recalled. "It was on Fox TV nationally on a Thursday night. While Fox may not have been NBC or ABC, it was still a big deal."

Later in the season, NIU upset No. 21 Alabama.

"That put a cap on it," Novak said. "The Maryland game opened people's eyes, but to win on the road at one of college football's meccas?

"I don't want to blow this out of proportion, but the way we were treated was amazing. There were 50 to 100 Alabama fans waiting for us outside our locker room afterward who applauded us. It wasn't like the Big Ten, believe me. I've had beer poured on me in the Big Ten.

"When we got back to DeKalb I had 50 to 75 e-mails from Alabama fans, and they were all positive."

Northern, which had also beaten Iowa State, captured national attention.

"When the first BCS poll came out, we were 10th in the country," Novak recalled. "Then, we started to get nicked up (with injuries). When (linebacker) Nick Duffy was lost, we really took a hit."

Despite the Huskies' strong season, NIU was left out of the bowl picture. Novak—the American Football Coaches Association Region 3 Coach of the Year—was naturally upset.

"I don't think a .500 team should get in over a team that won 10 games. Are you telling me they had a better season than us? Baloney," Novak said afterward of a 6-6 Northwestern team that received a bid to the Motor City Bowl.

More than half a decade later and retired, Novak's sentiments remained the same.

"There were 60 bowl teams that year," he said. "We may not have been BCS material, but if we weren't one of those 60 teams, then something was wrong."

Though the Huskies would garner bowl invitations in future years, Novak noted that "some of our later bowl teams were lesser football teams (than 2003)."

With no bowl to take his team to, Novak accepted an offer to coach in the 2003 Blue-Gray Classic.

With success came an upgrade in the program's facilities and TV and radio contracts to carry games to Huskie fans across the nation. NIU football found its way into features in the likes of *The New York Times, USA Today* and *Sports Illustrated.*

Yet, through it all, Novak remained true to his beliefs. Rather than taking bows when he retired at the end of the 2007 season, Novak recalled his roots.

"I owe so much to so many people," he said.

A three-sport letterman at Mentor High School in Ohio, Novak earned a football scholarship to Miami University. When he got to

Oxford, his football coach was Bo Schembechler, a Miami alum who later became a Hall of Famer at Michigan.

"My freshman year was Bo's first year," Novak said. "He was a wild man."

He added that many of the basics of the game he learned under Schembechler became a constant in his career.

"There was hard work and discipline," Novak said. "Bo and Bill (Mallory) were from the same school. It also came from (legendary Ohio State coach) Woody Hayes. They were all cut from the same cloth."

Following graduation from Miami, Novak coached at Warren Western Reserve High School in Ohio. It was there that he coached future Notre Dame star Ross Browner.

"Coached? I got him on the bus on time," Novak joked. "He was one of three brothers who played for me. There was Ross, Jimmy and Willard. They all could play."

Novak led Western Reserve to a 12-0 record and Ohio's large school division title to earn 1972 Coach of the Year honors. A year later, his team was 11-1 and back in the state title game.

Novak began his collegiate coaching career back at Miami under Dick Crum. The Redskins won two conference championships and appeared in two bowl games.

Joe Novak resurrected the NIU program during his tenure. His 2003 team recorded victories over Maryland, Iowa State and Alabama in a 10-win season.

From there he spent three years as defensive line coach under Gary Moeller at Illinois.

Novak recalled an incident that may well have summed up those years.

"I remember one year (1978) we opened with Northwestern," he said. "One of the newspapers, it may have been the *Chicago Tribune*, said nobody can win this game in its prediction. And, sure enough, we tied 0-0 with Northwestern."

Then, he joined Mallory's staff—first at NIU (1980–1983) and then at Indiana (1984–1995).

"Joe was an excellent defensive coordinator for me," Mallory said. "He's the kind of guy you'd want to be your coordinator."

Novak nearly returned to Northern in 1985, but lost out on the head coaching job to Jerry Pettibone.

"I was excited for the opportunity," Novak said. "Sure I was disappointed, but Jerry was a great choice."

Northern didn't pass on Novak a second time. When Novak was finally hired to take the Huskie helm ten years later, he remained true to his roots.

Every freshman had to learn the NIU fight song and sing it in the locker room following a victory. Players were required to wear coats and ties when the team traveled. A sign was hung in the locker room that read: "Those Who Stay Will Be Champions."

"That came from Bo," Novak said.

While many things may have come from others, it was Novak who blended them into a perfect combination during his time at Northern.

"Coach Novak was old school," said former NIU receiver P.J. Fleck. "He taught me that if you respect your players, they will listen."

Today, Novak and his wife Carole are enjoying the fruits of retirement.

"I do whatever I want," he said. "I was 62 when I retired. After 40 great years of coaching, it's time for other things. We live on an inner harbor, so we boat. We travel. We went to France and Italy.

"I watch college football on the Game Plan package. I've been asked to be part of the Harris Poll."

Novak has also found time for one of his favorite hobbies—reading.

"I finally finished James Michener's 'Hawaii,'" he said. "I never had time when I coached. I'd look at it and see it was over 1,000 pages and realize there just wasn't time. Now I have (Michener's) 'Texas' and 'Mexico' on my docket."

So, a new era goes for Joe Novak, but the same old rules still apply.

FOUR-DOWN TERRITORY

Favorite Football Movie—"Remember the Titans." First, it's a true story. Also, I could relate to coaching minority kids from my high school coaching.

First Car—It must have been a 1966 Pontiac LeMans. It was deep green with a black interior. I was fortunate to have had a full scholarship at Miami. My parents had saved the money to pay for my schooling. Since they didn't have to use it for my education, they bought me the car when I was a senior.

Worst Summer Job—There were two of them. I worked for Manpower. It was something different every day. One day I'd dig ditches, another I'd load moving trucks. I remember trying to fill cases of cookies. They were coming out faster than I could load them. The other was painting houses during the summer when I was a high school football coach. It was in Warren, Ohio. They were these old three-story houses. You had to get up high on a ladder, scrape first and then paint. It made me appreciate my job.

Favorite Subject in School—Math. That's what I taught.

RYAN DIEM

While the general football-loving public might not recognize Ryan Diem, his quarterback does.

"Ryan Diem has just been a rock out there at right tackle," future Hall of Fame quarterback Peyton Manning was quoted in a *Daily Herald* story by Bob LeGere prior to Super Bowl XLIV. "He has had a great year. He really had kind of an unspoken outstanding year last year. I love those five guys in front of me. I love their effort. I love their attitude. I'm looking forward to playing behind them on Sunday."

For Diem, who played at NIU from 1997 to 2000, the feeling is mutual.

"We throw the ball quite a bit and we've got the best quarterback in the league, so that's what we're going to base our offense around," Diem said.

Diem, who played right tackle for the Colts, is a key part of Manning's success. During the 2009 season, Indianapolis led the National Football League with the fewest sacks allowed.

"As a group, we work real well together," said Diem, a starter since his rookie season of 2001. "You've got some older veteran leadership with (center) Jeff Saturday and myself, and (left guard) Ryan Lilja."

That trio has been the core for more than half the decade.

"As a group we just function well," Diem said. "When Peyton's back there, he can read the defense and point us in the right direction, which always helps."

The Colts' 2010 appearance marked the second time in his career that Diem had played in the Super Bowl. The first came in 2006 when Indianapolis played the Chicago Bears, Diem's hometown team.

His Super Bowl experience has proven to be bittersweet. While the Colts defeated the Bears, Diem was injured in the game's second quarter.

In his second appearance, Diem and the Colts lost to the New Orleans Saints.

Diem was born in Carol Stream and played at Glenbard North High School. In addition to excelling on the football field, Diem was an All-State track performer. He set Glenbard North records in the indoor and outdoor shot put. Diem finished first in the shot at the state meet. Meanwhile, Diem was an honor roll student.

After being named to the *USA Today* All-America team as well as a *Chicago Tribune* All-State defensive lineman, Diem was exactly the type of player NIU head coach Joe Novak was seeking to rebuild the Huskie program.

"I was surprised he wasn't recruited more (by other programs)," said NIU head coach Joe Novak. "One thing in our favor was that four Big Ten programs were in the midst of coaching changes at that time. That really helped us."

When Joe Tiller was named the head coach at Purdue, the Boilermakers really went hard after Diem. However, Novak and the Huskies won out.

"He came in at 6 foot 6 and about 260 pounds," Novak said. "A kid that size who throws the shot that well has some explosiveness that really carries over into football."

Yet, it wasn't just pure physical abilities that caught Novak's attention.

"He was a great worker," Novak said. "He was smart. He was of high character and came from a wonderful family."

Four years later, Diem had added 60 pounds to his frame. He also became one of the greatest offensive linemen in NIU history. He lettered all four seasons and served as captain twice. Diem started the final 35 games of his Huskie career. Moreover, he did not allow a sack in his final two seasons.

"Ryan was just so dominant," said David Kaplan, the Chicago-based broadcaster who saw Diem play firsthand many times. "He just overpowered people."

Ryan Diem played in two Super Bowls with the Indianapolis Colts. (Photo by Scott Walstrom)

Diem was a three-time All-Mid-American Conference honoree, landing on the first team his final two years. In addition, he earned Academic All-America accolades as a mechanical engineering major.

All of this combined to make Diem the first NIU offensive lineman since Todd Peat to be drafted by an NFL team. The Colts selected the 6 foot 6, 320-pound Diem with their fourth-round pick.

"I thought that he might go higher than he did," Novak said. "The only question (NFL personnel had) were his feet. Were they good enough?"

As Diem developed, Indianapolis became one of the premiere teams in the NFL.

Off the field, Diem has partnered with "Allie and Friends" to host a charity golf outing to raise funds for the Children's Neuroblastoma Cancer Foundation. In 2008, Diem was selected as NIU Outstanding Young Alumnus.

JUSTIN McCAREINS

The Big Ten's loss was Northern Illinois football's gain.

According to his father, Justin McCareins easily could have wound up running pass patterns across the fields of the Midwest's largest and most prestigious conference.

"(Northwestern head coach) Gary Barnett knew us real well. He came to a bunch of Justin's basketball games," said John McCareins. "We were very close to signing with Iowa. Illinois showed some interest. (Wisconsin assistant) Brad Childress was high on Justin. Brad had recruited (McCareins' Naperville North teammate) Scott Kavanagh."

However, as the recruiting process played out, Justin McCareins found himself on the outside of the Big Ten looking in.

"Barnett took a wide receiver named Teddy (Johnson) from Elgin instead," John McCa-

reins said. "Iowa went with Kahlil Hill. They wanted Justin to come on as a preferred walk-on. (Head coach) Lou Tepper got fired at Illinois. Wisconsin signed (future NFL receiver) Chris Chambers."

The University of Wyoming also expressed interest, but then head coach Joe Tiller left Laramie to become the head coach at Purdue.

"That's when Northern came knocking," said John McCareins.

The Huskies had actually been recruiting Justin McCareins all along. Yet, with the Big Ten schools lurking about, NIU's chances of signing the talented McCareins seemed remote.

Justin McCareins left NIU as the Huskies' career leader in receptions (204), yards (2,991) and touchdown receptions (29). McCareins was a fourth-round draft pick by the Tennessee Titans.

Assistant coaches Mike Sabock and Mike Mallory had been hot on McCareins' trail during his prep days at Naperville North. McCareins had been a star on both the basketball court and football field.

"Mark Lindo, my broadcast partner, was Justin's head basketball coach at Naperville North," NIU play-by-play man Bill Baker said. "We knew just how talented Justin McCareins was."

"There were a lot of connections with Northwestern," said then-NIU head coach Joe Novak. "Justin is a great kid and comes from a wonderful family.

"(Assistant coach) Mike Mallory got a little impatient with him. We felt maybe perhaps he was holding us off for a better offer from a Big Ten school. His parents and I had a meeting. He has great parents who are of high character.

"He's another example of the kind of player we wanted. You never saw his name in the paper (for being in trouble)."

In the end, McCareins signed with NIU.

"A lot of it came down to, did Justin want to walk on somewhere else and red-shirt or did he want to have a good chance to play right away?" said John McCareins.

Justin McCareins did play right away. In just his second game as a true freshman, McCareins caught a touchdown pass against nationally ranked Kansas State. It was the lone Huskie score of the day. NIU went winless that season.

"Going 0-11 was not a lot of fun," said John McCareins, "but Justin was getting playing time."

By his sophomore season, McCareins became the primary receiver for the Huskies. He led NIU in receiving for three straight years.

Novak noticed McCareins' drive to improve himself each day on the practice field.

"Justin was very self-critical. He could be so hard on himself," Novak said.

National Football League scouts began to watch McCareins closely in his senior year at NIU.

On September 23, 2000, McCareins caught 11 passes for 189 yards and a touchdown against nationally ranked Auburn.

"He was right on the brink (of greatness)," Novak said. "He had a fantastic game. They couldn't cover him. He caught everything thrown his way."

According to his father, much of McCareins' success stemmed from a trip to former NFL receiver Cris Carter's speed camp in Boca Raton, Florida that included the likes of Randy Moss.

"That was at the end of Justin's junior year," said John McCareins. "He came home from that and said, 'You know, Dad, I think I can do this.'"

McCareins left NIU as the Huskies' career leader in receptions (204), yards (2,991) and touchdown receptions (29).

When the NFL Draft rolled around in April 2001, the McCareins family gathered around the television in their home to hear Justin's name called.

"It was just immediate family," John McCareins said. "We really didn't have any idea when he was going (to be taken)."

The Tennessee Titans drafted McCareins in the fourth round as the 124th overall pick.

"People started coming over to the house after that," John McCareins said. "Within 15 minutes, there were cakes and balloons everywhere."

McCareins played eight seasons in the NFL. His best years came as a member of the Titans before signing as a free agent with the New York Jets.

"New York is a tough place to play," said John McCareins. "Half of your games are late (four o'clock starting times) because TV doesn't want the Giants and Jets playing at the same time. Justin was living on Long Island, commuting to Hofstra (University) for practice and then out to The Meadowlands for the games in that traffic."

The New York media was also another factor.

"Justin is a pretty quiet kid," his father said. "That New York media can be pretty relentless."

Yet, McCareins played on teams that made the playoffs five of his eight NFL seasons. He finished his career with 240 catches for 2,676 yards and 16 touchdowns.

Mike Heimerdinger, son of NIU Hall of Fame quarterback Bob Heimerdinger, was McCareins' offensive coordinator for half of those eight NFL seasons.

"I learned how to be a pro under Coach Heimerdinger, and that stays with you," McCareins said in a 2008 interview on a Nashville newspaper Web site.

Heimerdinger said, "Justin really tried to better himself as time went along. He became a better route-runner over the course of his career. When he returned here (to the Titans in 2008), he was teaching some of the younger guys things about becoming a better receiver."

Yet, McCareins had no interest in coaching when his playing career ended. Instead, McCareins enrolled in the Coral Springs Police Academy in Florida. He graduated in December 2010.

"It's regimented, and there's a camaraderie and a little element of an adrenaline that compares to football for him," said John McCareins.

FOUR-DOWN TERRITORY

Favorite Football Movie—"Remember the Titans." You see a team that overcomes so much adversity. You see great leadership. They turn a negative situation into something so awesome.

First Car—It was a Plymouth Voyager minivan. I'm not sure of the exact year, it may have been a 1994. The sliding door had to be welded shut to keep it from coming open. It had a lot of character.

Worst Summer Job—I haven't had too many summer jobs, but I'd have to say baling hay. It's so hot. You use your legs a lot. The hay cuts you up. When you're up in the barn putting the hay away, it's like 140 (degrees). It's so dusty. It's the most physically demanding thing I've ever done. Even more so than football? For a single moment in time, yes, even more than football.

Favorite Subject in School—I've always liked math. I've always loved numbers, but I don't mean in a geeky way. I'm a business guy. I love dealing with numbers and money.

NIU FOOTBALL BY THE DECADE: 2000s

NIU ENROLLMENT—20,928 (2000)

IN-STATE TUITION PER SEMESTER—$1,575 (2000)

ROOM & BOARD RATES PER SEMESTER—$2,113 to $3,202 (2000)

NIU PRESIDENTS—John E. LaTourette (1986–2000); John G. Peters (2000–present)

CONFERENCE—Independent, Mid-American Conference

IN THE NEWS OF THE DECADE—9/11; Iraq; Hurricane Katrina; Global warming; Rising gas prices; Barack Obama

NOTABLE MOVIES OF THE DECADE—"Napoleon Dynamite," "Borat," "Lord of the Rings" trilogy, "Brokeback Mountain"

NOTABLE BOOKS OF THE DECADE—"Fast Food Nation," "The Da Vince Code," "Harry Potter" series, "The Kite Runner," "The Tipping Point"

NOTABLE MUSICAL ACTS OF THE DECADE—Black Eyed Peas, Kelly Clarkson, Snoop Dogg, Kanye West, Tim McGraw, 50 Cent

THOMAS HAMMOCK

The final carry of Thomas Hammock's NIU career will always be with him. Unlike so many other stories, however, that carry didn't come on Senior Day or in a bowl game. It came in the very first game of the season, which also turned out to be his last. "It was the last game I would ever suit up as a Huskie," Hammock said in an e-mail.

Hammock burst into the end zone to score the touchdown that gave NIU a thrilling 42-41 road victory against Wake Forest of the Atlantic Coast Conference.

"It was a 'Bone Yard Victory,' which is what we called victories over BCS opponents," he said. "My 38th and last carry was the one to win the game in a hard fought overtime match.

"I remember the team putting so much preparation into that game because the year before we had played the last game of the year, which was a makeup date from earlier in the season when they cancelled all games that week because of 9/11."

Hammock rushed for 172 yards and two touchdowns against Wake Forest. However, he experienced breathing problems and chest discomfort.

Soon after, Hammock was diagnosed with a heart condition. Doctors found an enlarged muscle mass near the left side of his heart.

"Everybody was just in shock," NIU head coach Joe Novak said. "One week he's diving in from the three with the winning score and the next week he can't play."

Hammock said, "I was told to decondition my body for six months and then go back to the doctors and get checked out again. My thought process was I would be back the following year after taking a redshirt.

"After six months when I went back and they informed me it was over, it really hit me hard because I never had a chance to experience a senior year. My parents never had a

chance to go through Senior Day and all those things. That's what really hurt the most because my parents made a lot of sacrifices for me in my life and Senior Day is always a time to show appreciation to the people who have been there since the beginning."

Rick Armstrong of the *Aurora Beacon-News* said Hammock was "like a bowling ball" when he ran.

"He was awfully strong and fast," said Armstrong. "It's just unfortunate that he didn't get to finish out his career. Who knows how far he could have gone?"

Hammock's beginnings were at Bishop Luers High School in Fort Wayne, Indiana. He earned varsity letters in football, wrestling and track. Hammock earned Athlete of the Year for his area following an All-State season in football and a third-place finish in the state wrestling tournament at 189 pounds.

Hammock described his recruiting process as "normal at the time before Rivals and all those recruiting services."

According to Novak, Hammock was recruited by the University of Kentucky as a linebacker.

"He was a real fine back," Novak said. "The one thing Thomas may have lacked was speed (to play in the pros), but he could really take it inside between the tackles and get those tough yards."

Hammock also had offers from other Mid-American Conference schools, but chose NIU because "I wanted to be part of a program that I could help turn around."

Northern was just that. Early in Novak's tenure, the Huskies were in the midst of a long losing streak.

"I took an unofficial visit to the Central Michigan game when the game was delayed twice because of rain (and lightning) when NIU won and broke the streak," Hammock said. "It was a great time, and I wanted to be part of a new tradition they were trying to build."

Running back Thomas Hammock had his collegiate career cut short by a heart ailment.

Hammock quickly became one of the key laborers.

"We had our top two returning backs (Ivory Bryant and Bill Anders) flunk out," said Novak. "Everybody asked what we were going to do. I said that we'd be fine because we had Thomas Hammock."

Whether it was wishful thinking or full confidence in Hammock, Novak wasn't disappointed. Despite missing those final 11 games of his senior year, Hammock ranked No. 8 on the NIU career rushing list with 2,432 yards. Moreover, the two-year captain ran for 100 or more yards 12 times in 32 varsity games.

"Thomas is one of the most, if not the most, hard-nosed players I've ever been around," said former Huskie teammate P.J. Fleck. "His actions spoke louder than any words. He's the best tailback I've ever been around."

When his heart ailment ended his playing career, Hammock became a student coach and mentor to the rest of the NIU running backs, especially backup Michael Turner, who took his spot in the starting lineup. Turner wound up rushing for a MAC-record 1,915 yards.

"It meant that I kept the tradition going of being a leader and showing the younger guys how to grow up and be professional just like I was taught when I was the young guy in the group," Hammock said.

Hammock, a first-team All-MAC pick, also performed well in the classroom. He graduated in three and a half years with a degree in marketing. Hammock earned Arthur Ashe Jr. Sports-Scholar honors and was runner-up for the Playboy Anson Mount National Scholar-Athlete Award in 2001–2002.

In 2003, Hammock landed a position with the University of Wisconsin football program under head coach Barry Alvarez. He spent two seasons with the Badgers.

"When we played Wisconsin (in 2002), Thomas and Barry had a little chat. Barry told him how badly he felt that he couldn't play. He wound up as Barry's graduate assistant the next year," Novak said.

Hammock returned to his alma mater in 2005 as running backs coach under Novak.

"It's funny because Thomas always used to say that he'd never be a coach," Novak said. "He started out in business, and I'm sure that he would have done very well for himself because he's so intelligent, but once he started coaching that was that."

Hammock came to a few realizations about coaching.

"The thing that goes through my mind was how hard those (NIU) coaches pushed us (as players)," Hammock said. "And I even noticed it more when I coached under Coach Novak. Things were a lot different."

One of the Huskie running backs that Hammock worked directly with was Garrett Wolfe.

"We had a very unique situation," Hammock told GopherSports.com. "When I was a senior at Northern Illinois, Garrett was an incoming freshman, and he was a guy that kind of wanted to hang with the older guys and he thought he was one of the older guys. I left that program for two years and went to Wisconsin to coach.

"When I came back, we definitely had a different relationship. As a player and coming back in my early stages of development as a coach, we were able to have an open relationship and talk. I could critique him hard and he took it and knew that what I was saying was coming from a perspective of having done it, and not as, 'You need to do this or that.' It worked best for the team and worked best for us."

After two years at NIU, Hammock made his way back to the Big Ten when he joined the University of Minnesota staff. Initially, he was the running backs coach. In 2010, Hammock added co-offensive coordinator duties. When Jerry Kill was hired as the Minnesota head coach late in 2010, Hammock was initially kept on the Golden Gopher staff. However,

Hammock later left to coach running backs at the University of Wisconsin.

Regardless of where Hammock is at, Fleck remains thrilled for his friend.

"Thomas is hard working and one of the brightest men you'll ever meet," said Fleck. "I hope he and I get on the same coaching staff someday. One of his best attributes is that he's honest. Thomas will always give you a pure answer. It may not always be the answer you're looking for or like, but he'll tell you what he thinks. Rarely do you get that from a friend."

Hammock clearly sees his future.

"My goal is to become a head coach where I can have the opportunity to be a leader of men," Hammock said. "I am very passionate about that and feel I can coach and recruit at a high enough level to compete for championships."

No matter where his career path takes him, Hammock forever remains an NIU Huskie at heart.

"I am very proud to have played at Northern Illinois University," he said. "I had an awesome student-athlete experience. I met my wife at NIU, and I always root for the Huskies except if the team I happen to be coaching has to play them."

NIU football fans will always remember LeShon Johnson. Wolfe and Turner sit atop the Huskie career rushing list. Does Thomas Hammock ever feel lost in the shuffle?

"I never feel I am lost in the shuffle because I never had a chance to finish my career," he said. "I had three great years and one great game that will last a lifetime. If people remember me as a fierce competitor, I am fine with that."

FOUR-DOWN TERRITORY

Favorite Football Movie—I love "Jerry Maguire." It happened to be the hip movie when I was growing up. I really liked "The Program" too because I thought that was how college was going to be.

First Car—My first car was a Dodge Plymouth. I remember I paid $250 for it from a guy that came into the restaurant that I worked at all the time because he was getting a new one. That car was in great shape but my insurance at the time was three times what I paid for it. I was a busboy; I couldn't afford that, but my parents helped out.

Worst Summer Job—The worst job I ever worked was when I was at NIU. We got summer jobs at Johnson Controls working on the assembly line making Neon cars. Let's just say that was some hard work. I may have shut the line down a time or two.

Favorite Subject in School—My favorite subject was always math, and I am sure that played a part in me getting a business degree. But my passion has always been football. You just can't beat it.

MICHAEL TURNER

Sometimes you have to roll the dice in the recruiting game. Fortunately, everything came up 7s and 11s when the Northern Illinois Huskies took a chance on Michael Turner.

"His story is an interesting one," said former Northern head coach Joe Novak. "He played at North Chicago High School. He was a hard kid to judge because there were three ballcarriers in that backfield."

Since Turner had to share the carries with the two others, many college recruiters didn't catch the player destined for National Football League stardom.

"We were fortunate we were so close (to Chicago)," Novak said. "We got to see him five, six, seven times. I told our staff that he'd be a great player or a bust, and I really didn't know."

By the time Turner's collegiate career wrapped up in 2003, Novak and his staff more

Michael Turner ranks among the greatest running backs in NIU history. Turner later starred for the San Diego Chargers and Atlanta Falcons.

than had their answer. Turner finished with 4,941 rushing yards and 48 touchdowns.

Four years earlier, Turner was more than happy to accept NIU's scholarship offer.

"I'm happy I came here," Turner told sports information director Mike Korcek in an on-line story. "This was the first scholarship offer. I wanted to go to the team that wanted me."

The NIU coaching staff liked what they saw from the get-go.

"He was a backup to Thomas Hammock," said Novak. "He rushed for over 900 yards as a backup as a freshman.

"He had the biggest thighs I've ever seen. Michael is so much faster than people think."

By his junior season, Turner was an established star. He finished second in the nation with 1,915 rushing yards. Five times he rushed for more than 200 yards in a game and twice that season he scored five touchdowns in a game. He also caught the attention and admiration of friends and foes alike.

"The honors that Michael received were well deserved," said Novak.

"We needed 15 guys to stop Turner. Eleven wasn't enough," said Toledo head coach Tom Amstutz.

"He is a big back, six feet, 228 pounds, and runs a 4.4," said Maryland head coach Ralph Friedgen. "This guy will be playing on Sundays. Their offense revolves around giving him the football. They play-action fake off of him and get some really big plays. Most teams have to put an extra guy in the box to stop him, but they still have trouble stopping him with eight or nine people in the box. That is how good he is."

As a senior, Turner again finished as the NCAA's runner-up in rushing (1,648 yards). Turner left NIU as the school's all-time leading rusher.

"He was a phenomenal player," said former teammate Dan Sheldon. "He was constantly proving himself over and over. Michael had a low center of gravity and balance like no other

player. He had the speed of a defensive back. He'd turn the corner and nobody could catch him."

The San Diego Chargers selected Turner in the fifth round of the 2004 NFL Draft. He was the 154th player taken.

Turner spent four seasons in San Diego, mostly backing up All-Pro running back La-Dainian Tomlinson. The Chargers elected to allow Turner to leave as a free agent following the 2007 season.

He landed in Atlanta when the Falcons signed him to a six-year, $34.5 million contract with $15 million guaranteed.

Turner quickly made an impact in Atlanta. In his very first game in a Falcons' uniform, he rushed for a franchise-record 220 yards against Detroit. He finished the year with 1,699 yards and a Falcons' record 17 rushing touchdowns. The spectacular season earned him a trip to the Pro Bowl. In 2010, Turner rushed for 1,371 yards and again played in the Pro Bowl.

With his pro career shifting into high gear, Huskie fans can smile. So too can Joe Novak, the man who rolled the dice and came up a big winner.

P.J. FLECK

Suppose you could play in your backyard and then get to coach there as well. For P.J. Fleck, that's precisely what happened.

Fleck grew up in Sugar Grove, Illinois, a short trip from DeKalb and Northern Illinois University. He grew up following the career of local football hero Don Beebe, who played at nearby Kaneland High School, then Western Illinois University and Chadron State before an NFL career with the Buffalo Bills and Green Bay Packers.

"Donnie's nieces and nephews all grew up with me," Fleck recalled. "At Kaneland, Don is all you ever heard about. Plus, he came back and gave back to the community in so many ways. I remember giving his niece 10 football cards to get autographed. They all came back with his signature, No. 82, God bless."

Fleck followed in Beebe's footsteps at Kaneland where he was an All-State honoree in football, basketball and track.

The Knights twice went undefeated and won a pair of Class 3A state football titles. Fleck set a state record with 95 receptions for 1,548 yards and 16 touchdowns his senior year. He caught 199 career passes for 3,121 yards and 34 TDs with at least one catch in 40 consecutive games during his prep years.

Still, Fleck wasn't on anyone's recruiting radar initially.

"I was not recruited in football at all," said Fleck. "I was 5-9, 150 pounds and ran a 4.8 (time) in the 40. Track actually looked more like the route I'd take."

Fleck's duties as an assistant football coach at NIU included being the recruiting coordinator.

"I don't think **I'd** have recruited me," he said.

Yet, Huskie head coach Joe Novak saw something he liked in Fleck.

"The only football camp I ever went to was at Northern," Fleck said. "I didn't drop a pass the whole camp. I came away with turf burns, so maybe I opened Coach Novak's eyes. I guess he decided to keep an eye on me."

The NIU head coach kept more than an eye on the turf-burned receiver.

"The only reason we recruited him was that P.J. was laying out in camp," Novak recalled. "He caught everything. I told my coaching staff, 'I may be wrong, but I'm entitled one pick, and P.J. is my choice.'"

Novak wound up offering Fleck his last scholarship.

"It was the only offer I got," Fleck said. "There weren't any from Division II or Division III. Northern's was it."

Novak's faith in Fleck would be tested early. During the Huskies' first game in the 1999 season, NIU was driving for an apparent touchdown against Western Illinois.

"The play came in for a pass to me," Fleck explained. "We had so many good receivers that year like Justin McCareins and Darrell Hill, but the ball was coming my way.

"(Quarterback) Frisman Jackson (later an NFL receiver) threw the ball to me and it went right through my hands and wound up a pick-six (interception for a touchdown) the other way."

Doubt began to creep into Fleck's head as Jackson "stared a hole right into me."

Yet, Fleck's miscue proved to be one of the turning points of his career.

"Coach Novak came over to me and said, 'Don't worry, youngster, we're coming right back at you.' That meant so much to me," said Fleck.

The Huskies indeed came back to Fleck. By the end of his career, he had earned first team All-MAC honors in 2003. Fleck finished that season with 77 catches for 1,028 yards and six touchdowns. Against Ohio University, Fleck grabbed 14 balls for 234 yards and earned himself national player of the week honors from USAToday.com.

In that game, Fleck made a key fourth-down reception that kept a Huskies' drive alive.

"That may have been the biggest catch of the season," said former NIU assistant Mike Sabock. "People always talk about the Maryland and Alabama games and rightly so. But we almost lost to Ohio. It was fourth down and the play was designed for another receiver. P.J. told him, 'Switch sides with me. I'm running the route.' P.J. made a big catch to keep our drive going."

To Fleck, the season opener will always remain a shining moment in time.

"That Maryland game really stands out to me," Fleck said. "When I came to Northern, we had the nation's longest losing streak. We were lucky to get 2,000 fans in the stands. But for that game, tickets were being scalped. We wound up with over 30,000 and they were

Wide receiver P.J. Fleck arrived
at NIU from nearby Kaneland
High School. Fleck played with
the San Francisco 49ers.
.

yelling and screaming the whole game."

Fleck played a major part in the upset. The fifth-year senior had 12 receptions for 113 yards and a touchdown.

"To see that turnaround in our program was incredible. To be a part of it from the lows of the longest losing streak in the nation to winning on Alabama's home field really was special."

NIU play-by-play man Bill Baker enjoyed watching and broadcasting Fleck's games as a Huskie.

"There are still football fields across the country with marks on them from where he dragged his feet to stay inbounds or make big catches," Baker said. "He has more energy than anyone I've ever been around. He's just a good kid, top to bottom."

David Kaplan did the play-by-play for many NIU games during Fleck's career.

"P.J. is my guy," said Kaplan. "I loved him. Tom Waddle, my broadcast partner, loved him. Every game he'd run over and shake our hands and thank us for the kind words we'd said about him. Those 30 seconds say a lot about P.J. Fleck. He made a lifetime of impressions with those 30 seconds."

Fleck followed his illustrious NIU career by spending two seasons with the San Francisco 49ers. After signing as a free agent in 2004, he spent most of that season on the practice squad before making an appearance against the New England Patriots late in the year.

"When I was lining up on the kickoff team that day, I took just a second to realize that my dream had come true," Fleck explained. "I played on Sunday. Yes, it was only one game, but I played on Sunday."

Fleck had his 49ers jersey from that day framed.

"It's grass-stained and all," he said. "But that day was priceless."

In 2006, after being placed on injured reserve for the '05 season, Fleck retired from pro football.

"I learned so much from my time with the 49ers," Fleck said. "I got to be around coaches like Dennis Erickson, Mike Nolan, Mike Martz and Mike Singletary every day."

With his playing career behind him, Fleck made his transition into coaching. He landed a graduate assistant position at top-ranked Ohio State in 2006. The Buckeyes rolled through the regular season as Big Ten champions and faced off against Florida for the national

championship. It was there that he learned another valuable lesson.

"I had Coach (Jim) Tressel and his staff on a pedestal," Fleck said. "It's my first year (coaching) and we're going to be national champs."

But, Florida had other ideas. The once-beaten Gators trounced Ohio State 41-14 in the national championship game in Glendale, Arizona.

"The next day, Coach Tressel was back to business," Fleck said. "We didn't waste time (sulking over the loss). It was a great lesson to see how he handled it. This never stops. You can learn from yesterday, but you can't dwell on it. It helped me in my profession."

Fleck took those lessons into his next coaching job, back on the familiar turf at NIU under Novak. He was retained on the staff when Jerry Kill took over the Huskies in 2008.

"(Novak and Kill) are so similar that they're different," Fleck explained. "They're both cut from the same mold morally. Both put the players No. 1. That's something you constantly hear as a coach from both of them."

Kill was impressed with his young assistant.

"He's not going to be around here forever because he's young," Kill said. "He's bled on this field, he's played in the NFL. His future is very, very bright."

As Kill predicted, Fleck left NIU to take a position at Rutgers University in 2010.

Moving into the coaching ranks forced him to look at the game from a much different perspective.

"As a player, you look at things from a player's view," Fleck said. "As a coach, you have to be one step ahead of the defense. You don't watch the ball and cheer because you got a first down. A play ends and you're thinking three plays ahead. Your reward is when the game is over and you've done your job well."

So, for the time being, Fleck wants to continue to hone his craft as a coach.

"I want to be one of those coaches that play-ers want to play for, to lay it on the line for," he said.

Fleck has sought out the advice of Northwestern head coach Pat Fitzgerald, who took over the Wildcats at age 31 following the unexpected death of Randy Walker in 2006.

"I asked Pat how he knew when he was ready. His response was that he wasn't ready, but he convinced himself that he could do the job. Who knows when I'll be ready? I may be a young coach. I may be an old coach. (For now), I'll continue to prepare," said a 28-year-old Fleck.

Preparation and effort have never been a problem for Fleck. Neither has enthusiasm.

"P.J. is a catalyst," said Novak. "I remember when we beat Central Michigan. I got caught up doing an interview on the way to the locker room. Well, I get in there late. P.J. is up on top of one of the lockers leading the fight song. P.J. was a **freshman.**"

With all that Fleck has to offer, any football program that lands him will benefit.

"He's going to be a great coach," Novak said.

After coaching pro wide receivers for one season, Fleck was hired by Western Michigan as its head coach.

FOUR-DOWN TERRITORY

Favorite Football Movie—"We Are Marshall" and "Invincible."

First Car—1989 Pontiac Grand Prix.

Worst Summer Job—Shucking corn.

Favorite Subject in School—History.

RANDEE DREW

Randee Drew intercepted 15 passes in his Northern Illinois career. But none was bigger than the one that clinched the Huskies' 2003 upset of Maryland.

Leading 20-13 in overtime against the 15th-ranked Terrapins, Drew capitalized on a fortunate bounce. Maryland quarterback Scott McBrien fired a pass intended for receiver Latreaz Harrison. The ball struck NIU defensive back Rob Lee's leg as he fell backward. The ball shot in the air and into the waiting arms of Drew.

"Everything was in slow motion," Drew said afterward. "One of them fell and kicked the ball and it came right to me. I guess (they) just put me in the right spot at the right time."

Six years later, Drew was fighting to earn his way back from injury in the Canadian Football League. His confidence was buoyed by the events of that historic night when NIU's victory over Maryland marked the highest-ranked opponent the Huskies had ever beaten.

"There were so many great plays in that game. Mine was just one of many," said Drew in an e-mail. "I remember guarding my man and seeing the ball thrown over my head. I instinctively turned and ran to the ball. All coaches say if you run to the ball, good things will happen.

"It was a great play and even better because of a great win for our team against a great team."

The victory proved to be a sign of good things to come as NIU later defeated Iowa State and Alabama en route to a 10-2 season. The Huskies rose as high as 10th in the nation when the first Bowl Championship Series poll came out.

However, when bowl bids came out at the end of the season, NIU was nowhere to be found.

"I felt extremely ripped off," said Drew. "Our team fought so hard that year and shocked college football. It was upsetting, but I can say if I took anything from it, it's that I'm proud that we helped open up the eyes of the country and made it possible for NIU to go to bowls after that.

"We paved the way, which is always good and rewarding in its own right."

A native of Milwaukee, Wisconsin, Drew was a four-sport athlete at Glendale Nicolet High School. In addition to football, he was the starting point guard in basketball. Moreover, Drew earned state championships in soccer and track.

"I was always busy and motivated by sports," he said.

Yet, Drew wasn't highly sought after as a recruit. In fact, the only interest he garnered was as a walk-on.

"I had a lot of Division II offers (from schools like) North Dakota, South Dakota and so on," he said.

Drew met NIU assistant Matt Canada while attending a summer camp at the University of Minnesota.

"Randee was a great kid coming out of high school," said Canada. "He had a very competitive drive about him and a strong desire to play at the Division I level.

"We were not able to give him a scholarship coming out of high school. I was reluctant to talk him into walking on and turning down money from I-AA schools, but I did tell him that we would be true to our word, and if he was good enough to play, Coach (Joe) Novak would take care of him. Coach Novak had a proven track record of taking care of walk-ons."

Key to Drew's decision was the influence of his grandmother.

"She trusted me on that fact that he would be taken care of and that he would be forced to go to class," said Canada.

Drew accepted the Huskies' offer.

"I came into camp determined and fighting," Drew said.

The NIU staff took note.

"Randee came to camp and beat out the competition," said Canada. "He was a starter in the opening game against Northwestern."

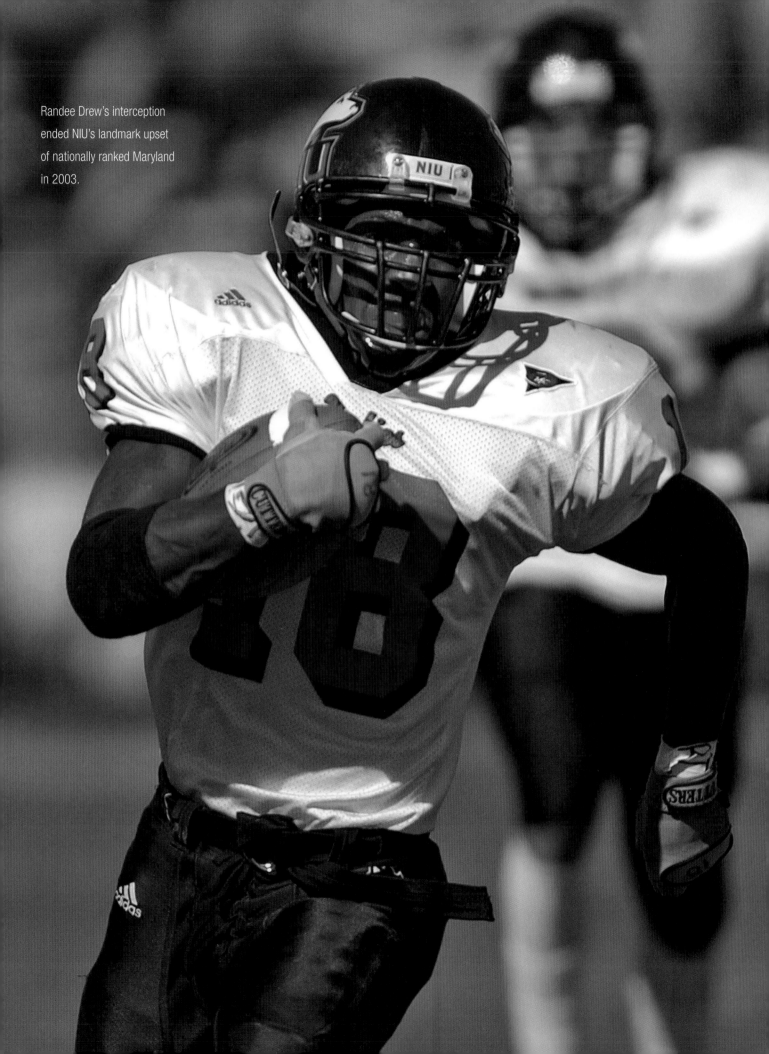

Randee Drew's interception ended NIU's landmark upset of nationally ranked Maryland in 2003.

Still, Canada had concerns, and they weren't all about Drew's on-field performance.

"The biggest concern was getting him a number that wouldn't stand out," the coach said. "I don't remember what the number was exactly that he was originally issued, but it was in the 90s. We had a concern he might stand out playing corner in a 90 jersey."

Thus, Drew ultimately donned the No. 18. He also earned something more valuable.

"They gave me a scholarship about five days before school started. It was a blessing and the rest is history."

That history translated into lettering all four years in a Huskie uniform. He started 36 times in his 44-game collegiate career. Included in those starts were two at wide receiver his freshman year.

As a junior, Drew became just the third player in Mid-American Conference history to lead the league in both interceptions (seven) and kickoff returns (26.1 yards-per-return average).

"Randee went on to be a great player and a great person," said Canada. "He should be very proud he trusted himself, but he was also blessed to have a family who supported his dream and allowed him to come to school."

Following his senior season, Drew joined teammate Michael Turner as a participant in the East-West Shrine Classic in San Francisco.

The venue for the postseason All-Star showcase delighted Drew.

"As a kid growing up I wanted to play for the 49ers," he said.

That dream became a brief reality when San Francisco signed the 5-foot-8, 185-pounder to a free contract in 2004.

Drew played the 2005 NFL Europe season with the Cologne Centurions in Germany.

"(I) loved NFL Europe," he said. "It was one of the best times in my life not only because of football, but the whole experience and culture shock was amazing. If I could do something again in my life, besides college, it would definitely be that."

Drew then spent two seasons playing in the Arena Football League. First came a season with the Orlando Predators in the AFL. That was followed by a year with the Green Bay Blizzard of af2.

"Arena was different, I won't lie," Drew said. "I wasn't too fond of the idea when I first started. But, as I played in 2006 with Orlando, I really started to like the game.

"When I played af2 in Green Bay, it was amazing. We made a championship run that I will never forget."

Drew plied his experience into a shot with the Canadian Football League. He landed on the practice squad of the British Columbia Lions in 2006.

In 2007, Drew had his breakout season. Signed as a free agent, Drew led the Montreal Alouettes with four interceptions. He added a fumble recovery, three sacks, four pass knockdowns and 67 tackles. As a result, Drew was nominated by Montreal for the league's outstanding rookie award. He earned CFL East Division All-Star honors.

Though the Minnesota Vikings of the National Football League expressed interest in him, Drew remained in the CFL. Midway through 2008, he suffered a season-ending knee injury.

In September 2009, he signed with the Edmonton Eskimos as a free agent. Drew fought his way back from the injury and joined the Eskimos' lineup in time for the playoffs. Edmonton reached the Western Conference final, falling to defending champion Calgary 24-21. Drew led the Eskimos with six tackles in the game.

"Playing in the CFL has been a great experience," Drew said. "It's given me the chance to experience new things."

Yet, perhaps none was bigger than that night in 2003 when his interception sealed NIU's victory over Maryland.

SAM HURD

The news was as stunning as any catch or special teams play Sam Hurd ever made.

On December 15, 2011, news broke that Hurd, who played at Northern from 2002-2005, was in federal custody, charged with trying to set up a drug-dealing network after authorities arrested him during a sting operation.

According to a *Chicago Tribune* story by Jeremy Gorner and Vaughn McClure, "Hurd was arrested outside a Chicago restaurant after he accepted a kilogram of cocaine from a confidential informant and an undercover federal agent posing as a drug supplier, according to federal charges filed in Dallas."

According to the charges, Hurd negotiated to buy "five to 10 kilograms of cocaine and 1,000 pounds of marijuana a week for distribution in the Chicago area, authorities alleged."

Federal authorities had been tracking Hurd since July 2011 when he was living in the Dallas area where he had played for the Cowboys since entering the NFL.

Hurd left the Cowboys as a free agent and had signed a three-year contract with the Chicago Bears. The contract carried a maximum value of $5.15 million ($4.15 million base total). The Bears gave Hurd a $1.35 million signing bonus.

Teammates, coaches and fans were shocked when the news broke.

"It's a situation I don't want anyone to be in, especially a close friend, a teammate that I played with now for four or five years now, especially a guy from Texas with a wife and daughter," said Bears receiver and former Cowboy Roy Williams. "So, it's tough for me just because I am not into drugs or anything like that. I know it has to be tough for him because he has his family. It's a choice he made and there are consequences with choices that you make."

Joe Novak, former NIU head coach told the *Chicago Sun-Times*, "(I'm) shocked. Disappointed that things even come to this point. You never think of those kids (who play for you) getting involved in something like this.

"He was a great player. He really loved to practice and play the game. That was never a problem. He was a little immature at times but that usually involved academics, where he needed a push or a prod.

"After six years (playing professionally) in the big city you figure they did a lot of growing up."

Garrett Wolfe, who played with Hurd at NIU, told the *Sun-Times*, "Sam has always been a great teammate and an even better friend. That's how I remember him. My thoughts and prayers as with him and his family in these trying times."

Hurd arrived at NIU in the summer of 2002. The native Texan was a late national letter of intent signee, committing to the Huskies in June 2002. Former Huskie assistant Jay Boulware had a hand in steering Hurd to Northern.

"It was a last minute choice," said Hurd in a Facebook response to this book's author in February 2011. "I was supposed to go to the University of Arizona, but NIU is a choice I'm glad I made. I met many friends and, of course, my future wife Stacey."

Hurd grew up in San Antonio, Texas. As a senior at Brackenridge High School, Hurd earned all-state honors with 20 touchdown receptions. He also played basketball and ran track as a prep athlete.

Listed at 6 foot 3 and 195 pounds, Hurd

Sam Hurd starred as the Huskies' big-play receiver prior to an NFL career (Photo by Scott Walstrom).

joined one of the most talented receiving corps in NIU history.

"Sam Hurd is a real talent, with tremendous potential," said head coach Joe Novak in 2004. "He is what I call a playmaker."

Hurd displayed his abilities from the beginning. He earned a letter as a true freshman. Hurd led the Huskies in yards per catch (23.2) and set the single-season receiving record for a freshman.

Hurd continued to get better as his collegiate career unfolded.

"When he finally got it and saw how good he could really be, he became special," said former Huskie teammate P.J. Fleck. "Nobody could cover him in the MAC. He was a step ahead of everyone else."

The Huskies clinched the 2005 MAC West title with a 42-7 blowout of Western Michigan the day before Thanksgiving. Hurd led NIU with four receptions for 119 yards that day. In addition, Hurd showcased his big-play abilities by hauling in a 53-yard touchdown pass from quarterback Dan Nicholson as NIU built a 28-7 halftime lead.

Meanwhile, Garrett Wolfe turned in a brilliant 277-yard, five-touchdown performance in the MAC West clincher.

"It feels great to go out and win and know we're going to Detroit (for the MAC Championship). I'm ready to get on that bus," Hurd said afterward.

When his Huskie career ended, Hurd's name could be found all over the NIU record book. He ranks second to only Justin McCareins with 2,322 receiving yards. Hurd's 21 touchdown catches trail only McCareins (29) and John Spillis (22). He is tied for sixth on the career reception list with 143 catches.

In addition, Hurd holds the NIU single-game record with a 266-yard effort against Central Michigan in 2005. Yet, he doesn't consider that game his finest Huskie performance.

"I would say the Miami of Ohio game (also

in 2005)," Hurd said. "The cornerback for Miami (Alphonso Hodge) was so high profiled and was supposed to go in the first round of the NFL Draft. I torched them for something like 220 yards (actually 223, a total that ranks third on the single-game NIU list)."

Hurd capped his Huskie career by leading the team with 65 receptions for 1,074 yards and 13 touchdowns.

Undrafted by the NFL, Hurd signed with the Dallas Cowboys in 2006. Ironically the first pass Hurd caught in the NFL was also Tony Romo's first pro completion.

"It was a good feeling," Hurd said of the 34-yard reception, "hopefully I will be able to catch more in the future."

Hurd made his first NFL start four weeks later and caught four passes for 42 yards and a touchdown against Arizona.

Yet, Hurd's performance on special teams was what caught both the Cowboys coaches' and fans' attention.

"Sam is a terrific special teamer who was elected captain of that unit last season (2010), which shows the respect he has from teammates," said Ken Sims of DallasCowboysStar.com.

Former Huskie teammate Randee Drew faced Hurd in practice and can attest to his talents as a receiver.

"First off, he has all the attributes of a good receiver," Drew said. "He is tall, (has) long arms, big hands and he used them all to his advantage. He is younger than me, but he was very interested in working hard and putting in the work. Sam's growth was tremendous. I'm not surprised that he is as successful as he is."

In 2007, Hurd began co-hosting a one-hour radio show for a Dallas radio station. A year later, he joined fellow wide receiver Terrell Owens on a local television show.

Moreover, Hurd also credited Owens for making him a better receiver.

"I learned a lot with Terrell Owens my first few years," he said.

When Owens left Dallas, Hurd turned to Cowboys' star Miles Austin.

"(Miles) has taught me a lot as well as me teaching him some things," Hurd said. "We both came in together as undrafted free agents. Miles Austin is one of my good friends on the team."

Joining Hurd on the Dallas roster was fellow NIU graduate Doug Free, the team's left tackle. Hurd continues to follow Huskie football.

"I have won some bets and lost some too with my teammates now," Hurd said.

Though he sponsored a celebrity weekend that benefited a number of San Antonio charities, it was Hurd's other off-the-field activities that grabbed national headlines as 2011 came to a close.

FOUR-DOWN TERRITORY

Favorite Football Movie—"The Waterboy" because it is a very funny football movie. My favorite serious football movie is "The Express." I liked it because one of my friends and ex-teammates at NIU, Lionel Hickenbottom, was in the movie. He did a lot of cool stunts in it.

First Car—A Chevy Tahoe. I really liked it because it was so durable. Rides like a tank.

Worst Summer Job—None.

Favorite Subject in School—Math, I was very good at it. I actually skipped a grade because my math scores were so high. When I first arrived on the NIU campus I had just turned 17.

DOUG FREE

Sometimes out of tragedy comes good.

Such was the case when Shea Fitzgerald died when a porch collapsed at a Chicago apartment in the summer of 2003.

"Doug (Free) was thrust into the picture when we lost Shea in the accident," said NIU head coach Joe Novak.

And what a situation to have thrust upon you. With Fitzgerald's family in attendance, the Huskies opened the season with an emotionally charged Thursday night game against nationally ranked Maryland. Starting at right tackle, Free and his Huskie teammates upset the Terrapins 20-13 in overtime.

"He handled that well," said Novak.

Free handled more than just that first game well. A three-time letterman from Lincoln High School in Manitowoc, Wisconsin, Free started 49 games in his college career.

Free earned first-team All-Mid-American Conference and Academic All-MAC honors as a senior. He also landed on the Outland

Doug Free emerged as one of the greatest offensive linemen in NIU history.

Trophy and Lombardi Award watch lists.

"Doug was about 6 foot 6 and 245 (pounds) as a tight end in high school," Novak said. "He was a basketball player too. When you watched him you noticed that he had pretty good feet."

With the University of Wisconsin asking Free to walk on, Novak pursued him with the idea of switching Free to offensive tackle.

"His eyes just about bugged out," Novak said. "Doug didn't think he'd put that much weight on."

By the completion of his Huskie career, Free moved up to the 315-pound mark and stood among the best ever to play on the offensive line at NIU.

"Doug was so athletic for his size," Novak said. "He had a nasty streak in him as well. Our players called him 'Doug Freak.' One of his real strengths is that he could block at the point of attack, come off his man, stay on his feet and get downfield to block another defender.

"I've heard people point that out in NFL games as well."

In addition, with a 3.24 grade-point average in industrial technology, Free was nominated for CoSIDA District V All-Academic honors.

Free was a semifinalist for the Draddy Award, which recognizes academic success, football performance and exemplary community service.

"(Free) may turn out to be the highest draft choice we've ever had. He's had a great career for us," said Novak during Free's senior season.

Free came close to fulfilling Novak's prophecy when the Dallas Cowboys selected him in the fourth round of the 2007 National Football League Draft. Free was the 122nd overall player selected. Six years earlier, Indianapolis had taken guard Ryan Diem as the 118th overall player. (Editor's note: To that point in NIU history, wide receiver John Spilis was the highest selection. Spilis, a third-round pick by Green Bay in the 1969 draft, went 64th overall. Larry English is the highest-ranked NIU player ever taken. English, a first-round pick by San Diego, was the 16th overall choice in the 2009 draft.)

Free spent his first three pro seasons in a reserve role. During that time, he learned from the likes of five-time Pro Bowl tackle Flozell Adams and former first-round draft choices Marc Colombo and Leonard Davis.

Free took over the starting right tackle position in 2009 when Colombo suffered through an injury-plagued season. Free took Adams' spot in a playoff loss to Minnesota.

Following the 2009 season, Dallas chose to let Adams leave as a free agent and inserted Free into the vacated starting assignment.

"Right now, we're going into it thinking that with Doug and these other guys, we're going to be able to keep doing what we've been doing," Cowboys' quarterback Tony Romo told Stephen Hawkins of the Associated Press at the time. "And hopefully the team can grow as an offense."

Meanwhile, Free told writer Calvin Watkins, "I got a lot of hard work to put in and I'm obviously excited. Last year, getting a chance to play, and I think playing pretty well, most people thought stuff like that, they definitely have some faith in me. It's the other side of the ball (going from right tackle to left tackle), but I think I've proven that I can play."

DAN SHELDON

A father's advice can go a long way in determining a son's future success. Take the case of Dan Sheldon.

"When I was being recruited, my dad told me to go where they want you and go where you will play," said Sheldon.

Tim Sheldon knew firsthand. He had played at Indiana University for two seasons back in the mid-1960s. When his son was being recruited by the likes of the University of Illinois

Dan Sheldon caught what proved
to be the winning touchdown in
overtime against Maryland
in 2003.

and Northwestern, the father drew from his own experiences.

"My dad always had my best interests at heart," the son said. "He and my mom made me the person I am today. They gave me every opportunity to be a success."

Success came naturally to Sheldon, a three-sport star at nearby Burlington Central (Illinois) High School.

"I played football, basketball and baseball," he said. "But football was always my calling. There's something about football that can't be matched. It's the excitement of the game. Everybody looks forward to Friday night. I loved performing in front of a large crowd."

After playing quarterback as a sophomore, Sheldon was switched to running back by Burlington Central head coach Dave Smith.

"He said I would get a lot more touches on the ball and would be more effective," Sheldon said. "It turned out that he was right."

Sheldon ran for 2,123 yards on 108 carries his senior season. He scored 43 touchdowns, 37 of those coming on the ground. In addition, Sheldon anchored the defensive backfield.

"He was clearly one of the best talents we've had in this area," said prep writer John Radtke. "He had the physical skills, but what really impressed you were his instincts. If you were a defender and had him in your sights, you'd blink and he'd be gone. He had lightning-quick instincts."

With college recruiters showing their interest, Sheldon had a difficult decision to make.

"People often get caught up in the persona of a Big Ten school and think they have to go there," Sheldon said. "Illinois wanted me as a defensive back. Northwestern was big on me early, but then I began to realize that maybe things weren't really the way they wanted them to seem."

Sheldon also drew the attention of Central Michigan, a Mid-American Conference rival of Northern.

"I figured if I were going to go to a MAC school, I may as well play in my backyard," Sheldon said.

P.J. Fleck, another NIU football player with local roots, also played a factor.

"P.J. was a guy who had gone a similar route," Sheldon said of the Kaneland High School star. "I knew him from competing against him in high school. He had enjoyed a lot of success. P.J. was part of the recruiting process. There were a lot of similarities between us."

Thus, Sheldon's decision came down to the Big Ten vs. the MAC.

"I had the same misconception that a lot of people had about bigger always being better," Sheldon said. "Some of it is ego. You think that to be appreciated you have to play for a Big Ten school. I was very close to going to Northwestern."

In the end, Sheldon's decision turned on his father's advice.

"Northern showed me the most interest all along," he said. "Northern didn't care that I was 5 (foot) 10. They didn't care that I didn't fit into a certain mold. They only cared that I was a football player who could help them be successful."

It was a decision that neither Sheldon nor NIU ever regretted.

"Danny was a kid who is a go-getter," said NIU head coach Joe Novak. "He could run."

Like Fleck, Sheldon played receiver for the Huskies.

"I was an offensive-minded player," Sheldon said. "(Running back) Michael Turner was the key part of our offense. He opened up our passing game. Teams were so intent on stopping Michael that we were left one-on-one as receivers."

Sheldon developed into a bona fide deep threat for the Huskies. In 2002, Sheldon caught 40 passes for 783 yards.

In addition, Sheldon served as the Huskies' punt returner.

"He was so electrifying," said Radtke. "He put people in the seats with his return ability. He was as important as Michael Turner or anybody else to Northern."

Yet, it's a pass reception that most people recall when Sheldon's name comes up.

"I've thought about that catch many times," Sheldon said. "It never plays out in my head as when I watch it on tape."

The play Sheldon described was his 30-yard touchdown reception that became the game-winner when NIU stunned Maryland to open the 2003 season.

"(In my mind) it was a quick five-yard hitch route that (quarterback) Josh Haldi delivered perfectly. I caught the pass and ran it in for the score," he said.

On tape, however, Sheldon saw himself catch the pass, shake out of the defender's grasp and then sprint into the end zone.

"That was a typical Dan Sheldon play," said Novak. "He scored a lot of touchdowns for us."

Making the play even more amazing is the fact that Sheldon appeared to be severely injured earlier in the game.

"I took a hit (in the third quarter)," he recalled. "I thought my career was over. I thought it was an ACL injury. They took me in and looked at it. Fortunately, it wasn't the worst-case scenario."

The Huskies' upset propelled NIU to a season for the ages. The Huskies won their first eight games. When the first Bowl Championship Series poll came out, NIU was ranked 10th in the nation.

Things came undone when injuries bit the team.

"We lost five starters, including me," Sheldon said. "We didn't have the same depth as other (ranked) teams. We went into our two biggest MAC games with key pieces missing."

In addition, those two games against Toledo and Bowling Green were on the road.

Despite losing both of those games, NIU still finished with a 10-win season. Yet, no bowl invitation came the Huskies' way.

"We all felt we deserved to go to a bowl game," Sheldon said. "We won at Alabama. We beat Iowa State. We played a tough conference schedule. It showed how poorly the system was run back then."

Just how poorly run were things in 2003? Northwestern, a team with a 6-6 record, received a bowl bid. Part of the reasoning went that the Big Ten school would bring more fans and attention to the bowl system.

"I have to believe that fans would have tuned in to the (bowl) game had we been a part of it," Sheldon said. "Anyone who loves the underdog would have tuned in. Fans want to see good teams play each other. They want quality bowl matchups."

Still, Sheldon managed to find a silver lining in NIU's bowl snub.

"What happened to us forced a change in the process," he said.

Sheldon eventually got a shot at a bowl game in 2004, his senior season. As things turned out, the experience turned out to be bittersweet. Though NIU defeated Troy State 34-21 to claim the Silicon Valley Bowl trophy, Sheldon's future was perhaps forever altered.

"I broke my collarbone in the bowl game," he said. "I still had two All-Star games ahead of me. I was projected to be a third- to fifth-round pick (in the NFL Draft)."

Missing the postseason All-Star games cost Sheldon exposure to NFL coaching staffs. He attempted to perform at the NFL Combine, but was a mere shadow of himself.

Undrafted, Sheldon signed as a free agent with the Arizona Cardinals.

"I felt like I performed well (in camp)," he said. "But there's a huge difference between a drafted player and a free agent. Teams have money invested in drafted players. I gave it my best shot. I wanted to be able to justify their decision."

Sheldon also got looks from other NFL teams, including the Chicago Bears and Indianapolis Colts. He played briefly with the Chicago Rush of the Arena Football League.

"Danny would probably be in the NFL today if he were bigger. Size was the only thing he lacked," said Radtke. "He had the skills, he had the smarts. Give him three inches and about 30 pounds more and he'd have made it."

Sheldon gave pro football one last shot with the Winnipeg Blue Bombers of the Canadian Football League.

"It was the best start of any preseason I'd had," he said.

However, Sheldon was plagued by a nagging hamstring injury he originally suffered while playing in NFL Europe.

"It was the last straw," he said. "When old ailments started to come back, I knew it was probably time to stop. I wasn't ready for the mental anguish of the practice squad. I'd been through that in the NFL."

Thus, Sheldon began to pursue a career in film.

"It's a whole other calling and passion," he said. "I'm working on feature films, writing and producing."

Hearkening back to his father's advice with recruiting, Sheldon has moved to California. He also values lessons learned at NIU.

"Northern was a big part of me growing as a person," he said. "It's not where you go, it's what you do."

FOUR-DOWN TERRITORY

Favorite Football Movie—I've written one that will hopefully become my favorite. I haven't found too many football and sports films in general that I haven't liked. Thinking back to high school days, it was "Varsity Blues." Maybe it was the time in my life, but that was a fun movie.

First Car—It was a purple 1987 Monte Carlo SS. It didn't last very long. My next car was a 1974 Corvette from my dad. He said the first one of us to get a scholarship got the car. I still have it and am getting ready to restore it.

Worst Summer Job—Roofing. There's nothing worse than being on a 110-degree roof.

Favorite Subject in School—I've always been fascinated by film. I always had an analytical, mathematical mind. I enjoyed problem solving.

GARRETT WOLFE

People who laid their eyes on Garrett Wolfe may not have expected the following statement from former Northern head coach Joe Novak.

"He's the best pure football player I've ever been around," Novak said of the player listed at 5 foot 7, 177 pounds his senior year.

Wolfe came to DeKalb from Holy Cross High School in Chicago. After being redshirted his freshman year, Wolfe began his NIU career as the No. 9 tailback on the depth chart.

"Even when I was No. 9, it wasn't a 'I hope' issue," Wolfe told Kevin Allen of *USA Today* in a 2006 feature. "It was, 'I will be successful.' Nobody ever hands you anything. You have to start at the bottom, no matter what you do in life. It's been an uphill battle my whole life to get any respect. It wasn't a big deal to me to be at the bottom."

Yet, the bottom was where he found himself in 2003. After working his way up to become Michael Turner's backup, Wolfe was declared ineligible by institutional academic guidelines.

"Pardon my French, but the kid got screwed," said Novak in a phone interview in the fall of 2009. "He got some bad advice (from the academic counselors) and was one credit short the next year."

Garrett Wolfe continued the Huskies' tradition of talented running backs. Following his days at NIU, Wolfe played for the Chicago Bears.

Novak thought he'd seen the last of Wolfe, for most players in that situation would have transferred out.

"It's a credit to him that he stayed," Novak said.

Thus, Wolfe gave NIU "three great years" according to Novak.

He stepped into the spotlight in the second half of an ESPN2 telecast on September 24, 2004 with 204 rushing yards against Bowling Green. Even more impressive, those yards **all came in the second half**.

"Wolfe just came out of nowhere and went crazy; everyone was wondering just who is this kid?" said NIU beat writer Rick Armstrong of the *Aurora Beacon-News*.

Huskie play-by-play man Bill Baker also recalled the performance.

"A lot of people forget A.J. Harris," Baker

said. "He was the starter who got dinged up and Garrett Wolfe had to come in. Who was that guy with Lou Gehrig? Wally Pipp. A.J. Harris got Wally Pipped because Wolfe took over from there."

Wolfe finished that sophomore season with a 210-yards-per-game average. Moreover, he scored 17 of his 21 touchdowns in the final seven games. His 325-yard performance against Eastern Michigan set the NIU single-game record.

In the Huskies' Silicon Valley Football Classic bowl game against Troy, Wolfe scored what was called a "momemtum-changing" 50-yard touchdown around left end in the first quarter. He was later forced from the game with a hip injury.

In 2005, Wolfe won honorable mention All-American acclaim and team Most Valuable Player honors for the second year in a row despite missing three late-season games. Wolfe seemed to play his best on the big stage. Going against the University of Michigan, Wolfe ran for 148 yards. Against Northwestern, he racked up 245 yards. Against Mid-American Conference foe Western Michigan, Wolfe ran for 277 yards and five touchdowns.

"(Wolfe) is electric," said WMU head coach Bill Cubit. "A charismatic guy who knows how to read a block and get through the hole. He finds little openings."

In the MAC Championship Game, Wolfe burned Akron for 270 yards and two touchdowns on 42 plays. That rushing total set a national NCAA Division I-A conference championship record.

Yet, in Novak's mind, the defining Garrett Wolfe play came back in the Big House against the Wolverines.

"He had a run against Michigan," recalled Novak. "Three defenders had an angle on him and were closing in. Garrett cut back, and they ran to where they thought he'd be. He made them miss and was gone."

By his senior year, the nation was paying attention. The little back once listed as ninth on the depth chart wasn't sneaking up on anybody. Yet, that didn't stop him.

In the season opener, Wolfe racked up 285 total yards (171 rushing and 114 receiving) against the then No. 1–ranked Ohio State Buckeyes.

By season's end, Wolfe had become the 12th player in I-A history to rush for more than 5,000 yards in his career with a school-record 5,164.

"Remember now, that was in just three years," Novak pointed out.

In addition, Wolfe was only the fourth player in I-A history to record three straight 1,500-yard seasons. Only Ed Marinaro, O.J. Simpson and Herschel Walker averaged more yards per game.

Wolfe also set NIU records for career touchdown runs (52), total touchdowns (57), 100-yard rushing performances (22) and 200-yard games (10). He ranks second in all-purpose yards and points scored. Wolfe was also the first player in MAC history to lead the league in rushing, scoring and all-purpose yards in three straight seasons.

"Garrett caught the ball out of the backfield," Novak said. "He could pass-block well too."

His former coach also liked his nose for the end zone.

"He was great on the goal line," Novak said. "He was stronger than people thought."

David Kaplan called a number of Wolfe's biggest games on TV broadcasts.

"He was unbelievable," Kaplan said. "He was so tough. Instead of losing three yards on a play, Garrett had the innate ability to keep his feet moving and pick up eight yards. You'd wonder how he did it."

When the curtain fell on his Huskie career, the Chicago Bears took him in the third round as the 93rd overall selection in the 2007 National Football League Draft.

He spent his first two pro seasons as a third-down back who also emerged as a key special teams contributor. Soon after scoring

Larry English became the highest drafted NIU Huskie when the San Diego Chargers selected him 16th overall in 2009.

his first NFL touchdown during the 2009 season, Wolfe's season ended when a lacerated kidney forced him to miss the remainder of the season.

"He's never going to be a star in the NFL," said Novak. "But Garrett Wolfe can be a dependable player who can do a lot of things well. There's more to him than meets the eye."

LARRY ENGLISH

One would not have expected Larry English, coming out of Aurora's Marmion Academy as a high school player in 2004, to wind up the 16th overall pick five years later in the 2009 NFL Draft.

"I can't say that I was expecting to be taken by any team," said English from San Diego

Chargers' training camp in August 2009. "Going into the draft, I understood that I could be definitely surprised and teams could come out of nowhere and draft you.

"I wasn't really looking at one team in particular, but more concentrating on the body of work that I was putting together."

English is the NIU highest player ever drafted by an NFL team.

English arrived at Northern on the heels of the Huskies' successful 2003 season. Under Coach Joe Novak, Northern's victories over Maryland, Alabama and Iowa State all caught his attention.

"I wasn't really highly recruited coming out of high school," said English. "Northern was the first team to offer me a scholarship. After going up there, I felt real comfortable with the coaches and team."

Larry English was the first defensive player to be selected as the MAC Most Valuable Player twice.

As the Huskies piled up those high profile wins, English committed to Northern.

"It was kind of an easy decision for me to play for Northern Illinois," he said.

His first season started out promising with a four-tackle effort in the rematch with Maryland on the Terrapins' home field. However, an injury ended his season and English wound up being granted a medical redshirt.

After rehabbing his injury, English found his way into the Huskie starting lineup. He led the team's defensive line with 78 tackles and a sack.

The 2006 season that followed made English a name to be reckoned with in the Mid-American Conference.

In Northern's Homecoming game against Temple, English set a school record with 4.5 sacks. He added a forced fumble and a fumble recovery.

"It was my breakout game," he said.

His breakout game soon developed into a breakout season. English ended the year with a school record–tying 12 sacks and first-team All-MAC honors. He had at least one sack in eight games and a tackle for loss in seven of the season's final eight contests.

Against TCU in the Poinsettia Bowl, English had two stops and a sack before leaving the game with a knee injury.

Still, English had arrived.

His junior year brought more prominence and more accolades. Playing 98 percent of Northern's defensive plays, English received the Vern Smith Leadership Award, which is annually given to the MAC Most Valuable Player.

So what did English do for an encore? He became the first defensive player to win the conference MVP twice.

"The greatest honor in an award as prestigious as this, and what makes it even better, is that it is selected by coaches in our conference," English said in a statement after the season. "It is chosen by the people who really know football and know our league, and it is great to be highly regarded by competition. Looking at the list of winners, I know that I am in really good company."

NIU beat writer Rick Armstrong of the *Aurora Beacon-News* said, "For Larry to win Player of the Year twice is really something, especially when one considers that he was coming off an injury from the Poinsettia Bowl. It just shows you how dedicated he was and how hard he works."

English also won the MAC's Defensive Player of the Year. He led the Huskies in sacks (eight), tackles for loss (15) and forced fumbles (three). English finished the 2008 regular season as the nation's active career sack leader with 31.5.

A three-time All-MAC performer, English holds the Northern career records for sacks and tackles for loss.

English was quick to credit Huskie defensive ends coach Mike Sabock with his development.

"I was a linebacker in high school, and he saw something in me in terms of having the ability to rush the passer," English said. "When I came up for my recruitment trip, he told me he wanted to move me to defensive end. From there, he taught me a lot about how to pass rush."

Sabock spent 24 years at Northern. He developed a special relationship with English.

"You always have relationships with your players, but most of the players you don't feel as strongly about as I did with Larry," said Sabock. "Larry is a terrific person and player with a wonderful family. He's a once-in-a-lifetime player."

When Novak retired heading into English's senior year, new Huskie head coach Jerry Kill did not retain Sabock.

"After I called my wife to tell her the news, Larry was the first guy I called," Sabock said. "There were tears in our eyes."

Sabock landed at Western Michigan, another MAC school. Despite being rivals, English and Sabock remained in close contact.

"There were a ton of scouts through here (Western Michigan)," said Sabock. "After we talked about our guys, I made sure to mention Larry. He was my favorite topic of conversation."

So what did Sabock tell those scouts?

"You're not going to draft a better person. He won't be a prima donna. He won't have an entourage. He won't be one of those guys wearing a ton of gold chains. He comes from a great family with a wonderful mom and terrific grandfather. He'll be someone your organization will be proud to have represent it," Sabock said. "On the field he will practice every day like it's a game. He only knows one speed."

According to Sabock, things weren't always that way. English's former position coach recalls a pivotal game at the end of the player's freshman year.

"We were playing Akron up at Ford Field in a game that would decide the MAC," Sabock said. "Larry hurt his ankle and came out. He was limping around and said he couldn't go. They taped it up at halftime, but Larry still said he couldn't play. We lost the game.

"(With the season over) I called Larry into my office. We met for about an hour and a half. We had a real heart-to-heart."

The main point of the meeting was that no one is ever 100 percent and players need to play through adversity. Sabock also emphasized that English could become a special player if he learned to play hard no matter the situation.

"To Larry's credit, he listened," Sabock said. "Come spring ball, he was a terror."

Just how special was Sabock to English and his family?

"My wife and I were at his house draft day," Sabock said.

Was his former coach surprised when he went 16th overall?

"I sure was," Sabock said. "I figured he'd go late first round and might even be one of those players who slipped into the second round. We've all seen those times when a player just keeps sliding in the draft. I was concerned that could happen to Larry."

Sabock need not have been concerned.

"I went out to the garage to get my wife a Diet Coke," Sabock said. "I was fishing through the cooler when I heard a big roar from inside the house."

That roar meant English was off the board and into San Diego's plans.

Those plans meant English would sometimes stand up as a linebacker and sometimes get down into a three-point stance as a rush end.

"(It's) outside linebacker in the defensive scheme that we run here (in San Diego). It allows me to do a lot of different things that I'm pretty excited about," English said. "It still allows me to rush the passer, which keeps offenses on their heels because they don't really know who's coming and who's not. I'm real excited about it."

And the excitement should only grow for the highest NFL Draft pick ever from Northern Illinois University.

FOUR-DOWN TERRITORY

Favorite Football Movie—"The Program."

First Car—A Mitsubishi Galant.

Worst Summer Job—I was a golf caddy one year. Man, I hated it.

Favorite Subject in School—Science.

THE JERRY KILL YEARS

(2008–2010)

JERRY KILL

Jerry Kill knows the value of hard work, commitment and loyalty. He learned it at an early age while growing up in Cheney, Kansas.

"I wouldn't trade it for the world," said the Northern Illinois head coach from 2008 to 2010. "I grew up on a farm outside of town. I was out there working at an early age."

Cheney, a town of approximately 2,000 people, is located about 25 miles west of Wichita.

Though he has grown to string together a successful coaching career in its third decade, Kill is still very much a product of his formative years. His father Jim worked two jobs while his mother Sonja ran the household.

"I was fortunate to have two parents growing up," he said. "I was the first one in my family to get a college education, but those two uneducated people taught me more than I'll ever know about life."

Many of those lessons came from long hours of work. Beginning at age 14, Kill worked on farms, in factories and at grocery stores.

In his spare time, he played whatever sport was in season.

"It was football and basketball during the school year and baseball in the summer. I played them all because it got me out of work," Kill joked. "Back in the day you didn't have any fancy uniforms. You played in blue jeans and cleats you got from K-Mart. The sponsor gave you a cap and t-shirt to wear."

Kill easily recalls the names of his high school coaches.

"Jack Thomas, Ken Disken and Roger Hilton," he said. "Being at a small school, those three did it all."

For Kill, one of the highlights of the 2009 football season was having Disken attend a Northern Illinois game.

"That was very special," Kill said. "He's in his 80s now."

As a high school football player, Kill worked his way into the starting lineup and eventually made the all-conference team. A two-time captain, he was named the team's most inspirational player as a senior.

With graduation fast approaching, Kill desired to keep playing.

"I maybe thought about baseball a little, but I was smart enough to look around and see that there were 22 players out on the football field so my chances were better," he said.

Kill landed at Southwestern College, an NAIA school in Winfield, Kansas. He met and married his future wife Rebecca there. He also played outside linebacker for coaches Phil Hower and Dennis Franchione, a man who would later coach at TCU, Alabama and Texas A&M.

"(Southwestern) was his first job," Kill said.

With a teaching degree in hand, Kill set out to begin his post-college life.

"We're in a different era today (with coaching careers)," he said. "All I wanted to do was get a job."

That opportunity came at Midwest City High School in Oklahoma. Mike Gundy, the future Oklahoma State head football coach, was the school's quarterback.

"I was making $20,000, my wife and I had a great apartment and I remember thinking, 'We're rich!'" Kill said.

Those feelings were short-lived when Franchione called to offer him an assistant coaching position at Pittsburg State, a Division-II school located in Kansas.

"I made about $250 a month," Kill said.

What he lacked in money, Kill soon more than made up for with experience.

"(Franchione) was tremendously organized," Kill said. "He always had a plan. He was classy, but he was very demanding."

Kill earned his way to offensive coordinator at Pittsburg State. In 1991, the Gorillas won the Division II national championship.

By 1994, Kill landed his first head coaching job at Saginaw Valley State in Michigan. His teams turned in five straight winning seasons, including consecutive 9-2 teams in 1997 and '98. Those final two teams also led Division II in rushing. In addition, Kill served as the school's athletic director.

All that changed when his father passed away from liver cancer in 1999. Kill and his family made the decision to accept the head coaching job at Emporia State in Kansas.

"It gave me the opportunity to come back towards home," he said.

While it also meant a $20,000 cut in pay and trading in a nationally ranked program for a losing one, Kill thought it more important to be closer to his grieving mother.

He coached at Emporia State for two seasons before the Southern Illinois job became open.

Saluki athletic director Paul Kowalczyk told Kill, "I'm looking for a guy who can turn the program around."

SIU had gone nine years without a winning record. During that period, the Salukis averaged fewer than four wins per season. SIU had not finished better than fourth in the Gateway Conference.

Kowalczyk took Kill on a tour of the SIU campus and facilities.

"It was dark, but I could see that the facilities weren't in too good of shape," Kill said. "I had some doubts (about taking the job)."

To help make his decision, Kill contacted Franchione and Gary Patterson, another trusted friend in the coaching profession.

"They both said you're not going to get a good job (to begin with)," Kill recalled.

When weighing whether to take an assistant coaching position elsewhere as another option, Kill was reminded that "as a head coach, you always control your own destiny."

Thus, Kill accepted the SIU offer. Things didn't start easy for him.

"I thought it would take at least five years to turn things around," he said, "but it was worse than I thought."

Kill's first Saluki team won only a single game in 2001. Unaccustomed to losing, Kill placed a phone call to Northern Illinois head coach Joe Novak.

"I didn't know him very well," Novak said. "He called me about his struggles and asked for some advice. I told him, 'You don't need my advice, you've had success. Stay with what you're doing.'"

And what Kill was doing was coaching an improving team. His second year at SIU brought a 4-8 record. Kill continued putting

Jerry Kill took the Huskies to three consecutive bowl games in his three years at NIU.

to use the old-fashioned work ethic he had learned growing up.

He was instrumental in reaching a deal with the local electrical union to install lights at McAndrew Stadium so the Salukis could again play night football. He and his team did community service work.

"I try to treat people like I want to be treated," he said. "It took time, but you've got to make kids realize it's not always about the game."

By the third year, it all came together. The biggest crowds in a decade flocked to see the new-look Salukis. SIU rolled to a 10-2 season, tied for the conference title and earned a trip to the Division I-AA playoffs.

Things were just getting started. Before Kill arrived in Carbondale, SIU had never worn the Gateway crown. Starting in 2003, the Salukis captured the conference championship three straight seasons.

By 2005 the Salukis qualified for the play-offs a third consecutive year. However, Kill suffered a series of seizures. He was diagnosed with kidney cancer. Following the season, Kill had surgery to remove the cancerous tumor.

While being treated, Kill met other southern Illinois residents battling the same illness. Because he realized many of them did not have the same financial resources he did, the Coach Kill Cancer Fund foundation was created.

"Because I have seen firsthand what others have faced, I would like to give something back. I think the hardest moments in dealing with this disease are when I see children, middle-aged individuals and the elderly who may not have the opportunity to see another day," reads a Kill quote on the foundation's Web site.

The 2005 playoffs also marked a turning point for SIU. The Salukis weren't just glad to make the tournament field, they wanted victory. That goal became a reality when SIU defeated Eastern Illinois 21-6 in the first round.

Thus, SIU earned the right to take on perennial power Appalachian State in the quarter-

finals. Though Kill's team lost to the eventual champions 38-24, the stage was set for even more Saluki success.

Despite slipping to fourth place in conference play, SIU again advanced to the playoff quarterfinals in 2006. A year later, SIU won 12 games, the most since the Salukis' 1983 national championship. This time around, Kill's team made it all the way to the national semifinals before falling 20-17 at Delaware.

Along the way, Kill's SIU teams caught the attention of the Northern Illinois University administration. In 2004, Kill made the decision to gamble on a two-point conversion that would have pulled off an upset at Huskie Stadium. While the decision failed and SIU lost 23-22, an impression was made.

Three years later, SIU returned to DeKalb and claimed a 34-31 victory. A season earlier, the Salukis had shocked Indiana University of the Big Ten with a 35-28 victory.

When SIU's 2007 season ended, Northern came calling—literally.

"(NIU athletic director) Jim Phillips called me on his way down to Carbondale," Kill said. "I can't remember if he was halfway there or how far into the trip he was, but he had (retiring head coach) Joe Novak and Tim McMurry with him."

When the NIU contingent met with Kill, it wasn't just the coach who came away with a good feeling.

"My wife was really impressed with Jim Phillips," Kill said. "He's a pretty persuasive guy. In the end, it was a family decision. (Staying in Illinois) also allowed me to still be active with my cancer fund organization."

Thus, Kill took over the NIU reins from Novak on December 13, 2007. He finished with an impressive 55-32 record at Southern. His teams went to the playoffs five straight seasons. Twice, he was selected as I-AA Coach of the Year, and he won the Eddie Robinson Award in 2004.

"I was fortunate to be around good players," Kill said. "You also have to give credit to your coaching staff."

Former NIU assistant coach Mike Sabock knows a Kill-coached team when he sees it.

"Jerry Kill's teams just don't give up, they don't quit," Sabock said. "I remember one time when he was at Southern Illinois, we had them down 28-7. They scored, recovered two onside kicks and the next thing you know they had us beat."

Later an assistant at MAC rival Western Michigan, Sabock faced the Kill-led NIU Huskies.

"I told my guys they better come ready to play for 60 minutes," he said. "It doesn't matter if you're up by three points or down by seven, Coach Kill's teams will just keep coming at you."

Jack Pheanis has been around NIU athletics since 1950. He played football and later coached football and golf for the Huskies. He ranks Kill among the best coaches he has ever seen.

"He is tremendous," Pheanis said. "I see the things he does with his team firsthand. I would have loved to have been an assistant under Jerry Kill."

Northern play-by-play broadcaster Bill Baker shares similar sentiments.

"Jerry is a class act," Baker said. "He is so level-headed. He has a sense of humor and a sense of business about him. The two never cross. He can be having fun one minute, but when it's time to get down to his job, Coach Kill is serious about what he does."

Veteran Chicago radio and TV personality David Kaplan was immediately impressed with Kill.

"I'm a huge fan," Kaplan said. "He gets exactly what Northern Illinois University is all about. Jerry Kill is as honest as the day is long."

Like Kill, Kaplan has dealt with threats to his personal health.

"Everything is in perspective with Jerry," Kaplan said. "Sure, he wants to win and is as intense as anyone. But he realizes that fourth-and-inches isn't the same as life and death."

Kill knew his work was cut out for him. Phillips and Novak warned him that the team he was inheriting might only win three or four games. In addition, Phillips left NIU to take the director of athletics position at Northwestern University in February 2008.

"I was very disappointed when he left," Kill said.

Now, a cancer survivor, Kill knew that life goes on. NIU turned in a 6-6 regular season and landed in the Independence Bowl.

"I was in shock to be able to go to a bowl game that first year after all I'd heard," he said.

Yet, Kill had his past coaching experience to guide him.

"Coaching is coaching," he said. "You're fighting your life off. Being at a mid-major really isn't all that different from being in I-AA. The BCS schools have the resources. That's why they're the big boys. You're fighting your life off."

The Huskies continued fighting and returned to the postseason in 2009. Following a seven-win regular season, NIU accepted an invitation to the International Bowl played in Toronto.

Though the Huskies lost to South Florida, NIU had made school history by going to a bowl game in back-to-back seasons.

In 2010, the Huskies won the MAC West title and played in the Humanitarian Bowl. However, the same day NIU accepted its bowl bid, Kill announced that he was leaving DeKalb to become the head coach at the University of Minnesota, the very same Big Ten team his Huskies had knocked off during the season.

Kill left NIU after compiling a 23-16 record in his three seasons. He is the only Huskie coach to post two wins over Big Ten teams. In addition, all three of his NIU teams played in bowl games.

No matter where his career takes him, Kill realizes the past has made him the person and coach he is.

"You are who brought you up," he said. "I've also learned things along the way. It's harder to be a coach now than ever before with all the shit that's going on today. There's no discipline in our society. We're headed in a bad direction. And it's not the kids' fault. Some of them really don't know any better. They don't know the difference in right and wrong."

And coaches like Jerry Kill are just the sort of men to help them learn. Just like his parents did for him all those years ago in rural America.

FOUR-DOWN TERRITORY

Favorite Football Movies—"Remember the Titans" and "Brian's Song."

First Car—It was a Mustang, a 1967 that was blue. I paid around $800 and got it used.

Worst Summer Job—I don't know if I'd say any of them were the worst. I can tell you the hardest and the hottest. It was being up in the loft of a barn. You're the guy who's picking up all the bales of hay and stacking them. It's about 105 degrees up there. If I had my whole team out in that barn, there probably wouldn't be but two of them left.

Favorite Subject in School—Biology.

NIU FOOTBALL BY THE DECADE: 2010s

NIU ENROLLMENT—24,424 (2009)

IN-STATE TUITION PER SEMESTER—$3,975 (2010)

NIU PRESIDENT—John G. Peters (2000–present)

AFFILIATION—Mid-American Conference

NEWS OF THE DECADE—Haiti rocked by earthquake; WikiLeaks publishes sensitive government data; Chilean miners rescued; Osama Bin Laden killed by U.S. Special Forces

NOTABLE MOVIES OF THE DECADE—"Black Swan," "True Grit," "The Social Network," "The King's Speech," "Inception," "Toy Story 3," "Harry Potter and the Deathly Gallows: Part II"

NOTABLE BOOKS OF THE DECADE—"The Girl Who Kicked the Hornet's Nest," "The Ugly Truth," "The Hunger Games," "The Help"

NOTABLE MUSICAL ACTS OF THE DECADE—Lady Gaga, Justin Beiber, Zac Brown Band, Esperanza Spalding

MAC HEARTBREAK

Lightning struck twice, five years apart, on NIU in the Mid-American Conference Championship game in Detroit.

The first time came in the 2005 conference title game. For more than 59 minutes the game belonged to NIU and star running back Garrett Wolfe. In the final 10 seconds, Akron snatched away the MAC crown with a 31-30 victory.

Wolfe ran for a conference-game record 270 yards and two touchdowns as NIU appeared to be on its way to a victory.

Yet, it was yardage he didn't get that most stuck with Wolfe.

"In the fourth quarter, if I could have broken one more tackle or made one more move, maybe we could have gotten the first down we needed," Wolfe said. "We lost the game, so it doesn't matter how many yards I had."

Huskie head coach Joe Novak said, "We were two yards short of the first down that would have ended the game. We couldn't make the play when we needed one, and they did."

Akron did indeed. The Zips began their winning drive from their own 19-yard line with just 1:41 left. With no timeouts, Akron drove into NIU territory.

On the game's final play, Akron receiver Domenik Hixon grabbed a 36-yard touchdown pass from Luke Getsy.

Akron had not won a football title in any conference, dating to their joining the Ohio Athletic Conference in 1915. The shocking victory sent Akron to the Motor City Bowl, which was also played at Ford Field.

Five years later, NIU entered the MAC Championship on a roll. The Huskies had won nine straight games, cracked the Top 25 poll and were listed as 17½-point favorites against Miami (Ohio).

However, the Redhawks gave the Huskies everything they could handle. The game settled into a battle that saw the lead change hands six times.

Special teams proved to be huge for NIU. The Huskies blocked the extra-point following Miami's opening score. That play loomed as key when NIU took a 21-20 lead when Willie Clark caught a 39-yard touchdown pass from Chandler Harnish early in the fourth quarter.

With the game in its final two minutes, the Huskies were on the verge of shaking off the sting from five years earlier and grabbing their first MAC title since 1983.

Miami faced a fourth and 20 from its own 38-yard line. Redhawk redshirt freshman quarterback Austin Boucher dropped back, faced pressure up the middle and rolled to his left. Boucher then threw a pass into a trio of NIU defenders. The ball grazed off Huskie linebacker Tyrone Clark's fingertips and into the hands of receiver Chris Givens. The improbable play went for 31 yards and a Miami first down.

Two plays later, Boucher correctly read an NIU blitz and fired a pass to Adrian Robinson, who streaked into the end zone for a 33-yard touchdown. Only 33 seconds remained on the clock.

After holding on a two-point conversion attempt, the Huskies had one last drive to pull off a miracle. Tommy Davis returned the kickoff to the 30-yard line. Harnish completed three straight passes, moving the ball to the Redhawk 32-yard line.

With 10 seconds left, Harnish attempted to get the Huskies even closer and threw down the sideline for Clark. However, the pass was incomplete. That left NIU with just one chance at the end zone with five seconds on the clock.

Harnish dropped back and looked for a receiver. Clark was covered. With the Miami rush closing in, Harnish stepped up in the pocket and tried to keep the play alive. But the Redhawks' Austin Brown caught him from behind. The sack ended the game and NIU's MAC title dreams.

"They made plays and we didn't," said NIU head coach Jerry Kill afterward.

Kill and his players, none of whom were part of the 2005 team, refused to buy into any fate at Ford Field theories.

"This is the game of football," Kill said. "This isn't about fate and all this stuff. There's nothing to all those things. You win or lose a football game. Sometimes it doesn't go your way."

While Kill may not have looked at the loss with a sense of ill luck or bad karma, most NIU backers might not agree.

Jeremy Werner's lead for the *Northwest Herald* read, "Northern Illinois president John Peters and athletic director Jeff Compher stared blankly, the same dazed look of trauma worn on the faces of dozens of Huskies players and thousands of NIU fans who had the same thought."

COACH FOR A DAY

Questions and doubt were everywhere going into NIU's appearance in the 2010 Humanitarian Bowl in Boise, Idaho. The Huskies had lost the MAC title game, head coach Jerry Kill and perhaps even the confidence of their fans.

NIU assistant coach Tom "Tuke" Matukewicz led the Huskies to a stirring victory in the 2010 Humanitarian Bowl in Boise, Idaho.

In the end, there seemed little cause for worry.

As the clock ticked down on the Huskies' rousing 40-17 victory over Fresno State, celebrations replaced those questions and doubts.

As the game story on the NIU Web site reported, "Gatorade baths were freely given, coaches' names were chanted, the Huskie Fight Song was repeated, and repeated, and hugs, smiles and even tears were evident.... To cap it all off, as the final seconds were counted down, a torrent of snow—worthy of any Huskie postcard—fell on the Bronco Stadium turf, covering the beautiful blue field in white."

At the center of it all stood interim head coach Tom Matukewicz, a holdover from Kill's staff and a fellow Kansas native.

"Our motivation was through the roof," Matukewicz said afterward. "It couldn't have been better. We had a lot to play for. I feel sorry for Fresno because they hit the perfect storm. I tell you, we'd have run through those windows right there, that's how much we wanted this thing, because of how the thing ended and because everyone was talking about how we were going to fracture and fall apart. Instead, it was like fire to steel, it strengthened us."

Much of that strength came from the performances of quarterback Chandler Harnish, running back Chad Spann and defensive end Jake Coffman.

While all three were quick to give credit to the offensive and defensive lines, the trio proved to be more popular than the three wise men during the holiday celebration.

Harnish threw for a season-high 300 yards and ran for another 72. He scored a pair of rushing touchdowns and threw for another. The junior was named the game's Most Valuable Player.

Spann dominated the game's second half. The senior ran for two scores as NIU pulled away for the victory. Spann finished with 95 yards on 15 carries.

Coffman, the 26-year-old Marine Corps veteran who decided to play his final season after first deciding to retire the previous spring, racked up a career-best three sacks. In all, the NIU defense registered six sacks and 14 tackles for loss. Fresno State was held to just 74 yards rushing while NIU amassed 503 yards in total offense.

The bowl victory forced a rewriting of the NIU record book. The Huskies recorded their 11th victory, an all-time single-season best. NIU's 40 points were the most in a bowl game as a Division I school.

"(Since the MAC Championship game), the seniors stepped up, Coach Tuke stepped up and all the coaches and team came together," said Spann in the postgame.

"(Defensively), we just flew around, we wanted this one, no doubt," said Coffman. "(Defensive line) Coach (Jeff) Phelps brought us together. We were having so much fun out there flying around. The defensive line did a great job, so did the linebackers and secondary."

Matukewicz added, "Today, we were able to get everybody on the same page. Offense, defense, kicking game, we all came together. This was a team victory. You don't win nine games in a row without good players. We ran into some adversity and had to come back."

With the former coach (Kill) already in his new job at the University of Minnesota and the next coach (Dave Doeren) still at the University of Wisconsin preparing for the Rose Bowl, Matukewicz was the one left to celebrate and be celebrated.

"It was quite an experience," Matukewicz said. "I'd have done it for free. It should have been exhausting, but it was also energizing."

For Matukewicz, the two weeks he ran the NIU Huskie program served as a prelude to possible future head coaching positions.

"It was a job interview. That's the way I looked at it," he said. "Just like you tell the kids all the time, someday you're going to get an opportunity. You've got to be ready because you never know when that day will come. But when it does come, you've got to be ready.

"I've been practicing coaching speeches since I was 12 years old. I want to be a head coach some day."

Matukewicz began his two-week tenure as the Huskies' head man by holding a team meeting.

"That's the first thing we did," he said. "We told the team there was a choice to make. We could be the team who let all that was going on ruin all that we had done, or we could pull together and write a wonderful story. At the end of the day, our story was going to be told on national TV."

Whether the NIU record book records it or not, Tom Matukewicz was not only the Huskie coach for the day. Rather, Matukewicz stood atop the NIU Huskie throne as king for the day.

Most likely, he's got the national TV broadcast on ESPN to commemorate his coronation.

CHANDLER HARNISH

Perhaps it's symmetry in a sport that uses an oblong ball.

Don Fortunato and Bob Heimerdinger established themselves as top-notch NIU quarterbacks in the post–World War II era.

Fortunato, who passed away in 2009, signed with the NFL's Chicago Cardinals following his days as a Huskie. Heimerdinger, Fortunato's successor, led the nation in passing and total offense as NIU completed a 9-0-0 season in 1951.

Though Heimerdinger's jersey was retired by the university, other players have since worn the number 12. Chandler Harnish, also a quarterback, is one such player.

These Huskie standouts provide the bookends to six decades that saw more than its share of great NIU quarterbacks.

"He's one of the best I've covered," said beat writer Rick Armstrong of the *Aurora Beacon-News*. Armstrong's been around NIU football since the 1970s. He has been on the Huskies sports beat regularly since 1999.

"A lot of people will point to the numbers and it's hard to argue with that," Armstrong said of Harnish's place in Huskies history.

Statistically, Harnish left Northern as the school's single-season and career leader in total offense. On October 1, 2011, the senior passed the legendary Bork to become NIU's career passing leader.

"Chandler has a ton of talent," said Bork. "In fact, I would expect him to be playing (professionally) beyond his Northern days."

To be successful, quarterbacks constantly have to adapt to change. Harnish certainly faced more than his share of transition during his time as the NIU Huskies' starting quarterback.

"He is now playing under his third head coach and I've lost track of how many offensive coordinators/quarterback coaches he has had, but it might be four of each. It certainly appears he's taken the best of what each has had to offer and made the most of it. That's pretty impressive. I don't know that a lot of kids could have handled that," said Armstrong during the 2011 season.

"It's been a roller-coaster ride," said Harnish. "Many people would view it as a negative, but I'm very happy for the opportunity. I've learned something from all of them. My network is larger because of it."

Harnish arrived in DeKalb from Bluffton, Indiana, following a stellar prep career at Norwell High School. The Air Force Academy recruited him heavily and made a scholarship offer.

"They came after me pretty hard," Harnish said.

Meanwhile, the future Huskies star also had interest from Toledo, Indiana, Purdue and Michigan State. But in the end, Harnish said his decision to play at Northern was easy.

"Northern Illinois offered me first," he said. "Coach Novak is such an awesome person. I have always been realistic. I saw myself as more of a MAC quarterback than a Big Ten quarterback. People told me I was selling myself short, but I knew that I would have more time to develop in the MAC. Was my choice weakness or being realistic? I have no regrets. Northern would be my choice if I had to make the decision again today."

After sitting out the 2007 season as a redshirt, Harnish garnered nine starts for NIU in 2008.

Harnish responded by setting the NIU record for total offense by a freshman with 2,067 yards. He led the Huskies in rushing and won the Shea Fitzgerald Memorial Award, honoring the team offensive MVP, as well as being named NIU Offensive Back of the Year.

As a redshirt sophomore in 2009, Harnish ranked second in the MAC in passing efficiency with a career-best 137.9 rating and 11 touchdowns compared to just six interceptions. However, he was also sidelined for three games with a knee injury.

As a junior in 2010, Harnish put together one of the finest seasons in school history by a quarterback. The 6-foot-2, 220-pounder powered one of NIU's most prolific offenses. The Huskies went unbeaten in the MAC regular season and won a school-record 11 games.

In the Humanitarian Bowl, Harnish threw for 300 yards and a touchdown. In addition, he ran for 72 yards and two more TDs. Harnish was selected as the bowl game's Most Valuable Player.

"That's my proudest moment at NIU. We were able to overcome so much adversity with losing the MAC title game and then our coach (Jerry Kill, who accepted the head coaching position at the University of Minnesota)," said Harnish.

In his senior year, records fell on a regular basis. In September, Harnish broke Bork's 48-year-old school touchdown mark.

"We lost the game, so that really took away some of the excitement," said Harnish. "However,

in retrospect, it's something to be proud of. I'm very honored to have the record. Ten or 15 years from now, I'm sure it will mean even more."

Bork and Harnish first met at an NIU summer golf outing.

"He is an awesome kid," said Bork.

Harnish said, "He has been nothing but great to me. George Bork is a true icon and ambassador for NIU football."

In his final year as Huskies quarterback, Harnish landed on the watch lists for the Manning Award, the Maxwell Award, the Johnny Unitas Golden Arm Award, the Davey O'Brien Award and the Walter Camp Player of the Year. He won the Vern Smith Leadership Award as the top player in the MAC.

But football isn't just about numbers and awards.

"He's such a strong dual-threat QB, especially the past two years," said Armstrong. "Early in his career he was hurt several times and had to miss games. The way he was able to come back from his knee injury without surgery was key to that, although we've never been told, specifically, what the diagnosis on his knee injury was. His physical maturity has helped a lot in that regard. He's been able to take the beating a dual-threat quarterback has to endure."

Joe Novak was the Huskies' head coach when Harnish arrived on campus. Novak provided a historical perspective on the quarterback from his 12 years as NIU head coach.

"Our teams of the late 1990s and 2000s always had a quarterback that complemented our strong running game," Novak said. "While our program had several great running backs, we always had a QB—(Chris) Finlen, (Josh) Haldi, (Phil) Horvath—who could throw the ball well and were great leaders.

"Chandler Harnish has been the first QB in a long while who is capable of throwing for 300 yards and running for over 100 yards in the same game. He also has the great leadership

qualities that the others had. Chandler came into our program as a terrific runner and developed himself into a fine passer as well. He will certainly go down as one of the best quarterbacks in NIU football history."

Bill Baker has broadcast NIU football since 1980. He rates Harnish even higher than Novak.

"Every time I think I've seen the absolute best of in Chandler Harnish, he ups the bar on me," said Baker following Harnish's dazzling 2011 Homecoming performance against Western Michigan in which the senior quarterback ran for a career-high 229 yards and passed for another 203.

"Last Saturday's performance put him among the nation's elite," said Baker. "When you look at the era of Division I football at Northern Illinois, Chandler Harnish has officially earned my vote for the best to have ever played the game at quarterback, with all the best to George Bork and a few others, the best ever in DeKalb."

Baker's strong words weren't just about Harnish on game day.

"Having had the chance to be around him during practices, travel and the like over the last three years, I've been fortunate to observe what the average fan doesn't get to see: that Chandler Harnish is a leader, not just on the field, but in life as a whole," said Baker. "I've seen many student athletes do many things very well, but Harnish is the closest to having the entire package to ensure success in whatever he chooses to do once his days at Northern Illinois University are over."

Part of that entire package includes Harnish's performance in the classroom. He earned his undergraduate degree in business management with a 3.65 grade point average and began pursuing his MBA during his final season with the Huskies. Harnish was selected as a candidate for one of the 15 National Football Foundation Scholar-Athlete Awards. He was also named as a semifinalist for the Campbell Trophy, given annually for excellence on the field and in the classroom. Strong leadership and citizenship also factor into the award.

While Harnish was moving atop several NIU career lists in 2011, Heimerdinger, the original star wearing No. 12, recognized his fellow quarterback's talents.

"He has to rate as one of the great quarterbacks in Northern history. His leadership ability is evident every Saturday and his stats are not surprising when you see his talent. He has to rate up there with George Bork and Tom Beck," wrote Heimerdinger in an e-mail.

Bork said, "When I played I ran only out of necessity or fear. With Chandler, his running adds another dimension to the game. He really sticks his nose in there and barrels ahead. I would rate him right up there (among the best ever to play at NIU). He does so many things well."

For his part, Harnish recognizes the foundation laid by those Huskies who came before him.

"I feel so proud to be on the list (of all-time NIU greats)," Harnish said. "Bob Heimerdinger, George Bork, Mark Kellar, Michael Turner and all the others. The list goes on and on."

FOUR-DOWN TERRITORY

Favorite Football Movie—"Remember the Titans." You see a team that overcomes so muchadversity. You see great leadership. They turn a negative situation into something so awesome.

First Car—It was a Plymouth Voyager mini-van. I'm not sure of the exact year, it may have been a 1994. The sliding door had to be welded shut to keep it from coming open. It had a lot of character.

Worst Summer Job—I haven't had too many summer jobs, but I'd have to say baling hay. It's so hot. You use your legs a lot. The hay cuts you up. When you're up in the barn putting the hay away, it's like 140 (degrees). It's so dusty. It's the most physically demanding thing I've ever done. Even more so than football? For a single moment in time, yes, even more than football.

Favorite Subject in School—I've always liked math. I've always loved numbers, but I don't mean in a geeky way. I'm a business guy. I love dealing with numbers and money.

DAVE DOEREN
(2011–2012)

Dave Doeren became the 21st head coach in Huskie history in December 2010.

DAVE DOEREN

A Midwestern snowstorm wasn't about to stop Dave Doeren from taking the head coaching job at NIU.

"I knew he wanted the job because yesterday he spent two hours digging himself out of his driveway," said NIU Associate Vice President and Director of Athletics Jeff Compher. "Then he drove two hours through a blizzard to get here."

Before the drive began, however, Doeren faced yet another challenge.

"I had my wife and three sons in the car and my suit on," Doeren recalled, "I got out of the drive and got stuck. A guy came along in a truck and pulled us out."

Perhaps that story shows the drive and de-

termination of the 39-year-old former Wisconsin defensive coordinator who became the 21st head coach in NIU history on December 13, 2010. Doeren followed Jerry Kill, who left the Huskies to accept the head coaching position at the University of Minnesota.

Doeren was born in San Diego, the son of a Navy officer. As anyone who has grown up as a military child can attest, moving was just part of life. Doeren spent time in California, Tennessee and Kansas in his youth. He participated in virtually every sport growing up.

"In California I played soccer, swimming, baseball," he said. "I didn't play football until the fourth grade when we were in Kansas."

Basketball was also a big part of his life. His grandfather coached basketball and track in Kansas. He also worked four NCAA Final

Fours as a basketball referee.

"I call Kansas home, my mom still lives there," Doeren said.

A product of Bishop Miege High School in Shawnee Mission, Kansas, Doeren was a four-year letterman as a player for Drake University. He earned Academic All-American honors as a senior.

"I went to Drake wanting to become a doctor," Doeren said. "I studied biology and hoped to become an orthopedic doctor. That was the track I was on."

However, after having both his knees surgically repaired, Doeren was able to shadow a doctor as a preview to his future profession of choice.

"I found out it is also a profession of paperwork," Doeren said. "With all the lawsuits that go on, I found the medical experience wasn't what I expected."

Thus, with his Drake diploma in hand, Doeren decided to get his teaching certification and become a high school biology teacher and coach.

"My high school coach got me to coach the 7-on-7 team in the summer," he said. "The coaching bug got me."

That bug led Doeren back to Drake in 1995, where he began coaching linebackers. By the end of his third year, Doeren assumed the defensive coordinator position for the Bulldogs. Drake posted an impressive 24-7-1 record during his tenure.

Doeren left Drake to spend two years as a graduate assistant at the University of Southern California in the late 1990s. The Trojans led the nation in interceptions and turnover margin during the era.

Doeren landed a position as secondary coach and recruiting coordinator for FCS powerhouse Montana in 2000. Doeren spent two seasons at Montana, where the Grizzlies won a national championship and finished as the national runner-up.

"(Dave's) one of my favorites. I'll tell you that," said 35-year veteran coach Joe Glenn. "Dave came into my life when I became the head coach at Montana. When he joined us, he brought a new (defensive) attack with him, something that we wanted to move toward. He installed the defense as a young coach and away we went."

Doeren returned to Division I status when the University of Kansas hired him in 2002. Doeren coached linebackers and served as recruiting coordinator as the Jayhawks turned around their struggling program. Kansas received two bowl invitations in Doeren's four years in Lawrence.

Doeren left the Big 12 Conference for a position with the University of Wisconsin of the Big Ten Conference in 2006. The Badgers reeled off a 12-1 record and played in the Capital One Bowl during Doeren's first season in Madison.

By 2008, Doeren was Wisconsin's sole defensive coordinator. During his time with the Badgers, Wisconsin played in five consecutive bowl games. In his final season in Madison, Wisconsin ranked 22nd nationally in total defense.

Doeren said that he benefitted from coaching at five different universities in 16 years.

"I learned something valuable at each place," Doeren said. "Each (coach) was completely different from the next. Each had his strengths. Every experience you have lends itself to your coaching development."

That development eventually led to Doeren's landing in DeKalb.

"I value the fundamentals and technique," Doeren said. "I have many philosophies and beliefs in coaching, but those are the two that sum it up. If you have solid fundamentals and better technique than your opponent across the line from you, then you will do pretty well."

Like nearly all coaches, Doeren likes to have balance among his offense, defense and special teams.

"I believe in not beating yourself, being physical and also approaching the game from the mental perspective," he said. "I still believe that you can outwork people, not just from working more hours than others, but by working efficiently."

Wisconsin head coach Bret Bielema, Doeren's former mentor, showed genuine excitement for his good friend.

"Northern Illinois is getting not only a great coach, but a great family with Dave's wife, Sara, and their three boys," said Bielema. "Dave was one of my first hires at Wisconsin and he has been one of the major reasons we have had success. It was only a matter of time before Dave became a head coach."

O'Brien Schofield played for Wisconsin during Doeren's time there. Schofield later played linebacker with the Arizona Cardinals.

"When I first met Coach Doeren, I noticed how he knew exactly what he wanted and how he wanted it done. He is big on discipline. He wants his players to get it done in the classroom and carry that over to the field. As I spent more time around him, he opened up more. He's more of a player's coach. The biggest thing about him, though, is that he loves the game of football. He's going to give you the best chance to win," Schofield said.

Though he had a chance to join Kill's Minnesota staff, Tom "Tuke" Matukewicz instead opted to remain at NIU as Doeren's linebacker coach. The duo communicated on a daily basis while Doeren prepared the Wisconsin defense for the Rose Bowl.

"We texted back and forth three or four times a day," said Matukewicz. "I'm his new BFF."

Matukewicz, who guided NIU to its victory in the 2010 Humanitarian Bowl in Kill's absence, sees Doeren as a potential "rising star" in the coaching business.

"We've got an opportunity to continue to build things here," Matukewicz said. "We want to join the ranks of Boise State, Utah and TCU (as mid-majors who have become major players in the BCS)."

Doeren took over a Huskie program coming off an 11-win season, the most in NIU history.

"Coach Novak and Coach Kill did a great job laying the groundwork here," Doeren said. "I'm coming into a good situation. But we face a different challenge. Keeping a team on top is, in many ways, more challenging than getting there."

Doeren and his staff not only faced that challenge, they succeeded at it. NIU posted an 11-3 season, won the MAC Championship and triumphed in its bowl game. Just days before Christmas, Northern announced it had extended Doeren's contract by one year. His salary jumped nearly $50,000 to $420,000, the third-highest in the MAC.

A year later, the Huskies posted a 12-1 record and repeated as MAC Champions with a thrilling 44-37 double-overtime victory against 17th-ranked Kent State. The win sent NIU to its fifth straight bowl game and the first-ever BCS berth for a MAC school.

Yet, just a day later, Doeren left NIU to accept the head coaching position at North Carolina State. Reports listed his annual compensation in the range of $1.8 million.

FOUR-DOWN TERRITORY

Favorite Football Movie—The original "The Longest Yard." It was a great comedy that showed the funny side of football. I love Burt Reynolds. If I had to pick a movie for second place, I would go with "The Waterboy." I love Adam Sandler too.

First Car—It was a hand-me-down Honda, a 1981 if I remember right.

Worst Summer Job—I painted houses for six summers. I loved painting. I worked with one of my best friends who is a track coach at Texas A&M now. He and I painted St. Agnes Elementary in Kansas City. There are over

150 windows in that building. We had to re-sand, reputty, scrape and repaint every one of those windows. It took all summer long. It never ended. It was rough, but let me tell you, it looked really good when we finally finished.

Favorite Subject in School—It was definitely the sciences. Biology was probably my favorite. I was the kind of learner who always wanted to know why things were happening. That's why I didn't do as well in upper levels of math. I just didn't see where I'd ever use it. I liked seeing what made things work the way they do.

MAC TRIUMPH

The third time is the charm. The roles were reversed this time around. What a difference a year makes. The script had to be rewritten. Insert whatever cliché or angle you wish, but the bottom line is that NIU captured the 2011 Mid-American Conference Championship with a thrilling 23-20 comeback victory over Ohio University.

With NIU fans still stinging from MAC title game losses in 2005 and 2010, the West champion Huskies entered the December 2 showdown as slight favorites against Ohio, the East winner.

Virtually nothing went right for NIU in the first half. The Huskies committed three turnovers and also gave up a touchdown on a reverse pass play as Ohio built a 20-0 halftime lead.

The second half held an opposite story and outcome. NIU's defense shut out Ohio, holding the Bobcats to just 70 total yards and grabbed three interceptions. That stout defense allowed Chandler Harnish and the Huskies' offense to rally for NIU's first MAC title since 1983.

The game's real excitement began with 8:49 to play. Jimmie Ward intercepted Ohio quarterback Tyler Tettleton, the son of former major league catcher Mickey Tettleton.

NIU used just four plays to pull to 20-13 as Harnish, limited to just 13 rushing and 35 passing yards in the first half, connected with junior wide receiver Martel Moore for a 32-yard touchdown pass. While NIU kicker Mathew Sims missed the extra point, he would later get his shot and redemption and Huskie history.

After the NIU defense again held the Ohio offense in check, the Huskies quickly went 57 yards in six plays to tie the game. Senior wide receiver Nathan Palmer capped the drive with a 22-yard touchdown reception. Palmer, who a year earlier had fallen to the Ford Field in tears, earned the game's MVP honors.

Once again, NIU forced Ohio to punt. Taking over on their own 36-yard line with 1:18 left, the Huskies eyed potential victory if they could get into field goal range. Harnish and his receivers made that happen.

Junior Perez Ashford leaped backward to reel in a dazzling 27-yard reception. Harnish, who wound up with 250 passing yards, then fired a 15-yard pass to Moore. With the ball on the Ohio 19-yard line, Sims came onto the field for a 33-yard field goal attempt.

"I knew I wasn't going to let my team down twice," Sims said. "I just lost my focus on the extra point, but I was ready for that field goal."

Following a series of timeouts by Ohio head coach Frank Solich, Sims kicked the game-winner just inside the left upright with no time left on the clock. The Huskies raced onto the field while NIU fans, alumni and former players celebrated everywhere.

"That is a great feeling, to be celebrating on the field with these guys," NIU head coach Dave Doeren said afterward. "For one single moment, you are the best and no one can ever take that away from you. I am so proud of our team. We've fought through a lot of tough things. These guys have dealt with a lot of transition. They lost this game a year ago; they lost their coaches after the game; they took me and my staff and my family

into their lives; and I couldn't be happier."

Meanwhile, the victory helped Harnish cast aside any memories of the painful 2010 MAC title game.

"What happened last year?" Harnish said with a smile. "Like I said yesterday, this is where our senior class would leave our legacy, and why not go out the hard way? The only history worth a damn is the one we create today. We had some bad demons we wanted to avenge from last year, but this feels good."

HUSKIES RALLY FOR SECOND STRAIGHT BOWL GAME VICTORY

In a bowl game that was relatively new on the scene, the matchup was familiar to NIU football fans.

From 1993 to 1996, Northern and Arkansas State battled each other in the Big West Conference, an ill-fitting collection of lost souls that also included the likes of Louisiana Tech, Southwestern Louisiana and Nevada. During those days, Arkansas State went by the nickname Indians before changing it in 2008 to meet the NCAA's desire for political correctness. For the record, the Huskies won six of those seven games in the series.

The GoDaddy.com Bowl didn't stray from history. After spotting Arkansas State an early 13-0 lead, NIU rallied to stake a 38-20 victory at Ladd-Peebles Stadium in Mobile, Alabama.

"Our guys never flinched," said Huskies' head coach Dave Doeren afterward. "It was a lot of fun. I am proud of the Huskies, the entire team, our fans and how we represented Northern Illinois. We started to run our plays better and stopped beating ourselves. The coaches called an aggressive game. Two scores is nothing for us."

The pregame hype centered on quarterbacks Chandler Harnish of NIU and Ryan Aplin of

Arkansas State. Each had won his conference's Player of the Year Award. Each team entered the game on a winning streak. For the Huskies, it was eight wins in a row; the Red Wolves had won nine straight.

However, when Harnish kneed down shortly after midnight DeKalb time on January 9, NIU celebrated its second consecutive bowl victory. The senior capped one of the greatest seasons in NIU history by earning the bowl game's Most Valuable Player Award. Harnish completed 18-of-36 passes for 274 yards and two touchdowns despite leaving the game briefly with an ankle injury.

Yet, there were plenty of accolades to go around. Junior receiver Martel Moore caught eight passes for 224 yards and a touchdown. The San Antonio, Texas native was named the game's Offensive MVP.

Meanwhile, the Huskie defense shook off its early-game rust to stymie Aplin and the Arkansas State offense. Five times NIU forced the Red Wolves into turnovers. Redshirt freshman Dechane Durante sealed the NIU victory by returning an interception 36 yards for a touchdown with 8:19 left. While Durante was named Defensive MVP, there were numerous other candidates, including Rashaan Melvin, Kyle Jenkins, Alan Baxter and Pat Schiller.

Punter Ryan Neir grabbed Special Teams MVP by pinning the Red Wolves inside their own 20-yard line four times. Only one of his eight punts was returned.

When Harnish left the field in the second quarter with his injury, sophomore Jordan Lynch directed a seven-play, 78-yard touch-

NIU head coach Dave Doeren and his Huskies celebrated their victory in the GoDaddy.com Bowl in Mobile, Alabama. (Photo by Scott Walstrom)

down drive that put NIU ahead for the first time. Lynch completed a 41-yard pass to Moore and later scored on an electrifying three-yard touchdown run.

Seldom-used running back Jamal Womble plowed for a one-yard touchdown on the final play of the first half when Doeren gambled by passing on a point-blank field goal attempt.

All of this combined to lift NIU to its ninth consecutive victory, ending the year with an 11-3 record. The 19 seniors finished as the most successful class in school history with 35 wins and four consecutive bowl appearances.

Harnish finished the season with 3,216 passing yards. He threw for 28 touchdowns while being intercepted only six times. Harnish rushed for 1,379 yards and 11 touchdowns. His 4,595 total yards led to 39 scores.

"This was a storybook ending," said Harnish, the holder of 23 NIU single-season and career records.

JORDAN LYNCH

Jordan Lynch's blockbuster 2012 season may have come as a surprise to many people, but don't count Bill Baker among them.

"Jordan Lynch was not a surprise," said Baker, the Huskies' play-by-play broadcast since 1980. "We'd seen plenty over the past few years. A few scripted series here and there; meaningful snaps while the game was on the line under both Jerry Kill and Dave Doeren. And then, his appearance in the Go Daddy.com Bowl when (starting quarterback Chandler) Harnish limped to the sidelines and most Huskie fans found it difficult to draw a breath."

Most of those same Huskie fans had to wonder what the 2012 season would hold with the departure of record-setting Harnish and the starting offensive line that protected him. Enter Lynch and a revamped line.

The results were staggering. They were mind-boggling. Lynch, like Harnish, before him, emerged as a record-setter and won the MAC Player of the Year Award. The junior also won third-team All-American honors behind Heisman Trophy finalists Johnny Manziel of Texas A&M and Collin Klein of Kansas State. He was named second-team All-Purpose by the Associated Press and honorable mention quarterback by *Sports Illustrated.*

Lynch finished seventh in the Heisman balloting, second only to LeShon Johnson's 1993 sixth-place finish in NIU history. Lynch received three first-place votes.

"Jordan Lynch had a remarkable season," said Terry Boers of The Score 670 radio. "I had him third on my Heisman ballot. He is one of the five or six best quarterbacks in the country."

Former Stanford defensive back turned TV analyst Rod Gilmore compared Lynch to Klein and former Heisman winner Tim Tebow during the MAC Championship pregame.

"(Lynch) is not as tall as those guys, but he is just as talented," Gilmore told a nationwide audience.

Ivan Maisel, the lead college football writer for espn.com, compared Lynch favorably to the Heisman winner.

"He really, in style and size and output, he is a lot like Manziel. He didn't have that SEC platform," Maisel said. "His ability to create something out of nothing and his ability to both run and pass. He is very much like Manziel, but he didn't come up with the same kind of nickname. Jordan Football just doesn't have the right ring to it."

Coming out of Frank Lenti's highly regarded Mt. Carmel High School program, Lynch was projected as a defensive back by most recruiters.

"But all this young man wanted to do was play quarterback," Baker said. "Jerry Kill took the chance and Jordan Lynch took advantage. I wonder how many head coaches are still out there today reading the papers every

Sunday and wishing that they'd have had the vision, or was it just a plain old gut feeling that Kill had?"

That vision or gut feeling paid huge dividends for NIU. Lynch and his Huskie teammates won their second straight MAC Championship and earned NIU's first trip to a BCS bowl, where the Huskies faced off against perennial national power Florida State.

"I always believed that Lynch actually had a quicker first and maybe even second step than did Harnish," said Baker. "The only real question in my mind driving to Soldier Field on September 1 was his offensive line. With the loss of the only returning starter in Logan Pegram, there was nary a 'start' to be had by this group.

"If Jordan Lynch proves to be the headline when the 2012 season's story is completed, the guys who carried out their blocks, protected him in the pocket and gave him that mental level of comfort to be able to, so confidently, go about his business week after week most certainly deserve a sidebar. That's a success story in and of itself that people may overlook."

Meanwhile, Harnish kept watch over Lynch and NIU from his place on the Indianapolis Colts practice squad.

"Words can't describe how proud I am of Jordan," Harnish told Fred Mitchell of the *Chicago Tribune.* "He really has put the team on his back. He has the perfect quarterback mentality. If a bad play happens, he forgets it and moves on. He doesn't care what the media says, he doesn't care about what people around him say about being in my shadow and all those kind of things. He just ... plays the game."

Wide receiver Perez Ashford discussed the differences between Harnish and Lynch.

"Jordan is more athletic than Chandler, running, breaking tackles, speed. Other than that, it's been the same. Jordan learned a lot from Chandler and took that into this game," Ashford said.

Lynch, meanwhile, was quick to acknowl-

Jordan Lynch led the Huskies to a second straight MAC title and a historic berth in the Orange Bowl. (Photo by Scott Walstrom)

edge his teammates.

"I didn't do this all by myself, make it to the Orange Bowl all by myself. It's a game plan, it's the coaches, it's the teammates around me, the playmakers around me," Lynch said.

While most of the attention to Lynch's game focused on his running, NIU assistant coach Bob Cole pointed out his passing ability.

"That's the thing people don't understand about him, he's a great passer. He has great mechanics. He gets the ball out of his hands quick," said Cole prior to the Orange Bowl.

Cole further commented on Lynch's durability.

"He's probably the toughest player we've seen (and) I've been coaching for quite some time now, 25 years now, and I've never seen a guy like this take the pounding he takes. He dishes it out too. Just a tough kid from the South Side of Chicago who loves playing football."

Former NIU and Indiana University head coach Bill Mallory admired Lynch's play, whether it was from the TV screen or in person at the MAC Championship in Detroit.

Mallory said. "He's what you want in a quarterback. He's a leader, a great athlete. And yet he's a humble person. I like the way he presents himself. He's a winner. I've always said, 'Show me a good football team and I'll show you a good quarterback.' He has a great impact on that team. He's the hub of that offense."

Lynch, a junior, became the first player in NCAA history to surpass 3,000 yards passing and 1,500 yards rushing in a season. During the first half of the Orange Bowl, Lynch passed, ran or punted on 28 of 29 plays.

"And he'll be back in 2013, Huskie fans!" pointed out Baker.

ORANGE BOWL

By now, everyone who follows Northern Illinois football knows that the Huskies defied the odds and earned a BCS berth in the Orange Bowl for the first time in school history.

But, just how significant was the achievement?

Mike Korcek has been associated with NIU since his days as a student in the late 1960s. Korcek spent 34 years in the university's sports information office and another three as the SID emeritus before retiring in 2009.

"The Orange Bowl, win or lose, is the most significant event in Northern Illinois athletic history—maybe the entire school's history," Korcek said in December 2012.

Korcek's reaction to the Orange Bowl bid

was "astounding, amazing, incredulous, mind-blowing, off-the-chart."

In addition, Korcek's knowledge is rooted in his longtime friendship with his predecessor Bud Nangle.

"Bud and I talked about this years ago and he thought the biggest event historically was NIU being elevated to University Division status in the late 1960s," Korcek said.

To fully understand the significance, one has to realize that Nangle attended Northern in the late 1930s and finished his schooling after World War II.

"Think about it, from the Northern Illinois State Normal School or Northern Illinois State Teachers College to Division I Northern Illinois University," Korcek observed. "Obviously, the academic growth preceded the athletic side with our institution gaining university status in 1957, I believe."

Thus, between Nangle and Korcek, their Huskie experience spanned nine decades. They have witnessed every major event in Huskie history from the unbeaten 1951 season to the George Bork national championship era of the early 1960s and building of Huskie Stadium in 1965 through the Baby Boomer explosion in the late '60s. Nangle and Korcek saw the NCAA University Division status in 1969 and the affiliation with the Mid-American Conference in the 1970s. They were around for the exploits of Huskie greats such as Mark Kellar, Dave Petzke, LeShon Johnson, Ryan Diem, Michael Turner, Garrett Wolfe, Larry English, Chandler Harnish and Jordan Lynch.

"For all the time we reminisced about the 73-18 win over Fresno State (in 1990) or our first grid triumph vs. the Big Ten (over Wisconsin in 1988), what did those games mean in the bigger picture? Short-time notoriety at best. Trivial by comparison. Neither resulted in a championship or national rankings. I'd say the Kent State victory Friday (in the MAC Championship) might be the most significant in the Huskie legacy," Korcek concluded.

Bork, quarterback of that 1963 national championship team, felt a strong connection to the success of the 2012 Orange Bowl-bound Huskies.

"No, I never thought the Huskies would be in the Orange Bowl, but I am proud and happy. What a thrill of all of us," said Bork from a family Christmas in Puerto Vallarta.

Terry Boers, radio host on The Score 670, was puzzled by the national backlash against NIU bursting the BCS bubble.

"Northern Illinois did nothing wrong," said Boers, a 1972 NIU graduate. "The team played within the framework of the rules that had been established. NIU earned the right to play in the Orange Bowl."

Boers also found disparity with the nation's view of the NCAA men's basketball tournament.

"When March Madness rolls around, every-

body loves the underdog. Everybody is more than ready to jump on the Butler bandwagons, but apparently, the same thing doesn't hold true in college football," he said.

ESPN analyst Kirk Herbstreit called NIU being selected a "joke." His comments inspired Huskie players to throw oranges at the TV screen when Herbstreit's face appeared. Pro-NIU, anti-Herbstreit t-shirts were a big seller among the Huskie faithful.

Yet, not all of the national media were critical of NIU landing on college football's big stage. Ivan Maisel has covered college football for 23 years, the longest unbroken run by any writer in the country. He has written for the *Dallas Morning News, Newsday, Sports Illustrated* and ESPN.

"You can say what you want about the BCS and everybody always does, but every year seems to have its own unique version of a perfect storm," said Maisel. "Crazy things happen

The Huskies celebrated their berth Bowl Championship Series and Orange Bowl bid on Sunday, December 2. Pictured are Zach Anderson (hat) and Sean Progar (hands raised). Jimmie Ward is on Progar's right, while Rasheen Lemon appears on the far right. (Photo by Scott Walstrom)

NIU fans did not let the 1,202-mile journey keep them from supporting their Huskies. (Photo by Scott Walstrom)

with unforeseen consequences and usually it's met with some delight. This year people seemed so frustrated with the system and took that frustration out on the Huskies, which I don't really understand . . . usually they vent at the BCS or the holy, unrighteous way they treated somebody. This year they somehow vented their spleen on Northern Illinois. After a day or so, everybody said, 'Oh yeah, it's not their fault, it's the BCS's fault.'"

Maisel compared NIU's 2012 season to Utah's 2008 surprise run into the BCS.

"After Boise (State) beat Oklahoma (in the 2007 Fiesta Bowl), they got the benefit of the doubt," said Maisel. "TCU has had a number of good seasons and so when they got there, Gary Patterson had built up a resume.

"It's probably closer to what Utah did in '08 in that nobody circled Northern Illinois and said, 'Yeah, Dave Doeren has got it going on there.' It was his second season. You graduated a quarterback (Chandler Harnish) who was drafted. He may have been the last pick, but he was still drafted. You lose the quarterback of

your defense in (linebacker Pat) Schiller, who was just a great college player. So nobody was sitting there going, 'Northern Illinois should get this done.'"

Also factoring into the national view of the Huskies was their season-opening 18-17 loss to Iowa at Soldier Field.

"(NIU) beat Iowa everywhere but the scoreboard. They somehow managed to lose that game and as Iowa's fortunes sunk, so did people's views of Northern Illinois," Maisel said.

Maisel added that the nation was slow to realize that NIU won the rest of its games and quarterback Jordan Lynch was a relative unknown for much of the season. The Huskies won their second consecutive MAC title by defeating 18th-rated Kent State 44-37 in double overtime. The victory gave NIU its 12th straight victory, tying the Huskies with Notre Dame and Ohio State for the nation's longest win streak.

"Kent State was also getting so much of the attention and then Northern beats them at the end (of the MAC Championship game),"

Maisel said. "When everything else happened, the computers spit out that result."

That result put the Huskies into the Orange Bowl, landing not only NIU, but also a MAC school, into a BCS bowl for the first time in history.

Unfortunately for NIU, the 12th ranked Florida State Seminoles defeated the Huskies 31-10 in the Orange Bowl. Florida State's defense, which entered the game ranked No. 2 nationally, held NIU in check for most of the game.

"Definitely the best defense we played all year," Lynch said in the post-game press conference. "They were always in the right spot at the right time, it seemed like. They were hungry out there."

Yet, the Huskies did have their moments on the national stage, including success with a pooch punt, fake punt, onside kick and a Lynch-to-Martel Moore touchdown pass. In fact, that score got the Huskies to within seven points of Florida State late in the third quarter.

Matt Millen, the former pro linebacker and executive, praised the Huskie defensive efforts by Ken Bishop, Alan Baxter and Sean Progar during the Orange Bowl broadcast.

Maisel said, "Bowl results, because they are the last game of the season, leave a stronger imprint than the regular season. They completely alter how fans, media and everybody view a season. Imagine if Oklahoma had beaten Boise State by a point rather than the way it turned out. Five years ago Hawaii made the BCS and Georgia just stomped them. Very few people remember that."

Yet, NIU and its fans won't soon forget the Huskies' trip to South Beach.

NIU running back and Florida native Akeem Daniels (3) gains yardage in the Orange Bowl. (Photo by Scott Walstrom)

ROD CAREY BEGINS
(2012–?)

ROD CAREY

Even after taking over the Huskies from Dave Doeren, many NIU fans still may be wondering just who Rod Carey is.

"I'm a Midwestern kid," Carey told Fred Mitchell of the *Chicago Tribune*. "I was born in Madison, Wisconsin, and I went to high school in Minneapolis. I've coached in the Midwest, married a Midwest girl (Tonya). I share a lot of the beliefs of the people around here.

"We're all Midwesterners. So, I think you get rewarded in life. You work hard, you put others before yourself. Then everything else kind of takes care of itself in life. That's kind of my model."

Carey's resume lists his playing as an offensive lineman for former NIU head coach Bill Mallory at Indiana University in the early 1990s. Moreover, Joe Novak was on Mallory's Hoosier staff at the same time.

"Joe knows Rod," said Novak's wife Carole, in an e-mail. "He's cut from the same cloth (as Mallory and Novak). Good man."

Joe Novak agreed with his wife's assessment.

"He was a very good player, starting center," recalled Novak. "He was very bright, very dependable. At IU at the time our offensive centers did many of the adjustments in our blocking assignments. Instead of our quarterback doing that, it was on our center. Rod made all the adjustments for us, depending on the looks he was getting from the defense. He always did a great job with that."

Like Novak, Malloy spoke highly of his former player-turned-NIU head coach.

"When (NIU athletic director) Jeff Compher called and told me they were leaning toward Rod, I told him he would be an excellent hire," Mallory said. "First of all, he's just a quality person. He was a good team person; it wasn't about me, it was about his teammates. He was a hard worker focused on doing well and helping his team do well. Academically, he was very focused on graduating. He came from wonderful parents."

Before taking over the Huskies, the 41-year-old Carey began as a graduate assistant at Minnesota in 1998. He also held assistant coaching positions at Wisconsin-Stout, Illinois State and North Dakota. Doeren hired him in 2011.

"The biggest thing I learned from Coach Doeren was being consistent—never too high, never too low. Do your job, and be great at it. I do believe this about leadership: It's not about what you say, it's about what you do," Carey said.

Novak said that Carey already possessed many of those skills.

"Rod was always an even-keeled kid. I'm very happy that he got the job and believe he will do a great job at it."

Meanwhile, the Huskie players welcomed Carey as their new head coach.

"He has a different personality," said senior defensive end Sean Progar. "I think he meshes well with the team. I think it was good for them to bring in someone that knows what we do, both individually and as a team, and knows what we're all about."

Huskie assistant coach Bob Cole spoke highly of the players during a pre-Orange Bowl press conference.

"The players on the team really deserve all the credit for all they've been through," Cole said. "If you take Coach Carey, for instance. He started off as the o-line coach and the run-game coordinator and then went into the offensive coordinator and now he's the head coach. That all happened in four months, I'm not sure that has ever happened before in college football. To the kids' credit, they've stayed focused and followed things through. It was a seamless transition."

Quarterback Jordan Lynch said, "Nothing really changes (with Carey calling the plays). We're going to do what we did for the last 12 weeks. Do what we did, and come out and play fast, how we normally do it."

Bill Baker, the longtime "Voice of the Huskies," noted that Carey will have added responsibilities and demands as a head coach that he did not have as an assistant.

"But, when it comes to the game itself, from preparation to execution, I have no doubt whatsoever that he's the right man to continue the progress this program has made over the past 10 years. Great things still lie ahead of the Huskies," Baker said.

Carey's debut came on the national stage of the Orange Bowl, with Doeren watching from the stands. Carey pulled out all the stops against 12th-ranked Florida State, including success with a pooch punt, a fake punt and an onside kick. Those decisions, along with a solid defensive effort, kept NIU in the game into the fourth quarter. However, the Seminoles, rich on speed and depth, pulled away for a 31-10 Orange Bowl victory.

"I'm upset," Carey said afterward. "Florida State is a well-oiled machine. They beat us, no doubt. That doesn't change the fact I don't like to lose."

Those are encouraging words to Huskie fans' ears.

GROWING GAINS

The growth of NIU football on the field has been mirrored by its growth off the field.

As Joe Novak turned the fortunes of Huskie football in the early part of the 21st Century,

The Jeffrey and Kimberly Yordon Center stands in the north end zone of Huskie Stadium. It has served the NIU athletic department since 2007.

NIU supporters Ken Chessick (left) and Jeff Yordon (right) flank Vice President Eddie Williams at the groundbreaking ceremony for the Chessick Center. (Photo by Scott Walstrom)

NIU began to upgrade its facilities. That success and growth continued under Jerry Kill and Dave Doeren.

First came the Jeffrey and Kimberly Yordon Center, which stands in the north end zone of Huskie Stadium. According to the NIU athletic website, construction on the $14-million privately-funded facility began in June 2006. NIU athletic staff members moved into the facility in August 2007.

The building is named for NIU supporters Jeffrey and Kimberly Yordon, who provided the university with a $2.5 million gift toward the project. Jeffrey Yordon, a 1970 NIU graduate, is a former letter-winner in football and track who has enjoyed a successful career in the pharmaceutical business over the past 35 years.

The Yordon Center features not only a 120-player locker room for NIU football, but also what the NIU athletic website terms "an informal gathering space and a comfortable area to relax and prepare before and after practice."

The website further states that the center "benefits 467 student-athletes and 17 athletic programs on campus." The 62,000-square foot facility is in the Frances and George Wilkins Academic Support Center, honoring Novak and his wife, Carole.

The Yordon Center features one-on-one tutorial rooms, a group study room and a fully equipped computer lab, as well as the offices for the academic support counselors. It also houses an athletic training room, two rehabilitation pools, an x-ray room and an equipment room.

The second floor houses the Huskie coaching staff and also provides the latest in video equipment. It contains three conference rooms, a head coaching suite and nine assistant coaches' offices while overlooking the Brigham Field playing surface. Moreover, there are a variety of meeting rooms along with a tiered classroom that seats 150.

"The end zone complex at Northern Illinois is one of the better ones I have seen," said Kill, now head coach at the University of Minnesota. "It gave us a great opportunity in recruiting at Northern Illinois."

Mike Sabock coached at NIU from 1984–2007. When Novak retired and Kill brought in his own assistant coaches, Sabock joined the staff at Mid-American Conference rival Western Michigan.

"Looking at Northern now, especially after being at Western Michigan, just walking into the Yordon Center is really something. It's amazing just how classy that place is. (You've got) the murals on the wall, the bowl games (listed) on the wall, the history on the wall," Sabock said.

With NIU enjoying a string of bowl game appearances, the Huskie Stadium complex grew even more impressive when the athletic department announced in September 2011 that a long-awaited indoor practice facility would be built.

NIU supporters Dr. Kenneth and Ellen Chessick donated $3 million toward the practice facility, which will bear their names. Dr. Chessick, a surgeon and attorney, graduated from the Northern Illinois College of Law in 1984.

Preliminary plans called for an 80,000-plus square foot building on the north side of the Yordon Center.

"The Yordon Center, number one, is an impressive building," said Sabock. "Now you go and add the new indoor facility and attach it to the Yordon Center, and that's going to be as big time as they come."

The indoor facility addresses one of NIU's major needs.

"The only shortcomings we had were that we did not have an indoor facility to practice in when the weather was bad. That hurt us in bowl and championship games," Kill said. "However, the commitment the university had made to build the indoor facility will make Northern one of the best jobs in the MAC."

When ground was broken on site, NIU head coach Dave Doeren said, "Another step in the right direction, obviously we're extremely excited. Not just to have the ability to go inside but the ability to train, the ability to set a schedule and keep a schedule."

The Chessick Practice Facility will showcase a surface that consists of an artificial turf field and a four-lane sprint track. The climate-controlled environment will allow for year-round training.

"What a great teaching environment it's going to be to have the indoor facility," said Sabock. "You can go in there at spring practice. You can go in there for fall practice. Instead of standing outside freezing and dealing with wind and rain and snow and all the kids are thinking about is, 'When's practice over?' you've got this indoor space."

The size of the indoor facility is another huge plus. It will house a 120-yard football field and will be 65 feet high in the center.

"At a lot of indoor facilities they crimp on the size and make them short," Sabock said. "This is going to be a full football field with a track around it. You can kick in there and punt in there. We couldn't do that in our previous practice space."

Meanwhile, batting cages and a retractable net will allow for multi-sport use.

"As soon as the football team walks out of there, the women's soccer team or the men's soccer team or the baseball team or softball team is in there. It's going to be used all day, every day by every sport," Sabock said.

The Chessick Practice Facility will also boost recruiting.

"Kids are very facility-visual driven. They are going to walk into that place and think about spending the next four or five years, and

The Chessick Center under construction in early Janary 2013. It is scheduled to open its doors in time for the 2013-14 Huskie athletic seasons. (Photo by Scott Walstrom)

that's powerful," said Sabock, the Huskies' recruiting coordinator under Novak. "That thing is going to be huge. The way they are attaching it to the Yordon Center with that mall area and all that glass, you take a recruit into that facility and there is nothing in the MAC that compares to that."

Huskie Stadium has been billed as "The House That George Bork Built" after the record-setting NIU quarterback of the early 1960s. Bork led the Huskies to the 1963 NCAA College Division national championship. Two years later, Huskie Stadium opened.

"We didn't have anything like these facilities of today," said Bork. "We didn't know any better. We thought we had pretty good facilities with a grass field that was outside to practice on."

Times have changed and Bork fully supports the growth and gains NIU has made.

"Once that indoor facility gets up and running, Northern will be the cream of the crop in the MAC," said Bork. "Joe Novak was the one who was really pushing for that ever since he took the Northern job. He knew we had to get these facilities improved. He pushed hard and it looks like we're going to have them."

The indoor facility is slated to open its doors for the 2013-14 athletic seasons.

"The Yordon Center and the Chessick Center are the two most significant athletics facility enhancements since the construction of Huskie Stadium in 1965," said Brad Hoey, Director of NIU Communications and Marketing. "In its fifth year of operation, the Yordon Center remains a top athletic and academic performance facility and rivals many similar facilities at high-profile institutions. I think it's not accident that Huskie football has enjoyed unprecedented success since moving into its new home in 2007."

Hoey added that the Chessick Center played a role in Huskie Stadium being selected to host the Illinois High School Association's state football championships in odd years beginning in 2013.

Huskie Stadium is also expected to add an upgraded digital video board for the 2013 season. The old video board made its debut in 2000.

Sabock said, "You walk into Huskie Stadium next year with that new video board system and you're in a big-time place."

Moreover, NIU may not want to stand pat in its quest to remain a Top 25-caliber program.

"The next step, in my opinion, is to build on to the stadium with luxury boxes, which will help them make some money," said Kill. "They are well on their way to having a real special program if they continue to invest."

EXTRA POINTS

HUSKIE HOCKEY

Jack Dean and his NIU teammates knew how to put things on ice.

"Hockey was actually a club team," said Dean, a DeKalb native and key member of Northern's 1963 national championship football team. "We played in a club team league based at the Elmhurst YMCA. (We) played mostly small colleges in the Chicago area like Elmhurst and Lake Forest."

At the end of the hockey season, NIU took part in a tournament that included the University of Notre Dame Fighting Irish.

"They came in a gold bus, (while) we carpooled," Dean said. "We ended up beating them pretty badly to win the tournament. The (NIU) athletic department gave us old football jerseys to wear. (Defensive tackle) Lynn McCann was our best defenseman."

Baseball players Bill Malinowski and Fritz Peterson, who later played with the New York Yankees, were also on the team.

"Being a club team we were able to drink beer with the other teams after the games," Dean said. "Notre Dame took their pucks and got in their bus and went home after we beat them. I think their school sponsored them."

"One of our players, Dennis Shannon, was our coach. He played hockey for years around the Chicago area and was a great player. We practiced on the lagoon on the campus when there was ice."

MIKE SABOCK

You don't last for 24 years and four head coaches at one university unless you're doing something right. In the case of Mike Sabock, he did many things right.

"I started back in 1984 under Lee Corso," said Sabock. "I was there with Jerry Pettibone, through the junior college years with Charlie Sadler and then worked with Joe Novak."

Though he is not as well known by Huskie fans as former head coaches Bill Mallory, Joe Novak or Jerry Kill, Sabock is a key figure in his own right.

"No one knows more about what NIU football went through from 1984 through 2008," Sabock said.

He was born in Lanshtul, Germany, where his father was stationed in the U.S. Air Force. However, his family settled in Columbus, Ohio, soon afterward, where his father was a nearby high school football coach.

As Mike entered ninth grade, the Sabocks moved to State College, Pennsylvania, home of the Penn State Nittany Lions. It was there that Sabock played both quarterback and defensive back on unbeaten teams his junior and senior years of high school. In addition to earning four football letters, Sabock also was a four-year letterwinner as a pole vaulter.

Sabock left State College and played at Division III Baldwin-Wallace. He started as a defensive back for a Yellow Jacket team that climbed as high as No. 2 in the 1976 rankings.

"I played for Lee Tressel, the father of Jim Tressel at Ohio State," Sabock said. "Lee Tressel is well known and admired in Ohio."

After graduation, Sabock coached for six seasons at the prep level in Ohio. During that time, he earned a master's degree from Kent State.

Sabock then returned to State College to work as a graduate assistant under Joe Paterno. He spent the 1983 season with the Nittany Lions.

After Penn State, Sabock found his way to DeKalb. Corso had been hired to coach the Huskies when Bill Mallory took the head job at Indiana University.

"I got the job because of a great recommendation from Joe Paterno," Sabock said.

Corso's time at NIU lasted just nine games before he bolted to take a job coaching the Orlando Renegades in the United States Football League.

Mike Sabock spent 24 years at NIU. His Huskie career ran from 1984 to 2007.

"He took Bill Lynch (who spent 2007–2010 as Indiana University's head coach) with him," Sabock said. "I almost went too. Lynch called me a few weeks later to see if I was interested in being their secondary coach."

Instead of joining the fast-fading USFL, Sabock remained at Northern, where he was added to the staff by new coach Jerry Pettibone.

"(NIU assistant coach) Ted Huber really went to bat for me with Pettibone," he said. "That was a real fun staff."

It was also an era in which Pettibone's wishbone offense kicked into high gear with quarterback Stacey Robinson leading the way.

"Stacey was a wishbone guru," Sabock noted.

Two games from Pettibone's time at NIU stand out in Sabock's memory.

"We beat Wisconsin 19-17 (in 1988) for the

school's first win over a Big Ten school," Sabock said. "Then, there was the win over Fresno State, who came in ranked No. 24 in the nation (in 1990)."

In that game, NIU steamrolled to an incredible 73-18 rout of the Bulldogs.

"Robinson had 289 yards at the half and we were up 48-15," Sabock said. "I told the team at halftime, 'Fresno is still scary. They could still come back on you.' The players were just shaking their heads and saying what was I talking about.

"We had three or four interceptions. We blocked a punt. My dad called me from Pennsylvania and asked three or four times, 'How did that happen?'"

Although it's been said that winning cures all evils, Sabock isn't so sure.

"Even though we won (with Pettibone), the boosters wanted to see the ball in the air," he said. "The fans never really bought into the wishbone."

Despite the thumping of Fresno State, 1990 was Pettibone's final year at the NIU helm. Enter Charlie Sadler.

"When Charlie came in, he had been the Oklahoma defensive coordinator," Sabock said. "A lot of people wondered about it."

Sabock appeared to be out of a job. Sadler had already promised Sabock's coaching position to someone else. However, the Huskies' new head coach was so impressed with Sabock that he waited to see what developed.

"Charlie was a straight shooter," Sabock said. "He told me he'd be in touch if something opened up.

"Well, he called me at halftime of the Orange Bowl," Sabock said. "We were just getting home. The answering machine picked up and it was Charlie Sadler. You remember how once those answering machines started, you couldn't stop them. My wife kept telling him to hold on and that we were home."

Sadler was calling to say that the person he had promised the job to had declined. The job became Sabock's.

"That was January 1 and we headed out recruiting the next day," he said.

Sadler's five years in DeKalb produced no winning seasons. In fact, the Huskies were just 18-37 during his tenure.

"It was a tough schedule," Sabock said. "We didn't have players of equal caliber (as our opponents)."

As a result, Sadler brought in a high number of junior college transfers—many from California and Oklahoma.

"The vast majority of those guys we got you didn't want. They were bad characters," Sabock said.

One of the exceptions was LeShon Johnson, who finished sixth in the 1993 Heisman Trophy balloting. Johnson ran for a nation's-best 1,976 yards.

"There just weren't enough players like LeShon," Sabock said. "Those bad characters caught up with Charlie. That's why he lost his job."

Sadler's dismissal brought out more questions about Sabock's own future. Still, his wife knew the wife of Joe Novak, Northern's new coach.

"Our wives were very involved in the American Coaches Association," Sabock said. "We went to the press conference that introduced Joe Novak as the new coach. I told my wife to be sure and smile really nice at Carole Novak."

Though the smile may have helped, most likely it was Sabock's reputation that brought interest from Novak.

"We got home (from the press conference), I took off my coat and tie for two minutes, and our sports information director (Mike Korcek) called and said Coach Novak wanted to meet with me back at the stadium," Sabock said.

Though he didn't have any idea what position Sabock would coach, Novak wanted him on his staff.

"He called on Christmas Eve to hire me back," Sabock said.

Sabock's wife quickly wrote a note detailing the news and wrapped it for her husband's parents to open.

Novak, Sabock and the rest of the new Huskie staff had their work cut out for them. The program was filled with those bad characters left over from the Sadler regime.

"Joe gave those guys a chance, but most of them weeded themselves out," Sabock said. "That really hurt us because we were left to play the games with mostly freshmen and sophomores."

Sabock credits both Novak and the NIU administration during that time.

"Joe stuck with his philosophy (of doing things the right way), and luckily the administration stuck with him," he said.

It wasn't easy. NIU won just one game Novak's first season and none the second. The losing streak had reached 22 games during year three.

"When we beat Central Michigan (16-6) in a rainstorm, it finally ended," Sabock said.

Buoyed with its own recruiting classes, the Novak-led program began to turn things around.

"Each year we got closer and closer," Sabock said.

After an 8-4 season in 2002, the Huskies proved they had arrived in 2003. NIU upset a ranked Maryland team 23-20 on a Thursday night to open the season.

"That game made Joe Novak," Sabock said. "It was the turning point. (Since it was a Thursday night), we were the only game in town. We were the lead story on (ESPN's) 'SportsCenter' that night."

The victory provided the catalyst to what Sabock called "a once-in-a-lifetime season."

Sabock woke each Tuesday morning to check the national ranking in the *Chicago Tribune*. The Huskies climbed as high as No. 12.

"I kept thinking, this probably won't happen again," he said.

Despite wins over Iowa State and Alabama, the 10-2 Huskies were not offered a bowl bid at season's end.

"That was the biggest injustice," Sabock said. "Not going to a bowl game was a bitter pill to swallow."

Still, the toughest defeat Sabock experienced in 30-plus years of coaching came in 2005. Northern lost to Akron in the final ten seconds in a game that decided the MAC title and a bowl berth.

"To a man, we were convinced that we'd go up there, win the MAC and head to a bowl game," he said.

When Novak retired at the end of 2007, Northern hired Jerry Kill as his replacement. After spending 24 years in DeKalb, Sabock's time at NIU was over.

"Sure, it hurt," said Sabock. "It was difficult. He (Kill) tried to work it out for me to stay. He and Jim Phillips offered me a job as director of football operations."

However, that position meant a big cut in pay and loss of a company car.

"I considered it because of the close relationship we had for just about everybody in town," Sabock said.

Complicating matters was the fact that Sabock's son Kevin had earned a spot on the NIU roster.

"My oldest son (Dan) plays for Elmhurst College," Sabock said. "I told Kevin it would have been fun, but it's truly in your best interests that it didn't work out."

Out of a job, Sabock faced the prospect of being unemployed or something he considered worse.

"My biggest worry was that I'd wind up somewhere I didn't want to be," he said.

After he'd been without a job for two months, three offers came in almost at once. Eastern Michigan head coach Jeff Genyk offered a position as linebackers coach. Western Michigan's Bill Cubit wanted him as special teams coordinator and safeties coach. Finally, Mike Stoops called to set up an interview for Sabock to coach special teams and defensive ends at the University of Arizona.

In the end, Western Michigan won out.

"I'm a Midwest guy. It was a pretty easy decision," he said.

Becoming a Bronco also led to an interesting bit of trivia. With Western Michigan's victory over NIU in 2008, the Broncos' sports information director pointed out to Sabock that no one else—head coach or otherwise—could claim wins over all the MAC schools.

"That's a pretty neat thing," Sabock said.

Yet, there's something more special to Sabock.

"I love what I'm doing," he said. "When the kids who you coached call you up and tell you that they're now coaching and doing things the way I taught them. You can't beat that."

Sabock retired from coaching following the 2011 season. He and his wife moved to Florida. However, when head coach Dave Doeren left the Huskies to become head coach at North Carolina State, NIU suddenly found itself short. Offensive coordinator/offensive line coach Rod Carey was promoted to head coach. Joe Tripodi, who spent the season coaching tights ends and fullbacks, took over the offensive line.

"(Mike) called (athletic director) Jeff (Compher) and said, 'If Rod needs somebody.' Jeff passed that along to me and I jumped at it," said Carey.

Thus, Sabock took over the Huskie tight ends and fullbacks as the NIU prepared for the Orange Bowl.

"I'm going to take Mike (Sabock) every day of the week. He's doing a great job," said Carey.

FOUR-DOWN TERRITORY

Favorite Football Movie—"Remember the Titans" because of the whole message of bonding a team of differences together, and "We Are Marshall" because I remember when that happened.

First Car—A 1963 Chevy Impala. I sold it to my fraternity little brother for around $200. One night he was driving home and thought he heard the muffler fall off. It turned out it was the gas tank that was falling off. Imagine how that could have turned out.

Worst Summer Job—I was pretty fortunate.

I worked for the Penn State athletic department when my dad taught there. We did odd jobs like painting the tennis courts and the numbers of the seats at Beaver Stadium.

Favorite Subject in School—Science, that's what I taught for six years.

BILL BAKER

Bill Baker's career as "The Voice of the Huskies" began with a bang.

Mike Pinckney returned the opening kickoff 97 yards for a touchdown against Long Beach State on a Friday night at Anaheim Stadium.

"It was the first game of Bill Mallory's coaching tenure at Northern," said Baker of the 1980 opener. "That was quite a way to start."

Mallory and the Huskies posted a 16-9 win on that September night. Baker has been calling NIU football and basketball ever since.

"It's been a lot of years and a lot of memories," Baker said.

When asked to summarize those years, Baker paused for only a moment.

"I think of how close this program has been to becoming a consistent big-time winner at this so-called mid-major level," he said. "We've been on the cusp of it over the years. It's had its ups and downs.

"Bill Mallory started it. His team went 7-4 that first year. They stumbled a bit in 1981 (with a 3-8 record) but soon had it back on track."

By 1983, Mallory's Huskies won the Mid-American Conference championship and the California Bowl, the first major bowl victory in NIU history.

Yet, with success, Mallory left DeKalb to accept the head coaching job at Indiana University of the Big Ten Conference.

"That's sometimes life as a mid-major," Baker said.

Lee Corso followed Mallory but lasted what Baker termed "the nine-game experiment" of 1984.

Jerry Pettibone became NIU head coach for the 1985 season.

"Jerry built things back up to the point where Oregon State University came knocking," Baker said.

Following a successful run using the wishbone offense with electrifying quarterback Stacey Robinson, Pettibone left NIU after the 1990 season to run the Beavers in the Pac-10 Conference.

"Again, we were right on the cusp," Baker said. "We would get right up to the edge (of consistent success) and then get pulled back again."

Charlie Sadler followed Pettibone at NIU. Sadler's Huskies stumbled to a disappointing 18-37 record in five seasons.

"It was much like the Corso debacle," Baker said.

Joe Novak, the defensive coordinator for Mallory at both NIU and Indiana, was hired to right the Huskie ship.

"He had his work cut out for him, that's for sure," Baker said.

Novak's first team won one game in 11 starts. His second team went winless. NIU managed just two wins in his third year.

"Fortunately for Joe and for Northern, (then-Athletic Director) Cary Groth stuck with him," Baker said.

Novak and the Huskies turned a corner with a 5-6 season in 1999. Then came a steady succession of winning seasons, highlighted by 2003.

"That year was so much fun," Baker said. "The opening win over Maryland set the tone."

Later came wins at Alabama and Iowa State.

"I remember walking out of the stadium (at Alabama) and those fans being such class acts," Baker said. "They were saying, 'Shake the Burner's (Michael Turner) hand for me and tell him how good he is.'"

NIU finished the 2003 season with a 10-2 record.

Bill Baker has been broadcasting NIU football and basketball since 1980.

Yet, the Huskies were not invited to a bowl game. Such is life as a mid-major struggling for respect and consistency.

Novak retired in 2007 following a 3-8 season.

"Cross that one off the books," Baker said. "That team was so decimated by injuries. They lost so many key players for the year."

While the past had often seen a successful coach followed by lean times, NIU passed the torch to former Southern Illinois University head coach Jerry Kill.

"He was handpicked by (former Athletic Director) Jim Phillips and Joe Novak," Baker said. "Jerry Kill is a proven winner. His staff has been together for years. One of his real strengths is that he gets kids to believe. He convinces them that if they stay the course the coaches have

designed the path to success. 'Stay with us and you'll be a winner. You're next.' That's his message, and it's gotten through."

Baker's message has also gotten through to Huskie fans for more than three decades. Moreover, his broadcast base grew larger when NIU signed a contract with Chicago sports radio station WSCR (The Score).

"The real winners in having our games on in Chicago via WSCR are the fans and followers of NIU athletics," said Baker. "While we have partnered and continue to work with some outstanding local facilities such as WLBK in DeKalb, those signals cannot reach into the heart of the metro area. WSCR does expand the reach of the program to areas we would not normally have coverage with our local affiliates. And, no, having the games on an outlet as large as The Score does not appear to hurt our other station's listenership-wise. Many, many times, people in the DeKalb area in conversation tell me they enjoy the broadcasts and mention WLBK in particular."

In 2009, Baker was inducted into the NIU Athletics Hall of Fame. He has been a recipient of the Distinguished Service Award for Broadcasting from the Illinois High School Association and is enshrined in the Illinois Basketball Coaches Association Hall of Fame. Meanwhile, he doubles as the manager of advertising placement for the Kane County Cougars, one of the most successful franchises in the Midwest League of minor league baseball.

FOUR-DOWN TERRITORY

Favorite Football Movie—My favorite movie of all time would have to be "The Longest Yard." It's a classic when it comes to the old tried-and-true storyline featuring a decided underdog having its day in the spotlight.

First Car—My first car was a 1961 Mercury Comet. It was outfitted with a CB radio complete with a 102-inch whip antenna. Even back then, I had to be broadcasting something someplace.

Worst Summer Job—The worst summer job ever was actually more like a seven-month job between the time I graduated high school at Lane Tech in January of 1966 and began college at Illinois Teachers College North in September. In those days in Chicago you either began school in September or January depending on your birthday. The job was a position as a "picker-packer" at Sears' catalog facility on the west side. I would grab a catalog order from the stack, wander through acres and acres of warehouse space to pick out the ordered items and then pack and ship them out to whichever store had placed the order. It

was hot. The hours were long and I was working with a bunch of 40-to-50-year-olds that I had nothing in common with; still they were fairly nice to me. The one thing I vividly remember was the big boss telling a group of us newbies just before we went to work that first day that we could, in time, earn as much as $5 an hour in this position.

Favorite Subject in School—I didn't really have a favorite subject in school. At Lane Tech, we were subjected to many, many different skill courses. My favorite there, which only lasted a semester, was aviation shop. It didn't really help me much during my time in the Air Force, but did arouse an interest which would later lead to my actually getting a pilot's license.

NICKNAME, COLORS & MASCOT—OH MY!

Northern Illinois University teams haven't always gone by the nickname Huskies, worn cardinal & black nor had a mascot that was a dog.

In its early history, Northern Illinois State Normal School was known as "The Profs." This was a common name given to most teacher colleges of the era.

According to the 2004 NIU Football Media Guide, NISNS originally adopted yellow and white as the school's official colors in 1899. And, according to the student newspaper *Northern Illinois*, Volume 1, Number 1, the official school song was titled "The Yellow and White."

However, seven years later the school decided to change its colors to something brighter. The main problem with yellow & white was that the uniforms were constantly stained with grass and mud and thus difficult to see.

By December 1906, the NISNS Athletic Association discussed "the plan of having an athletic monogram, and have finally decided on one they think will be appropriate. It is to be a cardinal monogram, N.I. on a black diamond, and it is to be for team members only."

Thus, the official colors were established.

"A round black background on which is a Wisconsin-red N.I.," read the then-monthly *Northern Illinois* in February 1907. "The red and black are very showy and much more suitable for athletic colors than yellow and white."

Mike Korcek, NIU's longtime sports information director, went so far as to make a notation to graphic artists and printers in the NIU media guides: "The NIU cardinal red is Pantone Matching System 1935."

Later, the team switched to the nickname Cardinals to match the school colors. While this moniker appears to have been commonplace in the 1920s, in the 1930s, Northern was tagged as the "Evansmen" in recognition of athletics pioneer George G. "Chick" Evans. However, references also were still made to the "Northerners" and the "Teachers."

In 1940, according to the 2004 NIU Football Media Guide, a four-man committee of Evans, Harold Taxman, Walter Lorimer and Harry Telman, all members of the Varsity Club, was appointed to search for "a term with a trifle more dash."

Following much debate, a decision was reached. According to the January 25, 1940 issue of *Northern Illinois*, "Not only does the term have color and meaning, but it is particularly apt as in regard to NI's varsity teams. From now on the word 'Huskies' will be used constantly in this paper and in other papers to indicate our athletics squads."

According to the ESPN College Football Encyclopedia, "A notable stipulation of the original name is that the team forever became known, in its singular collective, as Husk-IE instead of the traditional Husk-Y form."

Korcek addressed this issue in the 2004 Football Media Guide: "Further note to Noah Webster and copy readers: Evans made refer-

ence in that 1940 story to a Huskie dog, no H-U-S-K-Y. So the singular collective form is indeed H-U-S-K-I-E, as in Huskie victory, Huskie touchdown, Huskie basket, Huskie spike, and Huskie All-America."

As for the mascot, NIU has used everything from a series of real dogs to a "live" Victor E. Huskie in costume to several line drawing logo versions.

Again, according to Korcek's writing, "Probably the most popular logo among the Baby Boomer set would be the 'fighting' Hus-

Victor E. Huskie is the official mascot of NIU athletics.

Victor E. Huskie is flanked by legendary broadcaster Harry Caray on the left and DePaul basketball coach Ray Meyer on the right.

on the project in 1988."

Victor E. Huskie is part of the cheerleading squad. It was noted in the ESPN College Football Encyclopedia that the job "was not all milk bones and fire hydrants, though, especially in the dog days of summer."

According to the Encyclopedia, Laura Schlembach—the 2002 Victor E. Huskie—noted such on her first day on the job: "They just handed me this large bag . . . and it was the worst smell ever, . . . The next game I came prepared. I brought Febreze. I brought dryer sheets. I made that thing smell so nice."

At the 2010 home football opener, NIU debuted a new look for Victor E. Huskie. The newly updated mascot entered Huskie Stadium riding on the back of a motorcycle.

HOMECOMING

Tracking down the origins of Homecoming can be as elusive as any Heisman Trophy-toting running back.

For years the University of Illinois has either claimed or been given credit for establishing the Homecoming tradition. For example, the ESPN College Football Encyclopedia states, "Homecoming weekend originated at Illinois in 1910, created by undergraduates W. Elmer Ekblaw and C.F. 'Dab' Williams. The first celebration was held October 14–16, and the Fighting Illini beat Chicago 3-0 in a game that served as the weekend's main event. Other schools adopted homecoming . . ."

Furthermore, the University of Illinois Web site stated that homecoming at the school "is the longest continuously running such collegiate events, beginning in 1910 and marking its 100th anniversary in 2010. The occasion has taken place in each of those 100 years, with the exception of 1918, when the event was canceled because of the exigencies of World War I."

However, documented research by former

kie in the boxer's stance commissioned in the late 1950s. In 1985–1986, the dog's head—known to insiders as the 'wolf' Huskie—made its debut under the direction of (then) NIU marketing director Chuck Shriver. The recently 'decommissioned' running Huskie dog was designed by John Vieceli of McMillan Associates of Dundee, which worked with former athletics director Gerald O'Dell

NIU sports information director Mike Korcek showed that NIU played its first Homecoming game in 1903.

"What is a quick definition of the word 'homecoming'?" Korcek has asked on more than one instance.

According to Merriam-Webster's Collegiate Dictionary, "homecoming" is defined as "a return home" and "the return of a group of people usually on a special occasion to a place formerly frequented or regarded as home; **especially**: an annual celebration for alumni at a college or university."

Thus, through documented university archive records, Korcek dated the origins of the Huskie Homecoming celebration to an alumni football game played on October 10, 1903. In what was called "The Eventful Game" by the student newspaper, the Northern Illinois State

Normal School varsity shut out the Alumni 6-0.

Further research set the University of Michigan's homecoming beginning in 1897. In addition, Marshall University (1906), the University of Wisconsin (1908), Indiana University (1909) and Baylor University (1909) also were ahead of the U of I's "first" Homecoming.

"Let me make this also perfectly clear: Northern Illinois did not invent or create the first Homecoming," stated Korcek in an e-mail, "but ours (or our form) was prior to Illinois."

Meanwhile, the University of Illinois Web site also stated that "Homecoming's original concept—designed by two University of Illinois students, Clarence Foss Williams, Class of 1910, and W. Elmer Ekblaw, Classes of 1910 and 1912—was to offer an annual event geared specifically to alumni and centered around a football game. Its inaugural launch was an un-

NIU has been hosting Homecoming since 1903.

was completely renovated following a fire a couple of years ago, so the information is no longer in house. Generally, we reach out to schools for their information, which they provide for various exhibits, but we rely on their facts and figures and give them credit.

"I don't believe there was extensive research done on this subject, at least that I've been able to find, so we couldn't officially confirm that one school versus others was the first to host a Homecoming."

Dent also brought up schools at levels below Division I.

Dent wrote, "Since those schools don't get as much coverage as DI schools, it is possible they were also hosting 'official or unofficial' homecomings in years past. It is also possible that some schools held 'homecomings' for basketball too.

"That said, I'd suggest getting the comments for your project from our member schools directly, as opposed to the Hall of Champions. I'd also look at what was done over the years in Division II, which includes HBCUs, and in Division III. I hope that helps to some degree."

According to the 2004 NIU Football Media Guide, NIU's first formal Homecoming was the weekend of October 12–13, 1906, according to university historian Glen Glidemeister. The term "Homecoming" first appeared in the October 1906 issue of (then) monthly *Northern Illinois* (a forerunner of today's *Northern Star*). In 1907, the NIU Alumni Association's constitution stated, "there shall be a social meeting of the alumni and guests, following the annual football game, on the evening of the second Saturday in October."

Again, according to the 2004 Football Media Guide, the first 11 NIU Homecoming football games were against the alums.

"That continued until 1913, when the series was curtailed by the alumni team because 'few of the members (were) in condition,'" stated

qualified success, drawing more than 10,000 participants."

When asked to comment on Korcek's research, Robin Kaler, the associate chancellor and director of public affairs at the University of Illinois, sent an e-mail response.

Kaler's response read: "In 1910, the students who organized the first such celebration on our campus claimed 'Illinois may well pride itself on being the originator of the plan for drawing home the alumni.' Over the years, we have learned of similar and earlier efforts at other institutions, but the University of Illinois certainly has one of the longest college traditions called 'Homecoming.'"

Further complicating matters was an exhibit featured at the NCAA Hall of Champions in Indianapolis in the early 2000s. The exhibit claimed that Indiana University had invented the Homecoming concept.

In an e-mail response, Hall of Champions Associate Director of Public and Media Relations Gail Dent stated: "Unfortunately, none of the staff who worked on that project are with the NCAA today and the Hall of Champions

the media guide's article written by Korcek.

The following year, 1914, the first Northern Illinois game against an intercollegiate football opponent at Homecoming took place on October 24 when the hosts defeated Wheaton College 29-3.

Meanwhile, Princeton and Rutgers, the first two combatants in what has been recognized as college football's first game back in 1869, did not celebrate Homecoming for many years.

Princeton first had a Homecoming in 1918, 50 years after that inaugural game, to celebrate the landmark contest's anniversary.

Harvard, the nation's oldest university, held its first Homecoming in 2009. The Crimson began playing football in 1874.

HUSKIE RIVALS

College football history has been built on rivalries. Most rivalries began as regional matchups in the early days of the sport. Many of these rivalries have stood the test of time; numerous books have been written and insightful documentaries have been made chronicling these clashes.

With NIU, the rivalry aspect has been as mystifying as a well-run triple option. Unlike universities such as Michigan and Ohio State of the Big Ten, NIU has not remained in one conference throughout its history.

Northern spent the early years of its football history playing an independent schedule. When the Illinois Intercollegiate Athletic Conference formed as a football league in the Roaring Twenties, Northern became an early member, joining in 1922. This league became known as The Little 19, although its membership numbers often fluctuated.

Though it competed again as an independent for the 1926 and 1927 seasons, Northern remained a key member of the Little 19/IIAC for decades afterward.

League members that were private schools withdrew during the 1930s, until in 1942 only the five state schools—Northern, Eastern, Southern, Western and Illinois State—remained.

In 1950, the league became the "Interstate Intercollegiate Athletic Conference" when Central Michigan and Eastern Michigan joined, increasing membership to seven schools.

Thus, according to the ESPN College Football Encyclopedia, "Historically, Illinois State served as the Huskies' greatest foe. The schools began meeting in 1906 and have played 55 times since then."

However, the NIU–ISU rivalry became difficult to maintain. In 1966, NIU withdrew from the IIAC. By the close of the 1960s, the IIAC was nonexistent. The conference officially disbanded at the end of the 1969–1970 academic year.

While Northern became a Division I football program in 1969, the remainder of the IIAC schools from Illinois played at the Division II and then I-AA (now called the Football Championship Subdivision) levels.

Moreover, Northern and Illinois State have not met on the football field since 2000. NIU holds a 25-22-9 edge in the series. The schools shared the 1941 IIAC title.

After competing as a Division I independent from 1969 to 1974, NIU joined the Mid-American Conference for the 1975 season.

"Historically, our biggest rivalries—dating back to the days of the Little 19 Conference—were with the in-state schools. So the ultimate decision by Chick Evans and the university in the mid-1960s was either stay with our 'old' traditional and geographical rivals or head to the established Division I Mid-American Conference, which was dominated by the Ohio schools," said former NIU sports information director Mike Korcek. "It would've been fortuitous if Illinois State and Southern Illinois joined with us. But at the time in the late 1960s, ISU and SIU made decisions based

Rivals have changed over the years for the Huskies.

on men's basketball and Northern Illinois concentrated on football. Just look at the facilities at each school. Horton Field House and SIU Arena were better arenas for basketball. You can see the respective priorities. Even the one side, the west side, of our new football stadium was superior to ISU's or SIU's for years and years—and still is."

Korcek added that although ISU and SIU were members of the short-lived Midwestern Conference along with Ball State, Indiana State, and NIU, the Redbirds and and Salukis wanted no part of the top level of football.

"It's sad," Korcek said, "but with the current two-division setup, two great institutions and programs like Illinois State and Southern Illinois would really enhance the MAC West Division and help with publicity in the Chicago market. But I think they are really happy in the

Missouri Valley. That said, we are the western 'orphan' in the MAC. We might feel strongly about Toledo, but UT would prefer to beat Bowling Green or Miami or Ohio more than us. But Evans said it best in the 1960s, that the MAC was the best option for us in this region and—under the circumstances—it still is."

The Huskies remained in the MAC until 1986, when they returned to independent status.

However, these years were difficult at best for the program. With no conference affiliation, NIU's schedule featured the likes of West Virginia, Wisconsin, Miami, Northwestern, UNLV, Minnesota, Nebraska, Kansas State, Cincinnati, Iowa and Army. While these programs may have brought some level of prestige to NIU football, they did little to enhance rivalries.

"When you're an independent, it's difficult," said longtime NIU play-by-play broadcaster

Bill Baker.

In 1993, Northern joined the Big West Conference, a mixed bag of schools from all over the country. In the three seasons NIU competed in the BWC, the Huskies played Arkansas State, Nevada, New Mexico State, Pacific, Southwestern Louisiana, Louisiana Tech, San Jose State, Utah State and UNLV as conference foes. Interestingly, NIU finished each of its three Big West seasons with a 3-3 conference record.

"I might be the only one to think this, but I felt like our biggest rival in the Big West was Southwestern Louisiana," said longtime NIU assistant coach Mike Sabock, later a member of the Western Michigan staff. "We had some great games with them down there and up in DeKalb."

Southwestern Louisiana, now called Louisiana-Lafayette, featured six players during those years who later made NFL rosters.

Sabock remembers NIU star running back LeShon Johnson and Southwestern Louisiana safety Orlando Thomas having some great battles during those games.

"Southwestern's stadium was below sea level and you had to walk up a tunnel to reach the field," Sabock said. "I remember LeShon and the safety (Thomas) walking up that tunnel and saying, 'Here we go again, one final time.' It wasn't trash talk or bad blood, it was mutual respect."

However, that mutual respect didn't always carry over to those Southwestern Louisiana–NIU games. Brian Mitchell played quarterback at Southwestern Louisiana during the late 1980s and early 1990s before enjoying a solid career as an NFL return specialist.

Sabock recalled in an e-mail, "One time Brian Mitchell scored on a long run up the sideline on the west side of the (Huskie) stadium toward the north end zone and for the last 15 yards of the run, looked toward the crowd to his left—which used to be our student section—and gave everyone the finger for the last 15 yards of his run! I saw it during the game,

but it was also on the game film!! I think it was because of the rivalry of that game!"

NIU returned to independent status in 1996 before rejoining the MAC a year later. However, as Korcek noted, NIU remains the only MAC school in Illinois.

"It was hard, really hard (to establish a MAC rival)," said former Huskie head coach Joe Novak, a native of Ohio. "It was a little one-sided on our part and a little contrived at times, but I really felt it was important to the program to have rivalries."

Sabock said, "It's tough to establish a rivalry when you are located on the outskirts of the conference like Northern is. It's really difficult for Northern to establish a MAC rivalry because of geography and the already established traditions of the other schools involved. Toledo has always been a nemesis for Northern rather than a rival. Bowling Green and Toledo have a natural rivalry. Western Michigan has Central Michigan. Northern just doesn't have that."

Sabock noted that NIU tried to generate a rivalry with Western Michigan during Novak's tenure as Huskie head coach.

"We never really had a rival in the MAC so we tried to make it Western Michigan," Sabock said. "We created a bulletin board that read BroncoBull.com and posted things to try to create a rivalry."

However, when Sabock joined the Western Michigan staff in 2008, he saw things from the other side of the fence.

"Western Michigan looks at NIU as a tough game, but not like a rival like Central Michigan," Sabock said. "It takes two to have a rivalry. Both sides have to see it that way."

Novak agreed.

"Western Michigan recruited the Chicago area, which we looked at as our area too," Novak said. "It was logical for us to consider it a rivalry but not so much for them."

The ESPN College Football Encyclopedia suggests that perhaps an annual game with the University of Illinois could create a new tradition. In fact, the two schools played in Champaign in 2010. However, it appears that such a rivalry would have lukewarm interest to U of I fans.

"It would be natural for Northern, but I'm not sure Illinois would look at it that way," Novak said.

Moreover, since NIU's upset of nationally ranked Maryland to open the 2003 season, larger non-conference opponents have had little interest in playing the Huskies in DeKalb. Big Ten members Wisconsin and Iowa have played NIU, but these games have taken place at Soldier Field in Chicago.

"It was a huge deal for our program to get those games in Soldier Field," Novak said. "When I was at Northern we wanted to play either Northwestern or Illinois every year and get something going for the program in that regard."

Perhaps Baker summed up the NIU situation the best.

"Won't somebody out there hate us?" Baker said.

THE GREAT DEBATE: MARYLAND OR ALABAMA

Democrat or Republican? Cubs or White Sox? Plain or peanut? Maryland or Alabama?

Though it may not fall among the greatest debates in the history of the human race, the question of which victory was bigger for the 2003 NIU Huskies is still hotly debated.

Both wins brought national headlines to head coach Joe Novak's program. One came at Huskie Stadium; the other on the road at one of the most heralded venues in college football.

So, which one was more of a landmark victory for the Huskies, Maryland or Alabama?

"Maryland," said P.J. Fleck, who caught 13 passes for 116 yards and a touchdown against the Terrapins. "To see Huskie Stadium from

where it was (with) 3,000 people at games to sold out (with) scalping tickets, ThunderStix, a Top 25 team in our place and winning! That started it all, us believing!"

Mike Sabock, the Huskies' defensive line coach that season, agreed.

"Maryland!!" wrote Sabock in an e-mail. "That is the game that started the excitement over NIU football. Beating the then-13th-ranked team to start the season got everyone into NIU, including donors! Alabama was a continuation of that victory. It's still a crime we did not get a bowl game that year!!"

Rick Cerrone, who graduated from NIU in 1976 before beginning a long career in Major League Baseball media relations, also chose the Maryland game.

"I contend that game was the greatest ever in Northern Illinois history," said Cerrone. "First of all, it was at home. It was on national TV, Fox Sports Net. Secondly, it put us on the map."

Randee Drew ended the game by grabbing a deflected interception.

"They both were great wins but if any win sticks out to me, it is the Maryland win," Drew said. "It meant so much to us as a team. We had lost one of our teammates (Shea Fitzgerald) that summer in a tragedy. We were running high with emotion. It was the home opener.

"We played so well. We never backed down, and I played my ass off."

However, not everyone sees it that way. Mike Korcek has been around NIU athletics since his days as a student in the late 1960s.

"No contest, it's Alabama," Korcek stated in an e-mail. "Ideally, you might say both were equally important, and upsetting Top 20 Maryland in your home opener on national TV was unbelievable and set the tone for 2003, but to win at Alabama at the home of Bear Bryant (and the Tide was No. 21 in the country at the time, but slipped badly at the end of year).

"Both games (and wins) generated great, unprecedented interest in Northern Illinois.

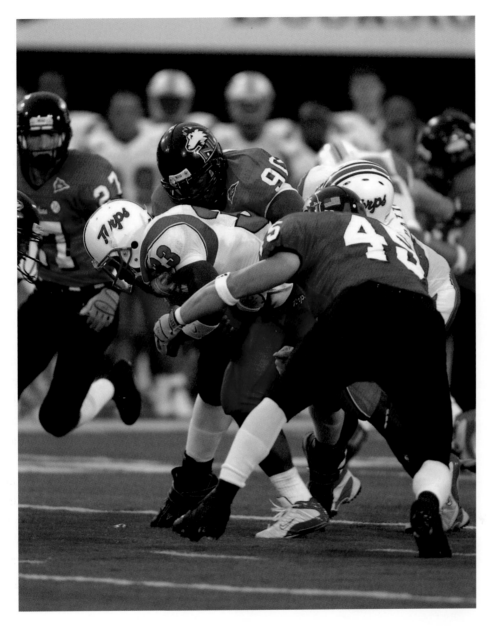

NIU began its incredible 2003 season by upsetting the Maryland Terrapins at Huskie Stadium.

But I didn't sleep the Sunday after Alabama and got called at home at 9 a.m. by *USA Today*. The combination of both (and Iowa State) gave a mid-major super credibility. As great as the Maryland game was, Alabama was even more electric and memorable."

Though he caught a five-yard pass and turned it into a 30-yard winning touchdown in overtime against Maryland, receiver Dan Sheldon sided with Korcek.

"The win over Maryland was an amazing game and kicked things off for us, but I think going down to Alabama and beating them on their field was more significant," Sheldon said. "Winning on the road is hard enough, then adding it was ranked Alabama at their place was pretty amazing."

Head coach Joe Novak said, "I have to say Alabama just because it's Alabama. Plus, it was played in Tuscaloosa. You looked around and saw there were 12 national championship banners, **12.** Those people down there had no clue who we were. To win down there with the ghost of Bear Bryant and everything that goes along with it was really something."

LeShon Johnson, the running back who finished sixth in the 1993 Heisman Trophy race, selected Alabama for similar reasons.

"I didn't play in that game. I was long gone. But if I have to choose, it would be Alabama because it's the SEC and all that great tradition," Johnson said.

Rick Armstrong of the *Aurora Beacon-News* sided with the victory at Alabama.

"Alabama just because of everything that goes with that name and tradition," Armstrong

Later in the season, Brian Atkinson and his Huskie teammates upset the Alabama Crimson Tide in Tuscaloosa.

said. "Before the game we toured the Bear Bryant Museum. It was like a cathedral. I wrote down NIU by three in the (museum's) guest book before the game. I remember everyone going nuts on the field afterward."

Armstrong's wife snapped a photo of the scoreboard that read: NIU 19, Alabama 16. Her quick action recorded a moment in history; Alabama officials shut the scoreboard off just seconds later.

David Kaplan did the play-by-play on the Fox Sports Net broadcast for the Maryland game.

"That was one of the cooler things I've ever called," Kaplan said. "It was just a surreal game. It had a bit of everything . . . a blocked field goal at the end of regulation, a quick touchdown to put Northern ahead, the wild interception at the end."

Kaplan recalls getting home from the game and turning on ESPN's "SportsCenter."

"This was a time when baseball races were heating up and the fall sports were all getting going and NIU is the lead story on 'SportsCenter,' **the lead story**," Kaplan said. "Three of the top 10 plays were plays from the game. They used my calls. It was such a thrill."

Thus, Kaplan picked the Maryland victory over Alabama.

"They were Alabama in name only (that season)," Kaplan explained. "It was a Mike Shula–coached team. (The win over Maryland was) a magical night in the cornfields."

NIU play-by-play man Bill Baker also chose the Maryland game.

"I really side with Maryland because it really set the tone for everything else," Baker said. "My memory of the days leading up to the game is so vivid. Joe Novak stood outside and told his players, 'I believe you can do it. You've got to believe you can do it.'"

Still, Korcek held firm with his choice.

"Alabama, 12 national football championships. Those title flags were on the field. Joe Namath, etc. How many SEC greats played on

The scoreboard tells the story.

that same field? Not putting down Maryland or Huskie Stadium, but this was the Crimson Tide. Big time!!!!" he wrote.

METEORIC GROWTH

Just as the 1960s were a time for change and upheaval in American society, so they were for NIU athletics.

The success of head coach Howard Fletcher's Huskies of the early-to-mid '60s provided a springboard for NIU's growth.

"It is my opinion that the real importance of the 10-0-0 1963 team was elevating our status regionally and nationally," said former sports information director Mike Korcek, a 1970 NIU graduate. "That '63 team was the linchpin. Winning the Mineral Water Bowl (1963) and that 1962–1965 era put us on the map and led to Division I, the MAC and the new stadium on west campus."

Fletcher's pass-happy style led by College Football Hall of Fame quarterback George Bork brought national headlines and attention for NIU.

When NIU opened Huskie Stadium in 1965, the facility became known as "The House That George Built."

Korcek's student days of 1966–1970 coincided with what he termed "the meteoric growth of NIU."

According to Korcek, NIU's enrollment went from 14,000 to 20,000 in his time as a student. With enrollment projections predicting Northern would reach 35,000 students by the mid-1980s, *Chicago Tribune* writer Dave Condon proposed the Big Ten Conference add NIU in the early 1970s.

While NIU's enrollment leveled off in the '70s, its athletic department continued to develop.

This transformation evolved from the Huskies' success under Fletcher to the move to Division I football in 1969.

"Chick Evans, Bob Brigham and my old boss Bud Nangle were instrumental in getting the Huskies University Division status," Korcek said. "That was Chick's vision and Brigham's duty, but Bud was the enabler, the key intermediary, the guy in the trenches that got it done."

The NCAA subcommittee that determined the major schools was chaired by Furman Bisher, the long-time sports editor of the *Atlanta Journal-Constitution.* According to Korcek, Bisher and Nangle were associated from Nangle's days as sports editor of the *Toledo Blade.*

While NIU never joined the Big Ten as Condon had proposed, the Huskies found a home in the Mid-American Conference in 1973.

"In the new D-1 era, Northern made a conscious effort to emulate the success of Miami (Ohio) heading into the MAC era," Korcek noted.

Thus, NIU hired Richard "Doc" Urich and Jerry Ippoliti in succession as its football coaches. Both men were Miami graduates as were later NIU head coaches Bill Mallory and Joe Novak.

"(Moving to Divison I status and joining the MAC were) two other key events in our history and development," said Korcek.

During the early '70s, NIU began to see some of its players drafted into the National Football League. In addition, an upset of MAC champion Kent State in 1972 brought further recognition.

"I played at a time when things were really changing at Northern," said running back Mark Kellar, the nation's leading rusher in 1973 and a Minnesota Vikings draft choice. "It was a great time to be there."

NIU also upgraded its schedules to reflect the "big-time" status of its program. The first of these games came in 1971 when the Huskies traveled to play the University of Wisconsin of the Big Ten.

"One of (Brigham's) most enduring accomplishments was convincing (Wisconsin AD) Elroy Hirsch to play the Huskies in football," said Nangle. "That got NIU into the so-called 'big-time' in football significance."

NIU continued to schedule larger opponents under the direction of Brigham.

"Over the years, we have played some tough major-majors," said Korcek.

Those "major-majors" include the likes of Northwestern, Kansas, Iowa, West Virginia, Nebraska, Kansas State, Florida, Indiana, Oklahoma State, Louisville, Cincinnati, Maryland, Alabama and Penn State.

When NIU left the MAC in 1986, a new era began for the Huskies. However, this time around, the changes weren't positive. NIU competed as an independent until joining the Big West Conference in 1993.

"Northern made a mistake when they left the MAC," said All-Century offensive lineman Randy Clark. "They didn't know which direction they were going."

Following three seasons in the Big West, the Huskies returned to independent status until rejoining the MAC in 1997.

During this era, NIU fell upon lean times. In fact, from 1986 to 2000, the Huskies experienced just two winning seasons (both of which came under Jerry Pettibone in the late 1980s). While the Charlie Sadler years (1991–1995) may be best remembered for LeShon Johnson, the era was marred by poor records and numerous character issues off the field.

The MAC formally extended invitations to NIU, the University of Buffalo and Marshall University on June 14, 1995. NIU officially voted to return to the MAC on June 21, 1995.

"We're thrilled about rejoining the MAC," said then-NIU Athletic Director Cary Groth. "The president (John E. La Tourette), our faculty and staff, and our alums believe this is the right fit for our program. One of our top priorities was to put the majority of our sports under one conference umbrella, and the MAC lets us do that."

RECRUITING

Recruiting is the lifeblood of any college football program. However, recruiting has changed just as much as any part of the game over the years.

"The biggest change (in recent years) is the pressure to commit before the senior year (of high school)," said Jerry Pettibone, who coached from 1966 to 1996 at six different universities, including Northern.

Today, Pettibone maintains a personal evaluation service for high school and junior college football players. The main focus of the service includes determining each athlete's playing ability level and helping navigate him through the college recruiting process.

"The rules as far as contact are completely different today (than when I coached)," Pettibone said. "Now, coaches can only have contact once a week. They only get to see them play or practice a limited amount.

"There's not as much time in the player's living room. There's pressure to make an offer as soon as possible these days."

Much of that pressure comes from the growth of technology into the recruiting process.

"The Internet has changed it all," said Mike Sabock, who coached for 24 seasons at NIU and served as the Huskies' recruiting coordinator under head coach Joe Novak.

"There are no secrets out there," Sabock said. "Kids and parents now see who's getting offered scholarships. It's natural for them to say, 'If so-and-so is getting an offer, what about me? I'm better than he is.'"

Prospective players are also now taking an active part in the process. Many of them make their own highlight DVDs or upload them onto YouTube for college coaches and recruiters to see their skills.

"It's hard on coaches," Sabock said. "It takes time out of your day (to watch everything). But, you've got to check them out because you don't want to miss out on someone. The kids now think it's easy to obtain scholarships."

Pettibone agreed.

"A lot (of recruiting) is done over the Internet and on Web sites," he said. "The official (campus) visit used to be the most important part of the process. Now, it's an afterthought."

Pettibone sees this as a huge negative.

"The personal side of it has been removed," he said.

As a result, the odds of coaches making mistakes in their offers have increased.

"The pressure to make those offers as soon as possible means the entire process is moved up," Pettibone said.

Thus, coaching staffs around the nation are spending much of their time focusing on high school players who are not only upperclassmen but rather sophomores.

"That's just crazy to me," said Pettibone.

While coaches have always needed to establish bonds with prospective players, that process has also changed in today's fast-paced, touch-of-a-button society.

"You have to think like an 18-year-old kid," said 28-year-old P.J. Fleck, the former NIU receiver who served as the recruiting coordinator at his alma mater before taking a similar position at Rutgers University.

"Texting, Facebook, Twitter, cell phones, that's how they communicate," said Fleck.

Thus, coaches often use any and all of these tools in their attempts to sign the next recruiting class.

Yet coaches have to make sure their communication isn't too impersonal.

"You can't just mass produce," Fleck said. "You have to be really careful."

One of Fleck's best friends from his NIU days is former Huskie running back Thomas Hammock, now an assistant coach in the Big Ten Conference.

"I enjoy the players," Hammock said. "They make it fun to watch kids you recruit develop under your tutelage and become good people and players. I enjoy recruiting and meeting different families and opening them up to my family.

"The best thing about recruiting is meeting new people and selling them on what you believe and value. The worst part of recruiting is the traveling and being away from my family."

Former NIU head coach Joe Novak looked for recruits who excelled in multiple sports.

"That was always attractive to me," Novak said. "That's not always true in today's game. Seasons have become 12-month ordeals. Coaches are leading athletes down that path."

Novak also wanted players who were concerned with things beyond football.

"We really liked high-character guys," Novak said. "When you look at some of our most successful players, they all came from quality families. Many of them had two parents with the same last name. You don't always find that these days."

No matter the era, no matter the school, recruiting will always dominate a coaching staff's time and energy. It was true when players wore leather helmets; it remains true today.

NORTH OF THE BORDER

During the Vietnam era thousands of draft-eligible college males fled to Canada. During the history of NIU football, a smaller number headed north of the border for nonpolitical reasons. Seeking to continue their playing days, these athletes signed with teams in the Canadian Football League.

In fact, Northern has sent a dozen players to the CFL. College Football Hall of Fame quarterback George Bork was the first former Huskie to play in Canada. The record-setting Bork spent fours seasons (1964–1967) in the CFL.

"The game is so different," said Bork. "There's the wider field, the extra receiver (on offense). There's unlimited motion. But the most difficult thing is the three downs. You really only have two downs because if you don't make the first down on your first two plays, you have to punt.

"It's a more demanding game than it is here (in the United States)."

Bork noted that he played for three different coaches in his four seasons with the Montreal Alouettes.

Bork played one of those seasons under fellow College Hall of Famer Darrell Mudra, who later coached at both Western Illinois and Eastern Illinois. Ironically, Mudra had coached Adams State to a victory over the Bork-led Northern Huskies in the 1962 Mineral Bowl.

"He was a great motivator and he was very intense," Bork said of Mudra. "He really worked at the psychological part of the game.

"He's had success everywhere he's gone. There were times when I thought he was a genius, and there were times when I would just shake my head. But, if you look at his record, you lean toward genius."

Mudra said, "George Bork was a brilliant passer."

Bork's brightest memory of his CFL days came when future Minnesota Viking Super Bowl quarterback Joe Kapp brought his undefeated BC Lions against Montreal.

"We were struggling along," Bork recalled. "They came in flying high, but we managed to beat them. It was really a thrill."

NIU sent the majority of its CFL-bound players north of the border during the tenure of head coach Charlie Sadler. Defensive back Eddie Davis proved to be the best.

Davis earned All-Star status five times in his 15 seasons in the CFL. Davis won the Grey Cup twice, first with Calgary in 1998 and then with Saskatchewan in 2007.

"It's still a dream you get to live doing a job you love to do," Davis said.

Davis also served as a player representative for the union.

"The NFL is more of a players' league," Davis said. "In our league the owners have more power."

Each team was bound to a $4.2 million salary cap in 2009, Davis' final CFL season.

"If a team has a top quarterback making $500,000 or $600,000, that's a big chunk," Davis explained. "So if you want to make more money, you may have to go to a new team (as a free agent)."

Davis should know. He left Calgary to join Saskatchewan as a free agent in 2001.

"Finances are the nature of the business," he said.

Following in Davis' defensive back footsteps

is former Huskie Randee Drew. A native of Milwaukee, Drew found his way to the Montreal Alouettes in 2007, where he earned All-Star honors.

"Playing in the CFL is a great experience," Drew said. "It has given me the chance once again to see the world and experience new things. It is professional football, and I am blessed to be a player in a wonderful league."

Like other American players, Drew has had to adjust to different rules in the Canadian game.

"Yes, the rules are different and the scheme is different, but at the end of the day it is a wonderful game of football," Drew said.

All the players and coaches listed above agree with one thing: It's great to be involved in pro football no matter the league.

"I still love to play after all these years," Davis said. "As long as a team was willing to have me, I was going to continue to play."

And as long as the CFL remains a viable option, NIU Huskies will no doubt appear on the league's rosters.

HUSKIES IN THE CFL

Andy Antoine, WR
Duane Arrindell, OG
George Bork, QB
Orlando Bowen, DE
Donnavan Carter, DB
Eddie Davis, DB
Randee Drew, DB
Farrell Duclair, LB
A.J. Harris, RB
Derek Sholdice, OT
Garett Sutherland, LB
Mike Sutherland, C

HUSKIES IN THE CFL DRAFT

1995—Derek Sholdice, Edmonton
1996—Mike Sutherland, Saskatchewan
1996—Duane Arrindell, Edmonton
1996—Farrell Duclair, Calgary
1996—Alton Francis, Saskatchewan
1996—James Eggink, Montreal
1997—Jamie Macdonald, British Columbia
1998—Garett Sutherland, Winnipeg
1999—Orlando Bowen, Edmonton
2000—Donnavan Carter, Toronto
Source: NIU Football Media Guide

MARCHING BAND

The marching band has been an integral part of Northern Illinois University football since the days a field goal and touchdown were both valued at five points.

According to its official Web site the Huskie Marching Band has been "defining collegiate life in DeKalb since 1899."

In today's world of electronically produced sounds, there is something special about a marching band. Moreover, the sounds produced by the precision of a quality marching band epitomize the pageantry and color that is college football.

"Certainly we contribute to the unique atmosphere of a collegiate sporting event," said Dr. Thomas Bough, the director of the NIU Marching Band in an e-mail. "We also support the football team, and many other teams, by performing at events and by actively cheering and supporting each team during the game.

"We also provide a special dose of Huskie Spirit at a variety of other events. On game day, those other events include the president's tent, the athletic scholarship tent and the tailgate area. During other times, the band or portions of the band perform at various NIU functions throughout the year."

The Huskie band performs at all home games as well as select road games. In addition, the marching band accompanies the Huskies when the team earns a bowl bid. The band also entertains crowds at select parades

The NIU Marching Band first appeared in 1899.

and university events.

According to Bough, the marching band practices seven to ten hours per week. Moreover, the band practices an additional eight hours on game day.

"In essence, marching band is a part-time job that does not pay," Bough said. "Very few of our students receive scholarships of any sort. Most do it simply because they love to perform and they love NIU."

Much like a football coach, Bough gets thrills from the experience.

"Getting to work with outgoing, talented young people from almost every major on campus (is gratifying)," Bough said. "Since most of the band have a major other than music, I get to know a lot of very interesting students. A close second to that is the sincere appreciation shown for the band and the band members across this campus. From athletics to Altgeld Hall, hundreds of NIU faculty and staff have voiced their support for the Huskie Marching Band."

Some of that appreciation has come from the NIU football staff.

"We have the best band in the land. They make game day a great experience. We feel they are a big part of our team," said NIU head coach Jerry Kill.

Former head coach Joe Novak said, "We really appreciate the enthusiasm and excitement the Huskie Marching Band brings to our football games."

Like Kill and Novak, Bough and other band directors also face challenges in their jobs. Many of those challenges involve finances, but there are additional factors.

"Scheduling and budgets (are the biggest challenges)," Bough said. "We plan every single rehearsal before the year even starts, to make sure that we can fulfill all of our obligations. There are lots of pieces of the puzzle . . . music has to be written for the winds and brass, then arranged for the drum line, then recorded and sent to the dancers and flag line. Much of the time, my job is to organize and manage a whole lot of very talented students and staff. Figuring out how to pay for it all is equally challenging."

Yet, all that hard work, planning and dedication pays off when the NIU Marching Band strikes up its music each autumn game day.

"The NIU Band has a core of students who are truly committed to the band and its long-term success. That core extends back into the Alumni Band as well. This level of commitment is one of the best things about the NIU band," said Bough.

DID YOU KNOW?

• **Victor Kays** served as the first captain under player-coach–team manager **John L. Keith** in 1899. NIU was then known as Northern Illinois State Normal School.

• **Paul Harrison** coached NIU for three seasons (1920–1922). According to *The Norther,* Harrison took his team to Lake Geneva, Wisconsin for its preseason training camp. This was several decades before NFL teams would follow suit.

• **John McNamara** was an All-Little 19 Conference offensive guard from 1927 to 1931. McNamara, an NIU Athletics Hall of Famer, later served as the president of M&M Mars, Inc. He is credited with inventing M&M peanut candies and was also the chairman of the board for Uncle Ben's Rice.

• Three Northern Illinois players have taken part in the Super Bowl. They are safety **Clarence Vaughan**, defensive tackle **Hollis Thomas** and offensive lineman **Ryan Diem**.

• **Bill Anderson** scored a school-record seven touchdowns in a 1912 game against Wheaton College. NIU won that game 114-7.

• In a 1963 game against Central Michigan, three NIU players caught 10 or more passes. **Gary Stearns** led the way with a Huskie-record 17 catches for 188 yards.

• Former NIU split end **Carl Aikens** was selected as the Arena Football League's 1989 "Ironman of the Year." The award was given to the player who best exemplified "two-way" toughness on both sides of the line of scrimmage. Aikens starred for the Chicago Bruisers as a wide receiver and defensive back.

• Kicker **Steve Azar** is the NIU career scoring leader with 370 points. Running back **Michael Turner** ranks second with 288 points.

• NIU has a history of national leaders. Three Huskie quarterbacks have led the country in total offense—**Bob Heimerdinger** (1950 and 1951), **George Bork** (1962 and 1963) and **Ron Christian** (1965). Bork was also the nation's passing leader in '62 and '63. Three NIU players have captured national receiving titles—**Jim McKinzie** (1952), **Hugh Rohrschneider** (1962 and 1963) and **Dave Petzke** (1978). A pair of Huskie running backs—**Mark Kellar** (1973) and **LeShon Johnson** (1993)—topped the national charts in rushing. Quarterback **Stacey Robinson** (1990) led the country in scoring. Receiver **Dan Sheldon** (2002) was the national leader in punt returns. Quarterback **Jordan Lynch** led the nation in rushing (1,771 yards) and total offense (4,753 yards) in 2012.

• Huskie Stadium became known as "The House That **George Bork** Built" in honor of the All-American quarterback of the 1960s who was featured in *Sports Illustrated.* The stadium later came to be called "The Doghouse."

• The current playing surface is called Brigham Field at Huskie Stadium in honor of **Robert J. Brigham**, a key figure in NIU athletics for more than 50 years.

• **Bob Brigham's** single-game rushing record of 242 yards set in 1948 lasted 25 years until it was broken by **Mark Kellar** in 1973.

• Prior to his days as a college and pro football broadcaster, **Brent Musburger** served a six-month stint as sports editor at the *DeKalb Chronicle*. After returning to the *Chicago American*, Musberger wrote a piece on the eve of the 1963 NFL Draft that said NIU quarterback **George Bork** would wind up in the NFL Hall of Fame. Bork went undrafted, played in the Canadian Football League and for the minor-league Chicago Owls before enjoying a distinguished career as a high school coach and teacher. "I was led astray by a member of the Bears coaching staff," Musberger told Jim O'Donnell of the *Chicago Sun-Times* in January 2010. "I'm sure they had a nice laugh over it, and Bork had a newspaper article that I hope he still has framed somewhere."

• New Orleans Saints head coach **Sean Payton** was offered a partial scholarship to NIU by then-head coach **Bill Mallory**. Payton instead opted to attend Eastern Illinois University, where he passed for more than 10,000 yards in his career.

• **Mike Mallory**, one of Bill Mallory's sons, served as an assistant coach on Sean Payton's New Orleans team that won the Super Bowl in 2010.

• NIU and rival Bowling Green were featured in the first ever **ESPN "Game Day"** appearance for a Mid-American Conference game in 2003.

• Former Huskies **Sam Hurd** and **Doug Free** were both members of the 2009 and 2010 Dallas Cowboys.

• The Huskies made back-to-back bowl appearances for the first time in school history in 2008 and 2009. Under head coach **Jerry Kill**, NIU played in the Independence Bowl and International Bowl, respectively. Kill's Huskies made it three straight by winning the Humanitarian Bowl in 2010.

• Defensive end **Jake Coffman** served two tours of duty in Iraq as a combat engineer for the Marine Corps after graduating high school. Coffman often led the Huskies onto the field carrying the American flag his parents flew at their house during his time with the Marines.

• When the Huskies won the **MAC West title** outright in 2010, they did so in dominating fashion. NIU crushed Eastern Michigan 71-3 in the final game of the regular-season conference schedule. The Huskies racked up 544 rushing yards and eight rushing touchdowns. Incredibly, NIU had five touchdown runs of more than 60 yards (71, 81, 61, 61 and 74).

• Following the announcement that the Huskies would face Florida State in the Orange Bowl, sales of NIU items jumped 274%, according to fanatics.com, an online retailer.

WHAT IF?

The world of sports often revolves around debate that takes place everywhere from the schoolyard to the water cooler to the tailgates of America.

It seems everywhere one turns there is a list or rankings of some sports-related topic. Who is the greatest player in school history? Who was the best quarterback? Which defense was the toughest? NIU football is no different.

Since football is a team game, let's examine the question of the greatest Huskie team ever.

There are a number of candidates to wear the all-time champion crown. Three great NIU football teams have been inducted into the Huskie Hall of Fame: 1951, 1963 and 1983.

The '51 Huskies posted a 9-0-0 record and won the Interstate Intercollegiate Athletic Conference title under head coach George "Chick" Evans.

"We felt Chick was many, many years ahead of his time," said Huskie Hall of Fame quarterback Bob Heimerdinger in the 2004 NIU Football Media Guide. "He liked the throwing game, studied it, watched the pros . . . we had a T (formation) with a flanker or slotback. It was a pro set, except you didn't call it that then."

The 1952 *Norther* yearbook said, "NI's Huskies of 1951 were a passing team first, last and three out of four times. As a team, the Huskies threw more and completed more passes for more yards than any other college team in the nation."

Like the 1951 team, the 1963 NIU Huskies also turned in a perfect season and captured the Interstate Intercollegiate Athletic Conference crown. Coached by Howard Fletcher and led by College Football Hall of Fame quarterback George Bork, NIU was voted the NCAA College Division national champion by The Associated Press and the National Association of Intercollegiate Athletics (NAIA).

And like its 1951 predecessor, the '63 Huskies also lived by the forward pass.

"We believe in putting the ball in the air and spreading out our opponents," Fletcher said.

The '63 Huskies capped their 10-0-0 season with a victory over Southwest Missouri State in the Mineral Water Bowl.

Twenty years later, head coach Bill Mallory's Huskies competed on the NCAA Division I-A level. Mallory's team won the Mid-American Conference championship and then defeated Cal State-Fullerton in the California Bowl.

"It was one of the most gratifying seasons," Mallory said afterward.

The '83 team went 10-2 en route to winning the school's first major bowl game. The team eventually produced seven National Football League draft picks, 19 professional players, eight All-Americas and five individual inductees into the NIU Athletics Hall of Fame.

"We were a bunch of overachievers," quarterback Tim Tyrrell said. "We felt we could play with anyone."

Len Ziehm has covered sports for the *Chicago Sun-Times* for over 40 years.

"That 2003 team was really good but I have to think that '83 team would have taken care of them," Ziehm said. "I just don't think that '03 team would have matched up defensively with that 1983 bunch."

Though not enshrined in the NIU Athletics Hall of Fame, the 1989 Huskies under the guidance of head coach Jerry Pettibone stand among the best in school history.

"This football team is what we've been building for the last five years," Pettibone said prior to the season. "You can just see over the last three seasons how we've developed."

Pettibone proved to be a prophet as the '89 Huskies went 9-2, losing only road games at Nebraska and Louisiana Tech. Quarterback Stacey Robinson led an explosive wishbone attack that averaged nearly 31 points a game.

The next candidate is the 2003 NIU Huskies, the team that no doubt will someday be inducted into the school's Hall of Fame. The season marked the culmination of the return of former Mallory assistant Joe Novak. The '03 Huskies shocked Maryland, Alabama and Iowa State en route to a 7-0 start and No. 12 ranking in the AP poll.

"Then we lost six or seven players to injuries," Novak said. "Losing (linebacker) Nick Duffy was a big blow to us. We also lost key players like Randee Drew, Akil Grant and Travis Moore. Losing those players really hurt us down the stretch."

Battered by those injuries, NIU dropped conference road games at Bowling Green and Toledo.

"It's unfortunate that we couldn't stay healthy for our games against those two MAC opponents," Novak said. "I really believe we had a legitimate chance to go 12-0."

Instead the Huskies finished the year with a 10-2 record. Unbelievably, NIU was not invited to a bowl game. Meanwhile, a 6-6 Northwestern team played in the Motor City Bowl.

The next candidate is the 2010 Huskies, which gets a slight nod over the 2011 team.

After losing its season opener at Iowa State when first-string quarterback Chandler Harnish was injured, NIU played solid football the rest of the way. The Huskies knocked off Minnesota, narrowly lost to Illinois and won the MAC West. However, NIU lost the MAC Championship 26-21 to Miami at Detroit's Ford Field. The Huskies capped the year with a 49-17 rout of Fresno State in the Humanitarian Bowl.

"Last year's (2010) Northern team was probably better overall," said former NIU defensive line coach Mike Sabock, who coached at MAC rival Western Michigan from 2008–2011. "They were better defensively and kicking game-wise in 2010. They won most of their games easily."

The final candidate is the 2012 Huskies, coached by Dave Doeren. After losing its opener to Iowa, the '12 team reeled off 11 straight victories, won a second straight MAC championship and earned a BCS berth. Quarterback Jordan Lynch passed for 2,962 yards and rushed for another 1,771.

So, there are the candidates. Which NIU Huskie team is the greatest of them all?

"Obviously, both the 1983 and 2003 were truly great Northern Illinois teams," said former sports information director Mike Korcek. "Where does 1951, 1963, or 1989 fall in that pecking order?

"Not to live in the past, but I still think 1983 and 2003 were better Northern Illinois teams (than 2010). Someone may say that 2003 gets an 'incomplete' grade with the bad finish and no bowl. (I) think Bill Mallory was a better overall and more experienced coach than Jerry Kill, and I don't think 19 professional players will originate from this year's (2010) group."

Korcek added that the MAC was not as good in 2010 as it was in 1983 and 2003.

"(The) Fresno (State) blowout win in the Humanitarian Bowl was impressive, though," Korcek added. "(However), Cal State-Fullerton had some decent NFL talent also in 1983."

Jack Dean played running back on the '63 national champions. The DeKalb native was later the head coach at Eastern Illinois.

"It is very hard to compare teams with regards to who is best," Dean said. "There have only been two undefeated (NIU) teams. Things have changed so much. I think we were probably (better) than the '51 team simply because the size and strength and 40 (yard) times were probably much better on our team.

"Teams 'past' us have changed so much it is also hard to say. They have some great players and great teams. However, we played a lot of the same opponents as now and fared very well. We only had 33 players so it is very hard to compare. We didn't have an organized weightlifting and off-season training program. Several of us played on the NIU hockey team in the winter. Only about six of us seriously lifted weights. However, we did have five guys on the '63 team that got pro contracts."

Novak, the head coach of the 2003 Huskies and the defensive coordinator of the '83 team, said, "No matter how I go I'd be making somebody mad. Our 2003 team had Michael Turner and guys like Danny Sheldon so we perhaps had a little bit more firepower. With the passing of 20 years, we got a little better. We were bigger and stronger. But that '83 team had real chemistry to it. Guys like (quarterback) Tim Tyrrell were real leaders.

"It would be interesting to see how it would turn out."

Beat writer Rick Armstrong of the *Aurora Beacon-News* attended NIU as a student in the 1970s. He served on the statistics crew in 1983. Armstrong, a Sycamore native, has covered NIU football on a regular basis since 1999.

"You have to rank this (2010) team either one or two in the school's Division I history," Armstrong wrote in an e-mail. "The 2010 team has the most wins in school history and a bowl win. The 1983 team has a MAC title and a bowl win."

When asked to compare the '83 team with the 2003 Huskies, Armstrong went with the more recent NIU edition.

"I'd lean toward the 2003 team for one reason," Armstrong said. "When the NCAA put the restrictions on scholarships (in the mid-1980s), it leveled the field. Players who would have been going to Big Ten schools or other major conferences are now going to places like Northern or other MAC schools. As a result, the 2003 team would have more talent and depth.

"Of course you run into the argument of comparing different eras and how difficult that is. I'm not sure you can truly get a picture, but it would be fun to match those great Huskie teams."

Mike Sabock spent 24 years as a Huskie assistant. He first joined the NIU staff in 1984, one year after the California Bowl team.

"Everything I've ever heard about that ('83) team was its will to win as a bunch of overachievers," Sabock said.

Sabock said the 2003 Huskies gets the edge over the '89 team because of its style of play and its strength of schedule.

"That ('89) was a good team," he said. "We ran the wishbone. But with that 2003 team we beat big-name people running a traditional offense. In my tenure at Northern, the 2003 team had to be the best because of who we beat."

The ESPN College Football Encyclopedia made some interesting choices. The book chose the 1963 Huskies as the best in school history. It also selected Fletcher as NIU's best coach. The '83 Huskies were lauded for winning the biggest game, the first major bowl victory in NIU history. Meanwhile, the Encyclopedia honored the 2003 Huskies with the school's biggest upset with their shocker over nationally ranked Maryland to open the season.

"I'm prejudiced, but I would say the '51 team was the best team," said Jack Pheanis, who played fullback that season and later coached under Fletcher. "After World War II ended you didn't really need scholarships because everybody had been in the service. The GI Bill was your scholarship. Nearly all of the teams were equal then."

Pheanis had transferred to Northern from the University of Illinois.

"It was not a step down to come from Illinois," Pheanis said. "In fact, Heimerdinger was a better quarterback than they had at Illinois by far. We had a great defense, a great offense and a great field goal kicker. We were solid all the way around.

"But, I really like the current team (2010)," said Pheanis. "They could have given our '51 team a run for our money."

Bill Baker has done play-by-play for NIU football since 1980.

"No, I cannot pick a greatest team," Baker said. "I can tell you my favorite team. Well, actually, it would be teams and it's dead even: The '83 Cal Bowl and the 2003 team."

So where does this leave us? Is there a way to determine the greatest Northern Illinois Huskie football team ever?

While none of these debates will ever be completely resolved, technology does provide some interesting possibilities.

Using a simulation engine designed by Lance Haffner Games, the author of this book set out to determine which NIU team stands as the greatest of all-time.

Lance Haffner Games of Nashville, Tennessee has been simulating college football games since 1983. Haffner's 3-in-1 Football has been used by many national media outlets, including major market newspapers and ESPN, to determine mythical matchups over the past three decades. Thus, Haffner Games is the means by which the All-Time NIU Huskies will be crowned as the greatest team in school history.

So, it's time to tee up the ball with the click of a mouse and the stroke of a keyboard . . .

The All-Time NIU Huskies Tournament was played out in a round-robin format, with each team playing the other on a neutral field in ideal

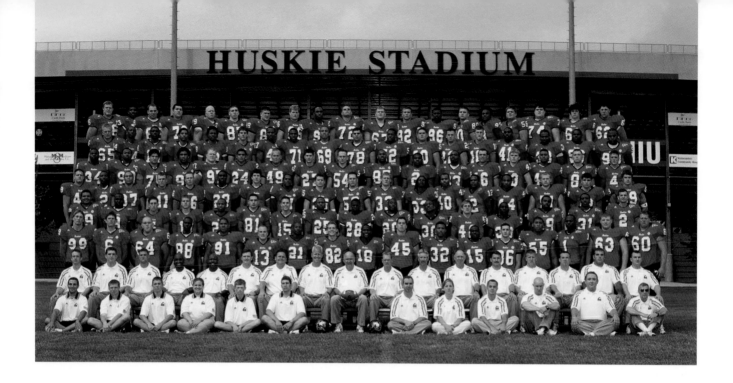

The 2003 Huskies were crowned the All-Time NIU Champions in a computer simulation.

weather conditions. For the sake of statistical reliability, each "game" was simulated 100 times. The results that follow are an average of those results and are presented as one game that represents the entire simulation.

Final Standings
2003 Huskies 6-0
1983 Huskies 5-1
2010 Huskies 4-2
2012 Huskies 3-3
1989 Huskies 2-4
1963 Huskies 1-5
1951 Huskies 0-6

In what turned out to be the game that determined the All-Time NIU Champion, Joe Novak's 2003 Huskies defeated Bill Mallory's 1983 team in 71% of the simulations. The average margin of victory was 19-12.

In that average simulated matchup, Michael "The Burner" Turner earned Huskie of the Game honors with 109 yards and one touchdown on 25 carries. Quarterback Josh Haldi completed 21 of 31 passes for 198 yards and a TD pass. P.J. Fleck and Sam Hurd caught eight and five passes respectively.

In the game that determined second place,

the '83 Huskies slipped past Jerry Kill's 2010 team 23-16. Mallory's '83 team ground out the victory with the three-prong rushing attack of Darryl Richardson (102 yards), Tim Tyrrell (91 yards) and Lou Wicks (62 yards). The '83 defense, coordinated by Novak, held Chad Spann to 71 yards on 26 carries. In addition, the Huskies sacked Chandler Harnish twice and intercepted him once. The '83 Huskies won 65% of the simulations.

Novak's 2003 team defeated Kill's 2010 edition by an average margin of 24-20. Turner ran for 128 yards and one TD. The '03 Huskies won 70% of the simulations against the '10 team.

Meanwhile, the 2012 Huskies went 3-3 in the tournament. Dave Doeren's team lost to the top three finishers in the All-Time NIU Huskies Tournament.

In the battle of the oldest teams, Howard Fletcher's 1963 Huskies toppled Chick Evans' 1951 team 24-14. College Football Hall of Fame quarterback George Bork threw for 310 yards and two touchdowns in the victory.

Thus, according to the computer, the 2003 NIU Huskies emerge as the greatest team in school history.

Let the debates begin (or continue) . . .

APPENDICES

NIU HUSKIE ALL-CENTURY TEAM

The Best of Northern Illinois University Football (1899–1998)

Offense	Years Lettered	Hometown
WR—John Spilis	1966–1968	South Holland, IL
WR—Dave Petzke	1977–1978	Fairbault, MN
WR—Hugh Rohrschneider	1960–1963	Burlington, IL
WR—Gary Stearns	1960–1963	Freeport, IL
TE—Jim Hannula	1977–1980	Elgin, IL
TE—Ken Moore	1974–1976	Chicago, IL
OL—Randy Clark	1977–1979	Mt. Prospect, IL
OL—Dan Rosado	1977–1979	Canton, GA
OL—Scott Bolzan	1980–1983	South Holland, IL
OL—Dale Berman	1958–1959	Grand Ridge, IL
OL—Todd Peat	1983–1986	Champaign, IL
OL—Tego Larsen	1936–1938	DeKalb, IL
OL—Ted Karamanos	1984–1987	Oak Lawn, IL
OL—Rich Barrent	1979–1982	Clinton, IA
C—Eric Wenckowski	1988–1990	Franklin Park, IL
C—Bob Evans	1960–1963	DeKalb, IL
QB—George Bork	1960–1963	Mt. Prospect, IL
QB—Stacey Robinson	1988–1990	Danville, IL
FB—Mark Kellar	1971–1973	Carpentersville, IL
FB—Adam Dach	1988–1991	Rockford, IL
HB—LeShon Johnson	1992–1993	Haskell, OK
HB—Reino Nori	1932–1935	DeKalb, IL
PK—Vince Scott	1980–1983	DeKalb, IL
PK—John Ivanic	1987–1990	Moline, IL
All- Fran Cahill	1948–1951	Utica, IL
Purpose Jack Dean	1961–1964	DeKalb, IL

Defense	Years Lettered	Hometown
DL—Larry Brink	1945–1947	Foley, MN
DL—Cary Caliendo	1987–1990	Brookfield, WI
DL—Doug Bartlett	1983–1986	Springfield, IL
DL—Jerry Meyers	1973–1975	Chicago, IL
DL—Scott Kellar	1982–1985	Roselle, IL
DL—Max Gill	1979–1982	Merrillville, IN
DL—Hollis Thomas	1993–1995	St. Louis, MO
DL—Steve O'Malley	1982–1985	Oak Forest, IL
LB—Frank Lewandoski	1976–1979	Muskegon, MI
LB—Mike Henigan	1960–1963	DeKalb, IL
LB—Larry Clark	1970–1972	Winnebago, IL
LB—Mike Terna	1977–1980	Wheaton, IL
LB—Bob Gregolunas	1973–1975	Calumet City, IL
LB—Clarence Vaughn	1983–1984, 1986	Chicago, IL
DB—Tom Beck	1959–1961	Chicago, IL
DB—Jeff Sanders	1982–1983	Kansas City, KS
DB—Brett Tucker	1985, 1987–1989	Sycamore, IL
DB—Dan Meyer	1964–1966	Arlington Heights, IL
DB—Dave Petway	1977–1980	Chicago, IL
DB—Lee Hicks	1981–1984	Rockford, IL
DB—Rich Marks	1971–1973	Chicago, IL
DB—Al Eck	1958–1960	Palatine, IL
P—Tom Wittum	1969–1971	Round Lake, IL
P—Todd Van Keppel	1981–1984	Valparaiso, IN
Return—Rodney Taylor	1985–1988	Davenport, IA
Return—Deon Mitchell	1995–1998	Ft. Wayne, IL

THE NIU HUSKIE ALL-CENTURY TEAM WAS SELECTED IN 1999 BY THE FOLLOWING COMMITTEE:

Mike Korcek, chair
Bob Brigham
Fran Cahill
Pat Culpepper
John Farney
Howard Fletcher
Bob Heimerdinger

Jerry Ippoliti
Tego Larsen
Bud Nangle
Joe Novak

NIU HUSKIE ALL-DECADE TEAMS

1899–1929 ERA:

Bill Anderson, HB (1910–1912)
Clarence "Boots" Cannon, HB (1916, 1920–1921)
Wes Concidine, E (1924–1927)
Navarre Edwards, HB (1909)
Charles "Wix" Garner, QB (1920)
Sanford Givens, HB (1900–1902)
Victor Kays, FB (1899–1901)
John McNamara, G (1927–1930)
Jack Mustapha, QB (1929–1930, 1933)
John "Red" Pace, E (1929–1932)
James Sawyer, E (1910–1911)
Kennard Seyller, QB (1913–1914)
Leland Strombom, HB (1927–1930)

1930–1939 ERA:

Roy "Flip" Allen, E (1935–1938)
Ed Behan, E (1938–1941)
Elzie Cooper, E (1934–1935)
Chet Davis, HB-QB (1935–1938)
Lou DeRango, G (1935–1937)
Howard Fletcher, T (1938–1939)
Karl Hein, T (1933–1936)
Bill Howard, T (1932–1935)
Ollie Krahenbuhl, FB (1937–1940)
Robert Price, E (1938–1940)
Alex Saudargas, G (1934–1937)
Leonard Skoglund, E (1932–1934)
Sam Smith, QB (1938–1941, 1946)
Frank Stegman, T-C (1937–1940)
John Young, E (1936–1939)

1940–1949 ERA:

Ed Arquilla, G (1941–1942, 1946)
Bob Brigham, FB (1947–1949)

Duane Cunz, G (1941, 1946)

Bob Duffield, FB-T (1940–1942, 1946)

John Farney, HB (1940–1942)

Don Fortunato, QB (1946–1948)

Bob Fowlie, C (1947–1949)

Harry Henigan, FB (1942, 1946–1947, 1949)

Floyd Hunsberger, HB (1947–1949)

Toimi Jarvi, QB (1938–1941)

Ed Mascal, T (1940, 1946)

Bill Minnihan, LB (1946–1949)

Jim Patterson, T (1939–1941)

Warren Reitzel, G (1946–1947)

Dick Williams, E (1944, 1948)

1950–1959 ERA:

George Acker, G (1949–1951)

Julian Brasini, E (1948–1951)

Lew Flinn, QB (1957–1959)

Bill Graham, HB (1951–1954)

Alex Gulotta, G (1954–1957)

Bob Heimerdinger, QB (1948–1951)

Al Jones, FB-HB (1949–1951)

Wes Luedeking, HB (1953–1954, 1956)

Jim McKinzie, E (1951–1952)

Gil Memmen, C-T (1948–1951)

Dan Mojica, HB (1950–1951)

Jack Pheanis, FB (1950–1952)

Bob Soltis, HB (1956, 1959–1960)

Ernie Wickstrom, HB (1949–1950)

1960–1969 ERA:

Ron Christian, QB (1963–1965)

Dan DeVito, DHB (1968–1970)

Jim Faggetti, LB (1966–1968)

Dave Herstedt, T (1962–1964)

John Lalonde, FB (1968–1970)

Lynn McCann, DT (1961–1964)

Dave Muderink, T (1960–1962)

Tom Rosenow, T (1965–1967)

Bob Stark, E (1964–1965)

Dave Weisendanger, OT (1968–1970)

1970–1979 ERA:

Mike Chelovich, OG (1978–1981)
Steve Claussen, TE-DE (1976–1979)
Jerry Golsteyn, QB (1973–1975)
Willie Hatter, SE (1970–1972)
Pete Kraker, QB (1976–1978)
Jerry Latin, TB (1972–1973)
John Nokes, DE (1970–1972)
Don Palochko, OG (1974–1976)
Allen Ross, TB (1977–1980)

1980–1989 ERA:

Ron Delisi, LB (1986–1989)
Brian Glasgow, TE (1979–1982)
Tim Griffin, LB (1982–1985)
Ted Hennings, DT (1986–1989)
Jim Latanski, TE (1977–1980)
Curt Pardridge, SE (1982–1985)
Mike Pinckney, WE (1979–1980)
Darryl Richardson, TB (1982–1985)
Pete Roth, TB-FB (1981–1982, 1984)
Gary Schlinger, DE (1981–1984)
Marshall Taylor, QB (1985–1988)
Tim Tyrrell, QB (1982–1983)

1990–1998 ERA:

Steve Henriksen, LB (1988, 1990–1991)
Mitch Jacoby, TE (1993–1996)
Gerald Nickelberry, LB (1991–1994)
Tim O'Brien, OG (1990–1993)
Chris O'Neal, C (1993–1994)
Raymond Roberts, TE (1990–1993)
C.J. Rose, DE (1992–1995)
Derek Sholdice, OT (1992–1995)
Mike Sutherland, C (1993–1995)
Charles Talley, TB (1993–1996)
Scott Van Bellinger, DE (1988–1991)
Larry Wynn, FLK (1989–1992)

Source: 2004 Northern Illinois Football Media Guide

1999–2009 ERA*:

Brian Atkinson, LB
Steve Azar, K
Kent Baker, P
Brandon Bice, DL
Brad Chieslak, TE
Ryan Diem, OT
Andy Dittbenner, P
Randee Drew, CB
Nick Duffy, LB
Larry English, DL
P.J. Fleck, WR
Doug Free, OT
Todd Ghilani, C
Josh Haldi, QB
Jermaine Hampton, SS
Lionel Hickenbottom, FS
Darrell Hill, KR
Ben Lueck, G
Justin McCareins, WR
Travis Moore, DL
Jake Nordin, TE
Jason Onyebuagu, G
Vinson Reynolds, DL
Dan Sheldon, PR
Vince Thompson, CB
Michael Turner, RB
Larry Williams, LB
Garrett Wolfe, RB

*Note: Era team selected in 2010. Ballots were sent to the following voters: Rick Armstrong, Bill Baker, Robert Collins, Brad Hoey, Mike Korcek, Glenn Krupica, Mark Lindo, Joe Novak, Eric Schultz, Phil Voorhis, Scott Walstrom

RETIRED NIU FOOTBALL JERSEYS
6—Dave Petzke
11—George Bork
12—Bob Heimerdinger
31—Mark Kellar

Source: 2004 Northern Illinois Football Media Guide

HUSKIES IN THE PROS
Huskies selected in the NFL Draft

Player	Position	Team	Round	Year
Larry Brink	DE-E	Los Angeles Rams	17th	1948
Fran Cahill	SE	New York Giants	19th	1952
Tom Rosenow	DT	San Francisco 49ers	16th	1968
John Spilis	SE	Green Bay Packers	3rd	1969
Tom Wittum	P-PK	San Francisco 49ers	8th	1972
Larry Clark	LB	Pittsburgh Steelers	5th	1973
Willie Hatter	SE	Miami Dolphins	7th	1973
John Nokes	LB	Philadelphia Eagles	9th	1973
Mark Kellar	FB	Minnesota Vikings	6th	1974
Rich Marks	LB	Denver Broncos	14th	1974
Jerry Latin	TB	St. Louis Cardinals	11th	1975
Bob Gregolunas	LB	Kansas City Chiefs	6th	1976
Jerry Golsteyn	QB	New York Giants	12th	1976
Jerry Meyers	DT	Chicago Bears	15th	1976
Ken Moore	TE	Minnesota Vikings	5th	1977
Randy Clark	OT	Chicago Bears	8th	1980
Jim Hannula	OT	Cincinnati Bengals	9th	1981
Scott Bolzan	OT	New England Patriots	9th	1984
Scott Kellar	DT	Indianapolis Colts	5th	1986
Curt Pardridge	SE	San Diego Chargers	6th	1986
Steve O'Malley	DT	Indianapolis Colts	7th	1986
Doug Bartlett	NG	Los Angeles Rams	4th	1987
Clarence Vaughn	LB	Washington Redskins	8th	1987
Todd Peat	OG	St. Louis Cardinals	11th	1987
Brett Tucker	CB	Houston Oilers	8th	1990
LeShon Johnson	TB	Green Bay Packers	3rd	1994
Ryan Diem	OG	Indianapolis Colts	4th	2001
Justin McCareins	WR	Tennessee Titans	4th	2001
Darrell Hill	WR	Tennessee Titans	7th	2002
Michael Turner	RB	San Diego Chargers	5th	2004
Garrett Wolfe	RB	Chicago Bears	3rd	2007
Doug Free	OT	Dallas Cowboys	4th	2007
Larry English (16th overall)	LB	San Diego Chargers	1st	2009
Chandler Harnish	QB	Indianapolis Colts	7th	2012

HUSKIES SIGNED AS NFL/AFL FREE AGENTS*

Player	Position	Team	Year
Reino Nori	HB	Detroit Lions	1936
Ed Behan	E	Detroit Lions	1942
Jim Patterson	T	Detroit Lions	1942
Toimi Jarvi	QB	Philadelphia Eagles	1944
Warren Reitzel	G	Los Angeles Rams	1948
Don Fortunato	QB	Chicago Cardinals	1948
Harry Henigan	FB	Chicago Cardinals	1949
Gil Memmen	T	Pittsburgh Steelers	1952
Ernie Wickstrom	HB	Chicago Cardinals	1954
Dave Mulderink	DT	Washington Redskins	1964
Gary Stearns	SE	Washington Redskins	1964
Bob Stark	DE	Miami Dolphins	1966
Lynn McCann	DT	Minnesota Vikings	1966
Roger Stark	DT	Dallas Cowboys	1966
Jack Dean	HB	Washington Redskins	1966
John Hoover	DT	St. Louis Cardinals	1972
John Spilis	WR	Chicago Bears	1972
Larry Clark	LB	Chicago Bears	1973
Greg Garton	OG	Miami Dolphins	1973
Byron Florence	FLK	Kansas City Chiefs	1974
Pete Miskov	PK	Seattle Seahawks	1976
Vince Smith	RB	Chicago Bears	1977
Bob Gregolunas	LB	Chicago Bears	1977
Ken Moore	TE	Denver Broncos	1978
Randy Shelton	OG	Cleveland Browns	1978
Jerry Latin	TB	Los Angeles Rams	1978
Tom Wittum	P	Detroit Lions	1979
Carl Fisher	FB	Kansas City Chiefs	1979
Rimas Kozica	DT	Dallas Cowboys	1979
Pete Kraker	QB	Chicago Bears	1979
Jack Wilson	CB	New York Giants	1979
Jerry Golsteyn	QB	Detroit Lions	1979
Scott Paplham	TE	Houston Oilers	1979
Dave Petzke	SE	Chicago Bears	1979
Allen Anderson	CB	New Orleans Saints	1980
Frank Lewandoski	LB	Seattle Seahawks	1980
Randy Clark	OT-C	St. Louis Cardinals	1980
Jerry Meyers	DT	Kansas City Chiefs	1980
Dave Petway	SS	Green Bay Packers	1981
Mike Pinckney	WR	Chicago Bears	1981
Allen Ross	RB	Chicago Bears	1981

Player,	Position	Team	Year
Larry Alleyne	LB	Dallas Cowboys	1983
Max Gill	DT	Detroit Lions	1983
Brian Glasgow	TE	Chicago Bears	1983
Tim Tyrrell	FB	Atlanta Falcons	1984
Vince Scott	PK	Buffalo Bills	1984
Steve Hirsch	DB	Minnesota Vikings	1984
Carl Aikens	WR	Indianapolis Colts	1985
Rastee Oce	CB	Dallas Cowboys	1985
Pete Roth	RB	Dallas Cowboys	1985
Todd Van Keppel	P	Dallas Cowboys	1985
Scott Bolzan	OT	Cleveland Browns	1986
Darryl Richardson	TB	Green Bay Packers	1986
Dan Rosado	OG-C	Miami Dolphins	1986
Steve O'Malley	NT	St. Louis Cardinals	1986
Curt Pardridge	WR	Green Bay Packers	1986
Ricky Mitchell	HB	Minnesota Vikings	1987
Reggie Sims	TE	Cincinnati Bengals	1987
Dan Graham	C-OG	Tampa Bay Buccaneers	1988
Reggie Harris	DT	Denver Broncos	1988
Ted Karamanos	OG	Washington Redskins	1988
Doug Bartlett	NT	Philadelphia Eagles	1988
Scott Kellar	DT	Green Bay Packers	1989
Todd Peat	OG	Los Angeles Raiders	1990
Ted Hennings	DT	Chicago Bears	1990
Stacey Robinson	HB	Philadelphia Eagles	1991
Brett Tucker	CB	Buffalo Bills	1991
Eric Wenckowski	C	Chicago Bears	1991
Adam Dach	FB	Chicago Bears	1992
Scott Van Bellinger	LB	New York Giants	1992
Rich Favor	SS	New York Jets	1993
Rob Wagner	DT	Dallas Cowboys	1993
Larry Wynn	FLK	Chicago Bears	1993
Raymond Roberts	TE	Detroit Lions	1994
Timmie Lewis	OT	Chicago Bears	1995
LeShon Johnson	RB	Arizona Cardinals	1995
Hollis Thomas	DT	Philadelphia Eagles	1996
Aaron Gilbert	QB	Tennessee Oilers	1997
Mitch Jacoby	TE	St. Louis Rams	1997
Charles Talley	RB	Dallas Cowboys	1997
Kent Booth	OG	Dallas Cowboys	1998
Duane Hawthorne	CB	Dallas Cowboys	1999

Player	Position	Team	Year
Deon Mitchell	WR	San Diego Chargers	1999
Mike Stack	FB	New York Jets	2000
McAllister Collins	C	Jacksonville Jaguars	2001
Jermaine Hampton	SS	Indianapolis Colts	2001
Lamain Rucker	DT	Miami Dolphins	2001
Cameron Saulsby	LB	Carolina Panthers	2001
Frisman Jackson	WR	Cleveland Browns	2002
Jon Pendergrass	WR	Seattle Seahawks	2002
Darian Tate	DT	Carolina Panthers	2002
Chris Finlen	QB	New Orleans Saints	2003
Tim Vincent	OT	Chicago Bears	2003
Steve Azar	PK	New York Giants	2004
Randee Drew	CB	San Francisco 49ers	2004
Nick Duffy	LB	Chicago Bears	2004
P.J. Fleck	WR	San Francisco 49ers	2004
Todd Ghilani	C	Dallas Cowboys	2004
Akil Grant	SS	Tennessee Titans	2004
Justin McCareins	WR	New York Jets	2004
Brad Cieslak	TE	Buffalo Bills	2005
Lionel Hickenbottom	FS	Cleveland Browns	2005
Rob Lee	CB	Buffalo Bills	2005
Sam Hurd	WR	Dallas Cowboys	2006
Phil Horvath	QB	Detroit Lions	2007
Jake Nordin	TE	New England Patriots	2007
Britt Davis	WR	New York Jets	2009
Matt Simon	WR	New Orleans Saints	2009
Eddie Adamski	OL	Minnesota Vikings	2010
Jason Onyebuagu	OL	Jacksonville Jaguars	2010
Mike Salerno	PK	Chicago Bears	2010
Chad Spann	RB	Indianapolis Colts	2011
Chris Smith	CB	St. Louis Rams	2011
Tracy Wilson	S	New York Jets	2011
Cameron Bell	FB	San Francisco 49ers	2012
Trevor Olson	OT	Tampa Bay Buccaneers	2012
Nathan Palmer	WR	San Francisco 49ers	2012
Pat Schiller	LB	Atlanta Falcons	2012
Scott Wedige	C	Arizona Cardinals	2012

*lists first team and year the player signed as a free agent

Note: This runs through the 2012 NFL season

HUSKIES SELECTED IN THE CANADIAN FOOTBALL LEAGUE DRAFT

Player	Position	Team	Round	Year
Derek Sholdice	DT	Edmonton Eskimos	2nd	1995
Duane Arrindell	OG	Edmonton Eskimos	1st	1996
Mike Sutherland	C	Saskatchewan Roughriders	1st	1996
Farrell Duclair	LB	Calgary Stampeders	1st	1996
Alton Francis	TB	Saskatchewan Roughriders	3rd	1996
James Eggink	DE	Montreal Alouettes	5th	1996
Jamie Macdonald	OT	British Columbia Lions	5th	1997
Garett Sutherland	LB	Winnipeg Blue Bombers	4th	1998
Orlando Bowen	DE	Edmonton Eskimos	6th	1999
Donnavan Carter	FS	Toronto Argonauts	1st	2000

HUSKIES IN THE WORLD FOOTBALL LEAGUE (WFL)

Player	Position	Team	Year
Dave Donaldson	OG	Chicago Fire	1974
Mark Kellar	FB**	Chicago Winds, San Antonio Wings	1975
Don Wnek	DE	Chicago Winds	1975
Jim Gilbert	P	Chicago Winds	1975
Rich Marks	LB	Chicago Winds	1975
Tom Plesha	DB	Chicago Winds	1975

**Kellar was drafted in the 7th round by the Chicago Fire in 1974.

HUSKIES IN THE UNITED STATES FOOTBALL LEAGUE (USFL)

Player	Position	Team	Year
Larry Alleyne	LB	Chicago Blitz	1983
Rich Barrent	OG	Chicago Blitz	1983
Carl Aikens	WR	Chicago Blitz	1984
Scott Bolzan	OT	Chicago Blitz	1984
Tim Tyrrell	QB	Chicago Blitz	1984
Jerry Golsteyn	QB	Orlando Renegades	1985
Pete Roth	RB	Orlando Renegades	1985
Curt Pardridge	WR	Orlando Renegades	1986
Steve O'Malley	DT	Arizona Outlaws	1986

HUSKIES IN THE XFL

Player	Position	Team	Year
Mitch Jacoby	TE	Chicago Enforcers	2000
LeShon Johnson	RB	Chicago Enforcers	2000

HUSKIES SELECTED IN THE UNITED FOOTBALL LEAGUE DRAFT

Player	Position	Team	Round	Year
Chris Smith	CB	Omaha Nighthawks	4th	2011

HUSKIES IN THE UNITED FOOTBALL LEAGUE

Player	Position	Team	Year
Jake Nordin	TE	Las Vegas Locomotives	2009
Chris Smith	CB	Omaha Nighthawks	2011
Garrett Wolfe	RB	Omaha Nighthawks	2011
Scott Wedige	C	Sacramento Mountain Lions	2012
Chad Spann	RB	Omaha Nighthawks	2012

HUSKIES IN ARENA FOOTBALL***

Player	Position	Team	Year
Steve O'Malley	DT	Chicago Bruisers	1987
Rickey Mitchell	HB	Pittsburgh Gladiators	1987
Gary Schlinger	LB-RB	Chicago Bruisers	1987
Sheldon Sobol	LB-RB	Chicago Bruisers	1987
Carl Aikens	WR	Chicago Brusiers	1988
Pete Genatempo	QB	Chicago Bruisers	1988
Ted Hennings	DT	Detroit Drive	1990
Stacey Robinson	HB	Tampa Bay Storm	1991
Eric Wenckowski	C	Albany Firebirds	1991
Corey Ray	HB	Cincinnati Rockers	1992
Larry Wynn	WR	Iowa Barnstormers	1993
C.J. Rose	DE-FB	Albany Firebirds	1997
Ralph Strickland	WR-DB	Milwaukee Mustangs	1997
Deon Mitchell	SE	Grand Rapids Rampage	2000
Kent Baker	PK-P	Iowa Barnstormers	2001
Rashe Hill	OT-DT	Iowa Barnstormers	2001
Buster Sampson	DB-WR	Pensacola Barracudas	2001
Trent Clemen	FB-LB	Quad City Steamwheelers	2002
Jon Pendergrass	WR	Indiana Firebirds	2003
Lamain Rucker	DT	Peoria Pirates	2004

***lists first team and year the player signed as a free agent
Source: Northern Illinois University Football Media Guide

BIBLIOGRAPHY AND RESOURCES

BOOKS

ESPN College Football Encyclopedia. Michael MacCambridge (ed.). New York: Hyperion, 2005.

Mandell, Ted. "Heart Stoppers and Hail Marys: The Greatest College Football Finishes." South Bend, IN: Hardwood Press, 2006.

Maxymuk, John. "Strong Arm Tactics: A History and Statistical Analysis of the Professional Quarterback." Jefferson, NC: McFarland, 2007.

Sanders, Charlie, with Larry Paladino. "Charlie Sanders' Tales from the Detroit Lions Sidelines." Champaign, IL: Sports Publishing, 2005.

The Sports Illustrated College Football Book. New York: Time Inc. Home Entertainment, 2008.

Whittingham, Richard. "Rites of Autumn: The Story of College Football." New York: The Free Press, 2001.

NEWSPAPERS AND PERIODICALS

Allen, Kevin. "The Little Running Back Who Could Emerges at Northern Illinois." *USA Today*, August 30, 2006.

Armstrong, Rick. "Spann named MAC Player of the Year." *Aurora Beacon-News*, December 1, 2010.

Asmussen, Bob. "For Peat's Sake, These Kids Can Play." *Champaign News-Gazette*, March 6, 2010.

Associated Press. "Robinson Runs Over, Around No. 24 Fresno State. 73-18, Bulldogs: Northern Illinois quarterback gains 308 yards and scores five touchdowns in the record-setting upset." *Los Angeles Times*, October 7, 1990.

Brown, Gwilym. "A Big Man in Any League." *Sports Illustrated*, November 11, 1963.

DeSimone, Bonnie. "The QB Who Put NIU on the Map." *Chicago Tribune*, August 14, 1999.

Frisk, Bob. "Bork Adds Basketball Honor to Career Football Achievements." *Daily Herald*, January 16, 2001.

Greenburg, John. "George Bork: Northern Illinois' Aerial Ace." *College Football Historical Society Newsletter* XII, no. IV (1999).

Huskie Illustrated, August 28, 2003.

"Illinois Intercollegiate Athletic Conference—IIAC—Little Nineteen." *NCAA News* (June 6, 1970).

Korcek, Mike. Northern Illinois 2004 Football Media Guide. 2004.

LeGere, Bob. "Former Illini teammates on opposite sides in Super Bowl." *Daily Herald*, February 5, 2010.

Morris, Mike. "Legendary Athlete Leaves Memories." *Northern Star*, October 12, 1988.

Mitchell, Fred. "It's a Soar Subject." *Chicago Tribune*, December 5, 2012.

Mitchell, Fred. "Grounded in the Midwest." *Chicago Tribune*, December 16, 2012.

O'Donnell, Jim. "Musburger Takes Chicago Roots to Highlight Game." *Chicago Sun-Times,* January 7, 2010.

Reed, William F. "LeShon Johnson." *Sports Illustrated*, November 20, 1993.

Warner, Jeremy. "No title for NIU." *Northwest Herald*, December 4, 2010.

Wieberg, Steve. "Looking Now and Then at the Golden Years of Every Team." *USA Today*, August 27, 2009.

WEB SITES

Carlson, Rich. "northernstar.info." November 3, 1993. <http://northernstar.info/sports/article_48977092-da5d-5a59-a7e4-aeacd71c93eb.html> (accessed October 12, 2010).

"Champaign Central Football History 1894–2004." <http://www.champaignschools.org/index2.php?file=history&header=./central/athletics/football/> (accessed October 22, 2010).

"Huskies Suffer Heartbreaking Loss in MAC Championship." December 3, 2010. <http://www.niuhuskies.com/sports/m-footbl/recaps/120410aaa.html> (accessed December 5, 2010).

"McCareins Appreciates Heimerdinger's Influence." June 23, 2008. <http://nashvillecitypaper.com/content/sports/mccareins-appreciates-heimerdinger%E2%80%99s-influence> (accessed October 30, 2010).

Merrill, Elizabeth. "espn.com." September 1, 2010. <http://sports.espn.go.com/extra/ufl/news/story?id=5519159> (accessed October 12, 2010).

<http://www.niuhuskies.com/>